PRAISE FOR
THE 4 LENSES OF
INNOVATION

"Rowan Gibson has done a superb job of 'unpacking' what it takes to innovate. His account of great innovators and his Four Lenses framework are bound to stimulate and inspire would-be innovators everywhere."

Philip Kotler, S. C. Johnson Distinguished Professor of International Marketing at the Kellogg School of Management at Northwestern University

"Can you develop an innovative mind? Yes, you can. And this book is the manual. Rowan Gibson's *Four Lenses of Innovation* opens the door to understanding innovation. It enables you to develop and nourish big ideas, and put them into practical applications. What an exciting journey!"

John and Doris Naisbitt, authors of *China's Megatrends* and *The Global Game Change*

"Rowan Gibson provides an insightful look at innovation—enabling the reader to look at the world through new lenses of discovery. This is an excellent piece of work for practitioners and organizations who seek to have innovation as part of their DNA."

Camille Mirshokrai, Managing Director of Leadership Development, and Partner, Accenture

"*The Four Lenses of Innovation* is a wonderful book—full of inspiring examples and practical advice, it is bound to become a reference book for innovators all around the world. Rowan Gibson has produced another gem on innovation!"

Costas Markides, Professor of Strategy and Entrepreneurship; Robert P Bauman Chair in Strategic Leadership, London Business School

"This book is a must-read for anyone who wants to look beyond mediocre, status quo ideas. At Mars Inc., I use the Four Lenses to help team members understand that nothing is impossible. It's a revolutionary thinking method that never fails to provide velocity and perseverance when navigating complex challenges."

Cedric Bachellerie, Mars University Regional Director, and former Innovation Capability Manager, Mars Incorporated

"Rowan Gibson's *The Four Lenses of Innovation* will inspire you to think big, look afresh at the challenges you face, and take bold action to change the world. I heartily recommend it."

Robert B. Tucker, author of *Driving Growth Through Innovation*

"*The Four Lenses of Innovation* offers leaders and their teams simply the most understandable and practical tool for catalyzing enterprise-wide innovation. It removes the mystery from the innovation process, providing a common language, system, and structure for spotting and capturing opportunities for radical change."

Jim Darroch, Vice President, Global Fulfilment, CMMSG Division, Foxconn

"Rowan Gibson shows us how to unlock the potential of innovation. With this book and the four lenses methodology, he encompasses the key perspectives that will help you take a more effective approach to your business challenges, harness new trends, open up new opportunities, and anticipate customer needs."

Markus Durstewitz, Head of Innovation Methods and Tools, Airbus

"*The Four Lenses of Innovation* will help you kindle the innovation energy within your company. The book, like the methodology itself, is both inspiring and practical. We use the Four Lenses as our main framework for looking at the world in an innovative way."

Felipe González Soto, Innovation Management Director, Cementos Argos

ALSO BY

ROWAN GIBSON

RETHINKING THE FUTURE

INNOVATION TO THE CORE (COAUTHOR)

THE 4 LENSES OF
INNOVATION

A POWER TOOL FOR **CREATIVE THINKING**

ROWAN GIBSON

AUTHOR OF **INNOVATION TO THE CORE**

DESIGN BY **ADRIANA MATALLANA**

WILEY

Cover image: Rethinking Group Design
Cover design: Rethinking Group Design
Book design: Adriana Matallana

This book is printed on acid-free paper.

For general information about our other products and services, please contact our Customer Care Department within the United States at (800) 762–2974, outside the United States at (317) 572-3993 or fax (317) 572-4002.

Wiley publishes in a variety of print and electronic formats and by print-on-demand. Some material included with standard print versions of this book may not be included in e-books or in print-on-demand. If this book refers to media such as a CD or DVD that is not included in the version you purchased, you may download this material at http://booksupport.wiley.com. For more information about Wiley products, visit www.wiley.com.

ISBN 978-1-118-74024-8 (paper); ISBN 978-1-1118-94730-2 (ePDF); ISBN 978-1-118-94731-9 (ePub)

Printed in the United States of America

10 9 8 7 6 5 4 3 2 1

For my Zulma, the wife of my dreams,

who is with me in everything I do, and is

the reason for everything I do.

CONTENTS

viii   **Preface**

xi   **Acknowledgments**

xii   **Introduction**

1   **PART ONE: THE MIND OF THE INNOVATOR**

2   The Elusive Source of Creative Genius

12   Challenging Orthodoxies

15   Harnessing Trends

20   Leveraging Resources

30   Understanding Needs

40   The Four Lenses of Innovation

46   Time for an Innovation Renaissance

58   *Lessons to Take Away*

61   **PART TWO: THE POWER OF PATTERNS**

62   Seeing Things from a Fresh Perspective

66   What's Wrong with Our Brains?

68   The Pattern-Recognition Principle

70   Why We Stop Noticing

72   The Pattern of the Crowd

74   Resistance to Change

78   Patterns and Innovation

80   Sharpening Our Perceptive Powers

84   A Power Tool for Creative Thinking

86   *Lessons to Take Away*

89   **PART THREE: LOOKING THROUGH THE FOUR LENSES**

92   "Here's to the Crazy Ones"

96   What Exactly Is an Orthodoxy?

102   Meet the Challengers

105   On a Path of Disruption

111   Innovation Means Shifting Assumptions

114   Ready to Rethink Everything?

117   *Lessons to Take Away*

118   Seeing the Future in the Present

120   A Global "Change Bomb"

122   The Race for Tomorrow

126   Learning to Ride the Waves

130   Meet the Trend Surfers

137   The Man from the Future

142   *Fast-Forward* Companies

144   It's Happening Now!

147   The Next Big Thing for Your Business

151   *Lessons to Take Away*

CHALLENGING ORTHODOXIES

HARNESSING TRENDS

152	Repurpose, Redeploy, & Recombine
155	How Would You Define Google?
159	Leveraging Resources in New Ways
160	Extending the Boundaries of the Business
163	Stretching into New Spaces
166	Unlimited Potential for Growth
168	Exploiting Underutilized Assets
170	What Else Could We Do with This?
174	Leveraging Resources from Others
177	*Lessons to Take Away*

LEVERAGING RESOURCES

178	Innovating from the Customer Backward
182	Do Customers Really Know What They Want?
185	What's Wrong with It?
189	Understanding Particular Customer Groups
191	Innovating for Local Needs and Tastes
194	Matching What Is Possible with
	What Is Needed
201	*Lessons to Take Away*

UNDERSTANDING NEEDS

203	**PART FOUR: HOW BIG IDEAS ARE BUILT**
204	The Archimedes Principle
208	Rethinking the Universe
214	8 Steps to Building a Breakthrough
216	Inventing the 20th Century
224	Unpacking the Creative Process
230	"Say Good Bye to the Bag"
232	Different Routes to Big Ideas
235	*Lessons to Take Away*
236	What Exactly Is an Insight?
242	Do Insights Come from Breakthrough Thinking?
	Or Does Breakthrough Thinking Come from Insights?
244	A Practical Definition of Insights
246	Understanding *Ideation*
248	Stepping Stones for Creative Thinking
250	Improving Your Capacity for Radical Innovation
252	How Powerful Are Your Insights?
254	Working with the Four Lenses
259	*Lessons to Take Away*
260	Notes
269	Image Credits
272	Index
284	About the Author

After my speeches and seminars, people often come up and ask me where they can find a book on what I just talked about. I always assumed that my last book, *Innovation to the Core*, in which I dedicated a whole chapter to the Four Lenses of Innovation, would be sufficient to cover the subject. But after hearing the same question from so many people in so many countries, representing such a broad range of companies and industries, it finally became clear to me that the remarkable innovation methodology I have been using, championing, and perfecting all these years has long been crying out for a book of its own.

I have to candidly admit that, for me, the bigger story—indeed, what I consider the most important business challenge of our era—has always been how to embed innovation as a deep, enterprise-wide capability inside our organizations, so that it becomes just as integral to what we do as other capabilities like supply chain management, customer service, or quality. Given that innovation is now recognized globally as the core driver of growth, strategic renewal, and long-term business performance, it's simply ludicrous for a company to hope that it will somehow happen just by chance, or with a minimum of management attention. I have therefore devoted most of my consulting and speaking career to helping organizations make innovation happen in a broad-based and sustainable way, and I have been wonderfully gratified to see the positive impact this has had on countless companies all around the world. A few years back I also cofounded an Internet portal called *Innovation Excellence* to help make innovation resources, answers, and best practices accessible for the greater good. Today, it's the world's most popular innovation website, and home to a huge international online community. In some small way, I like to think that I have tried to do for enterprise innovation what pioneers like Deming and Crosby set out to do decades ago for quality.

So my attitude toward innovation is that we need to approach it *systemically*. Generating a lot of good ideas is usually a waste of time if a company doesn't build the necessary leadership commitment, management infrastructure, business processes, tools, training and engagement programs, performance metrics, incentives, rewards, cultural mechanisms, and organizational values to nurture innovation all the way from the mind to the market. However, having said that, there remains of course a fundamental need to come up with ideas that are compelling enough to be worth developing and commercializing in the first place. And that is where I believe things are best done *systematically*—using proven methods, tools, and processes to dramatically enhance our creative thinking skills, and to significantly improve the odds of coming up with some radical breakthroughs. Nobody would deny that serendipity still plays an important role in the innovation process, as it very often has in the past. But what if there was a way to rely less on luck on more on the incredible creative power of the human mind, combined with the formidable execution power of the modern business organization?

In recent years, much of the writing on innovation has focused on the social environments, ecosystems, and networks that seem to best foster creativity, experimentation, and new thinking. This body of work has certainly made an important contribution to the field. But if are going to make innovation more systematic and less serendipitous, we need to do more than simply create the right kind of culture or network of connections and then sit back and wait for great things to happen. We need to learn how to use our creative thinking skills much more effectively—and more collectively—across and beyond our organizations, so that we can achieve a step change in our ability to spot and exploit innovation opportunities with revolutionary potential.

You and your colleagues may have already employed a systematic ideation methodology in the past to stimulate the flow of new ideas. Maybe it was some form of brainstorming. Or perhaps you used a popular creativity technique like the Six Thinking Hats, lateral thinking, SWOT, TRIZ, random association, SIT, or Design Thinking. Most of the business executives I interact with have tried some of these tools and techniques, often with a degree of success. So why do they get so excited when they learn about and start using the Four Lenses of Innovation? What could explain the wide and almost instant appeal of this simple yet highly powerful methodology? Why does it take so much of the mystery out of how to come up with breakthrough ideas? I invite you to find out on the pages ahead. Once you have tried the Four Lenses, you will see for yourself just how amazingly effective this methodology is for systematically stretching your thinking along new lines, discovering inspiring new insights, and producing a portfolio of high-quality ideas and radical new growth opportunities.

I have personally introduced the Four Lenses to hundreds of leading companies and tens of thousands of business people in 60 countries across the globe. Many of those companies have worked intensively with the lenses to come up with profitable new products, services, processes, strategies, and business models. Some have used this tool to produce innovations worth hundreds of millions of dollars. In fact, over the last two decades, the methodology has been embraced by a whole host of major players in a diversity of industries including automotive, consumer packaged goods, financial services, telecommunications, electrical appliances, fashion and beauty, pharmaceuticals, oil, industrial chemicals, computer software, energy, mining, architecture, construction, and many more. Now it's my great pleasure to introduce the Four Lenses to you. Or, if you already know something about the technique, to give you a deeper understanding about how it can drive the front end of the innovation process inside your company.

This is not a typical business book, as a quick glance through its pages will tell you. I wanted it to be more of an intellectual journey—one that will take you from the ancient past to the emerging future as it traces the elusive source of creative genius, and the particular thinking patterns that consistently lead innovators to their Eureka moments. It will examine what inspired great thinkers during the Renaissance era, and what inspires the most outstanding business visionaries in our own day. It will help you to better understand how your brain actually works, and why we find it so difficult to break existing patterns of thought that blind us to new ideas. It will take you inside the minds of a long list of luminaries from Archimedes, Albert Einstein, and Thomas Edison all the way through to Steve Jobs, Jeff Bezos, and Elon Musk, in an effort to illustrate how big ideas are actually built. It will dispel some of the myths that continue to surround innovation, and clarify the critical role that insights play in the process of producing breakthroughs. And it will give you some practical guidelines for using the Four Lenses inside your own organization to facilitate your search for new, innovative solutions.

In many ways, every book is a personal journey, both for the author and for the reader. I certainly found it enlightening to put this book together, and I sincerely hope that reading it proves to be equally enlightening for you.

ROWAN GIBSON
San Jose, Costa Rica
February 2015

ACKNOWLEDGMENTS

First and foremost, I'd like to thank my wonderful wife, Zulma, for her huge support with every part of this book. Often, an author will thank his wife for her great patience during the writing process, and I would certainly like to do that, but Zulma's support was not just passive. She was actively involved in every aspect and every single page of the book, in particular coordinating all the design and image-sourcing that was necessary to bring such a highly graphic book to life. I am deeply grateful for her love, companionship, guidance, and professionalism every day. I could never have written this book without her.

My children—Henry, James, Nicolas, and Camilo—have also been a real encouragement and daily inspiration to me, and my mother and father, June and George Gibson, are the ones who originally recognized my own creativity and gave me the wings to fly.

Unlike my previous books, *The Four Lenses of Innovation* was not just a writing project. It also turned into an epic design project. This is where I want to thank and applaud Adriana Matallana for her spectacular graphics and illustrations, her brilliant styling of the whole book, and her saintlike patience in the face of my seemingly endless changes. A word of appreciation, too, for her partner, Gustavo Valentino, for all his hard work behind the scenes on the graphic production. Thanks also to Peter Barratt-Jones and the team at Rethinking Group Design—especially Jan van Buul, Sabine Swinkels, and Bas Gruyters—for their preliminary design ideas and for the front cover illustration and graphics.

I'd like to express my deep gratitude to the publishing team at Wiley, first for reaching out to me initially to ask if I had another book in the works. That early display of interest truly catalyzed the project, and over its course I have had the pleasure of working with Brian Neill, Charlotte Maiorana, Elizabeth Gildea, John Maas, Tiffany Colón, Lauren Freestone, and Richard Narramore. Also a quick shout-out to independent writer Andrea Meyer for her helpful research.

Thanks to my fellow "book slaves" and dearest friends, John and Doris Naisbitt, for their unfailing support and experienced advice at all times. Thanks to my clients and audience members around the world who have helped me to refine the Four Lenses over the years. And thanks, finally, to the cute little hummingbirds here in Costa Rica that showed up outside my office windows every day to give me a few moments of welcome distraction from writing.

Ever wondered where big, breakthrough ideas come from?

How do innovators manage to spot the opportunities for industry revolution that everyone else seems to miss? What is it that enables them to imagine radically new or different ways of doing things that will fundamentally change customer expectations and behaviors, or break long-established industry paradigms, or shift the entire basis for competitive advantage? Where do they get the brilliant flashes of inspiration that lead them to their game-changing discoveries?

Building a social environment that is conducive to creativity and risk-taking is only part of the challenge

In recent years, we have learned a lot about the innovation process. We now know, for example, that big ideas tend to be born and nurtured in "fertile" environments—cities, markets, campuses, online networks, technology hubs, or industry clusters like Silicon Valley—where there is a rich ecosystem of connections to make recombinant creativity possible. We have seen that innovation thrives in corporate cultures where everyone is invited to submit or pursue their own ideas, and where nobody is punished for making mistakes or trying new things. And we have discovered that ideation can be supercharged by employing "open innovation"—a popular modern approach in which ideas are generated by external constituencies like customers, suppliers, dealers, strategic partners, universities, contract labs, entrepreneurs, or virtual networks of R&D problem solvers, and then captured and integrated into an organization's own innovation processes.

This important understanding is helping more and more companies create the cultural and constitutional preconditions that serve as catalysts for innovation. They are working hard to stimulate the innovation process by mixing people from inside and outside the organization with diverse backgrounds, talents, and perspectives, and then watching the sparks fly as they share and recombine different concepts, capabilities, and domains. They are encouraging all of their employees to use their imaginations, suggest new ideas, and even take risks, by fostering an environment where there is a high level of trust and support, and even tolerance for failure; where people are not afraid to speak out, think independently, or propose and try a different way of doing things. They are also changing the physical workspace to make it more open and interactive, and more inspiring for the people who work there.

All of this represents incredible progress. Yet there is much more to making innovation happen, because building a social environment that is conducive to creativity and risk-taking is only half the equation. At the end of the day, you can design the most pro-innovation corporate culture, the richest ecosystem of connections, and the coolest of workplaces, but it's the people who interact with these environments that actually produce the new combinations of thoughts and technologies that may lead to commercial success stories. Breakthrough ideas are not generated by social systems themselves—by cities, or campuses, or networks. They come out of the heads of *individuals* who are connected to these communities. So to truly solve the mystery of where new ideas come from, we need to understand not just the environments that enhance our capacity to dream up and introduce new things, but also the thinking processes inside the human mind that lead innovators to their "Eureka moments."

This book is about **THE SECOND HALF OF THE INNOVATION EQUATION.** It's about understanding particular patterns of thinking that unlock our ability to innovate. It's about learning how to emulate **THE MIND OF THE INNOVATOR.**

Part One

The mind of the innovator

The elusive source of **creative genius**

Everyone can name a few innovation heroes. Most people reflexively think of modern business icons like Steve Jobs, Sir Richard Branson, or Jeff Bezos. Others recall the "industry builders" of the nineteenth and twentieth centuries, such as Thomas Edison, Henry Ford, or Walt Disney. Some think back to the "great men" of the Renaissance era—like da Vinci, Galileo, or Gutenberg. And of course there are countless other individuals, many of whom are not well known, who have nevertheless earned a place in history's great "Innovation Hall of Fame." So we all seem to know what an innovator is. But what's been harder to define for thousands of years is how innovators actually come up with their ideas.

In ancient times, it was believed that creativity was not a human attribute at all, but solely a divine one. The Sumerians, who are credited with a large number of technological and social innovations at the very beginning of human history, believed that the many creative achievements of their civilization were not due to their own efforts, but rather were gifts from the gods. The Babylonians and Assyrians, who were direct descendants of the original Sumerian people and builders of mighty empires, believed in guardian angels that guided and blessed their famed inventiveness in architecture, astronomy, mathematics, medicine, philosophy, and literature. As an example, the Babylonian King Nabopolassar, father of Nebuchadnezzar the Great (who was renowned for constructing the Hanging Gardens of Babylon), once said: "He (Marduk) sent a tutelary deity (cherub) of grace to go at my side; in everything that I did, he made my work to succeed."[1]

In the Judeo-Christian tradition, human beings were likewise not considered to be "creative."[2] They were makers and users of things that God had created in the first place. Or, if they actually managed to invent something new, it was not thanks to the human imagination, but thanks to the grace, wisdom, and power of God. These "richly blessed" individuals functioned merely as conduits for the divine.

In ancient times creativity was viewed as a divine attribute

The ancient Greeks perpetuated the belief that creativity was not something intrinsic to human beings. In Greek mythology, for example, it wasn't humanity that invented fire, and thus initiated the rise of civilization. Instead, it was Prometheus the Titan, the champion of mankind, who stole it from heaven and gave it to them. As a punishment for this transgression, which was aimed at helping humans on the road to progress, Prometheus was sentenced by Zeus to eternal and agonizing punishment.

Perhaps the best known innovator in Greek mythology was Daedalus (meaning "clever worker"), who was supposed to have invented the crafts of carpentry and sculpture, as well as creating the first masts and sails for the navy of Minos, the king of Crete. He also built the famous labyrinth in which the monstrous Minotaur was kept, which made it almost impossible to slay this fearsome beast. But his most famous invention was human flight. He was the father of Icarus, who mythically flew too close to the sun and fell to his death

when the wax on his wings of feathers melted in the heat. These magical wings were designed and constructed by Daedalus, who used his own pair of wings to successfully fly away from a tower where he had been imprisoned by the king. Pausanias, the Greek traveler and geographer, pointed to the source of this great inventiveness when he later wrote of Daedalus, "All the works of this artist . . . have a touch of the divine in them." The moral of this mythical tale, which is a recurring theme in Greek mythology, is that human attempts to be inventive or creative (considered the exclusive province of the gods), as well as any pride associated with these attempts, can ultimately do more harm than good. David Landes, the renowned Harvard professor of economy and history, wrote that "the ancients were dreadfully afraid of this emulation of the gods, and not coincidentally the protagonists in each case were punished for their hubris."[3]

In the Greek story of Pandora, supposed to be the first woman on earth, each of the gods helped in the act of creation by endowing her with a unique attribute or capability, including physical beauty, the power of speech and music, the skills of needlework, weaving and gardening, and fatefully also the trait of curiosity (which is why she opened the fabled "box," releasing all manner of evil into the world). Pandora's name—which meant "all-gifted"—was given to her not because she had any inherent abilities of her own but because every Olympian had given her one of these special gifts. Similarly, the Greeks believed that creativity—the

capacity for imaginative or original thought—was an extrinsic power or gift that was imparted to people by divine spirits.

It was therefore customary for Greek philosophers, poets, and artists to seek their inspiration from mystical goddesses called "Muses." Another common belief was that at birth everyone was assigned a personal "daemon"—an invisible guardian angel—whose role it was to mediate sacred wisdom, guidance, and motivation from above. The dramatist Menander, the famous historian and essayist Plutarch, and great philosophers such as Plotinus and Plato held this belief. Plato, for example, wrote that these intermediary beings interpreted and transported "divine things to men." Socrates claimed he had a personal daemon—some form of spiritual oracle or "voice"—that spoke wisdom to him. Indeed, in Hellenistic culture and religion, people attributed even the heroic conquests of Alexander the Great not to the brilliant military acumen of the man himself but to the mighty daemon that guided him.[4]

This belief in a tutelary deity that would attend to a person from birth to death was also shared by the ancient Romans. Interestingly, they called this guardian spirit a "genius." That's where the word actually comes from. It is rooted in the Latin verb *gignere*—or, in old Latin, *gegnere*—meaning "to beget, to bring into being, to produce, to create" (it is obviously also related to the Latin word *genesis*). But whereas we use the term *genius* today to describe a particularly talented or intelligent person, the ancient Romans used it to refer to a person's spiritual guardian or divine patron. In other words, if Steve Jobs had been some great Roman innovator at the height of the empire, nobody would have called him a genius. Instead, they would have believed he *had* an exceptionally powerful genius that was inspiring his achievements from the supernatural realm. The idea of human creativity just didn't figure into the Roman mind-set. As Cassiodorus, the Roman statesman and writer, once put it, "things made and created differ, for we can make, who cannot create."[5]

When the Roman Empire collapsed in the fifth century AD, the church of the Middle Ages, with its center in Rome, became the heir to Judeo-Christian, Greek, and Roman traditions, including the belief in guardian angels, and the notion that any attempt to exalt human prowess was to be condemned because it represented a denial of mankind's complete dependence on divine grace, inspiration, and influence.

{ The Greeks believed that everyone had a personal "daemon"—an invisible guardian angel—whose role it was to mediate sacred wisdom and guidance from above. The Romans called this tutelary deity a "genius." }

Everything started to change with the European Renaissance of the fourteenth to the seventeenth centuries, and in particular with the birth of humanism.

That's when the belief began to spread that great creative or scientific accomplishments were the direct result of a person's own education and abilities, rather than the work of some external divine entity. Suddenly, it was the human being that was the genius. And in this exciting new age, as rationalism slowly eroded the power of mysticism, people were encouraged to tap into their own intellectual and creative capacities in unprecedented ways. Thus, the Renaissance ushered in an era of unleashed human potential, producing a slew of technological, artistic, and cultural achievements. It was an age in which invention and innovation could flourish.

Clearly, one of the main reasons for this remarkable upswing in technological and artistic creativity was the urbanization of Northern Italy, and in particular the emergence of powerful city-states like Florence, Venice, and Milan. In these busy centers of trade and finance, the richest merchants, bankers, and city officials fought to maintain their dominance in part by becoming patrons of the arts, competing with each other to fund the work of the greatest painters, sculptors, architects, writers, philosophers, and scientists of their day.

A prime example is the Medici family of Florence, which owned the largest bank in Europe during the fifteenth century, and which sponsored famous figures like Michelangelo, Leonardo da Vinci, and Bertoldo di Giovanni. The efforts of these patrons brought together a variety of highly talented people from the worlds of art, education, and science, who then had the opportunity to cross-pollinate ideas and insights from their different fields, disciplines, and cultures. This historic intersection point, writes Frans Johansson in *The Medici Effect*, "forged a new world based on new ideas."[6]

But while such a vibrant network of connections was undoubtedly a fertile breeding ground for innovation, what we primarily want to understand for the purposes of this book is the innovative *thinking patterns and dispositions* that became so prevalent in the Renaissance period.

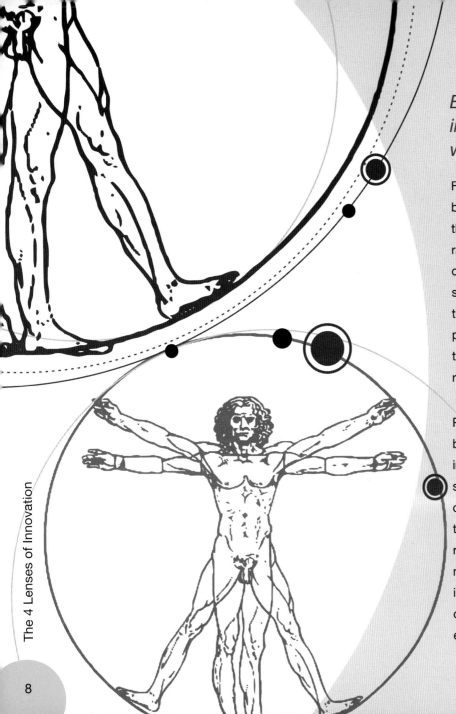

Essentially, what the Renaissance introduced was a completely new way of looking at the world.

For the first time in history, man—as opposed to deities—became the center of the universe. Humanism emancipated the human mind from the constraints of medieval supernaturalism, opening people's eyes to see, understand, and appreciate things that had previously been clouded by religion and superstition. Suddenly what mattered was maximizing life in the here and now, and working to make the world a better place in the future, rather than just putting up with things the way they were while waiting for some promised heavenly reward.

Prior to this point, individualism, curiosity, and creativity had been severely restricted by the medieval church. Instead of independent thinking, inventiveness, individual expression, and self-improvement, the church taught humble subordination, conformity, self-denial, and at times even self-hatred, asserting that individualism and ego were synonymous with arrogance, rebelliousness, and sin. Rather than fostering curiosity for the natural world and a desire to understand the individual's place in it, the clergy demanded that the laws of nature and of the church be accepted with blind faith and unquestioning obedience. Anyone who tried to challenge the dogmas, authority, or tradition of the papacy on any matter was threatened, punished, or completely done away with as a heretic.

Thus, there was generally very little motivation for suggesting a new idea or a new way of doing things, especially if it involved some attempt to better understand the mechanical forces of nature (which was God's domain, not man's) and then to manipulate these forces in an effort to improve quality of life. Any form of technological progress could potentially be viewed by the church, and by society, as a hubristic violation of divine order. The prevailing attitude in medieval times might be summed up by the old phrase, "If God had intended man to fly, He would have given him wings." In fact, when one Benedictine monk, by the name of Eilmer of Malmesbury, actually attempted to fly in the eleventh century by attaching Daedalus-like wings to his hands and feet and jumping off a tower at Malmesbury Abbey in England, this event only seemed to prove the point. Eilmer fell and broke both his legs, and was lame ever after.

We might even go so far as to say that during the Middle Ages there was no concept of human creativity whatsoever.

The Latin noun *creatio* ("creation") and the verb *creare* ("to bring forth, produce, beget, or create") were applied exclusively to God, as in the expression "creatio ex nihilo" (creation from nothing), which described God's original act of creation. Even when the word *create* first appeared in English in the fourteenth century (in Chaucer's *The Pardoner's Tale*) it was used solely as a reference to divine creation. So the notion that humans and their activities could be "creative" simply didn't exist in medieval consciousness. People were generally not expected to be inspired, imaginative, original, or expressive in their thinking and their activities, or to show any pride in their natural abilities. They were expected to be modest in their thoughts and actions, to be subservient to God and to the clergy, as well as to their rulers and masters, and to just get on with whatever they were supposed to be doing in life.

Whereas the medieval mind had been severely suppressed, the Renaissance mind was set free to discover the beauty and the wonder and the significance of every possible phenomenon. It vigorously embraced art, reason, and science in an unfettered search for new knowledge, meaning, and values.

Instead of simply accepting life the way it was, the Renaissance mind sought to improve it for future generations. It set out to demystify and define everything from anatomy to astronomy, with the goal of bettering all humanity. It recognized, for the first time in history, that creativity and genius—as personified by "great men" such as Michelangelo, Leonardo da Vinci, Nicolaus Copernicus, Galileo Galilei, or William Shakespeare—were based on human capabilities rather than supernatural powers.

This liberation of the mind had a profound impact on a world where free thinking and progress had been stifled for a thousand years. It introduced fresh perspectives that threw open a wide and beckoning door of new opportunity, experimentation, and discovery. In particular, we want to look at four of these mental perspectives—four patterns of thinking that were characteristic of the Renaissance mind-set, and that became the fuel for creativity and innovation in this exciting and highly transformational era.

 Challenging Orthodoxies

Harnessing Trends

 Leveraging Resources

Understanding Needs

Challenging Orthodoxies

Perhaps the first thing that comes to mind when we think about Renaissance innovators is their contrarian spirit. It was a time when people began to ask skeptical questions that had never been asked before, and to challenge deeply entrenched beliefs that had long been taken for granted. For example:

Copernicus, Galileo, and Kepler asked:
"What if the Earth is not the center of the Universe? What if it revolves around the Sun along with the other planets?"

Martin Luther asked:
"What if the papacy and the dogmas of the church are actually wrong? And what if we could read the Bible and listen to sermons in our own language, instead of in Latin?"

Petrarch asked:
"What if a person can achieve great things in this world without being ungodly? What if God wants us to use the intellectual and creative powers he gave us to their fullest potential?"

Andreas Vesalius asked:
"What if the dominant theories of human anatomy that have been unassailable for a thousand years are fully misguided? What if the human body functions completely differently than we have been taught? And what if we started dissecting some dead bodies to find out the truth?"

Paracelsus asked:
"What if everything we know about medicine is nonsense? What if certain chemicals and minerals, used in the right dosage, would be a far better way to cure illnesses than traditional practices? What if nature could teach us much more about medicine than ancient books from Greece and Rome?"

Machiavelli asked:

"What if politics has nothing to do with theology or morality? What if it's simply about using all means—fair and foul—to retain power?"

Descartes asked:

"What if all of our traditional systems of thinking, most of which are founded upon Aristotle's ideas, are false? What if we set out to build a new philosophical system from the ground up, by first doubting everything we think we know?"

Isaac Newton asked:

"What if conventional concepts of physics, gravity, and motion are inconsistent with reality? What if we need new laws and mathematical models for understanding mechanics?"

Filippo Brunelleschi and Leon Battista Alberti asked:

"Why can't a painting be less like wall decoration and more like a window into the natural world? What if we used mathematical and optical principles to imitate objects so accurately that they look entirely real?"

Christopher Columbus asked:

"What if we could get to the East Indies much faster by sailing west instead of east and circumnavigating the globe?"

Amerigo Vespucci asked:

"What if the Earth has a much larger circumference than we learned from Ptolemy's cartography? What if these lands Columbus has newly discovered are not the Indies at all, but in fact another whole continent—a New World?"

Almost by definition, these Renaissance revolutionaries were nonconformists who were willing to contest previously held truths—beliefs and assumptions that had been accepted as absolute gospel for perhaps a thousand years or more—and to reinvent their worldview completely from scratch. Many of them were branded as heretics or lunatics. Yet their propensity to break the chains of precedent and to challenge conventional thinking became the basis for a whole string of breakthrough discoveries and new philosophies that literally changed our world.

{ This capacity to challenge orthodoxies and to propose perhaps wildly antithetical alternatives is one of the fundamental driving forces for innovation. }

2

Harnessing
Trends

While Early Renaissance poet and scholar Petrarch looked back at the Middle Ages as a period of "darkness and dense gloom"[7]—a time of cultural and economic backwardness—he saw his own epoch as a time of "varied and confusing storms" at the dawn of a "better age."[8] Like a few of his contemporaries and many of his successors, Petrarch was intuitively aware of the revolutionary portent in these "storms" of change, and he grasped that they would herald a new era. The man they call the "Father of Humanism"[9] and the "Father of the Renaissance"[10] was obviously a man who had a deep sense for nascent discontinuities. Instead of adapting himself to the way the medieval world had worked for centuries, he focused his attention on the way the world would be, or should be, in the future. Indeed, he himself ignited the intellectual fuse that set off an explosion of change over the next three hundred years, laying the foundation for the modern age.

No doubt Petrarch's ability to recognize and catalyze the next "tide of history" was fed by his wide travels across Europe and within his native Italy, at a time when the longest trip most people made in a lifetime was to the local market. Petrarch has been called "the first tourist"[11] because his foreign travels were not just for diplomatic business (he served as an ambassador), but often simply for the sake of pleasure and curiosity. He paid close attention to what he encountered in other lands, carefully noting the customs of the people he observed, and showing intense interest in the characteristics of countries or cities he was visiting for the first time. He met with scholars, senators, nobles, cardinals, bishops, authors, poets, politicians, and diplomats, and corresponded with some of the most important figures of the fourteenth century. Petrarch's extensive travels and connections must have given him a very wide-angled lens through which to view the world, revealing all kinds of new and inspiring insights to feed his imagination.

Petrarch didn't just see a big shift coming. He was a pioneer and prime mover of that shift. He triggered a massive reappraisal of writers and philosophers from ancient Greece and Rome, personally searching for and collecting old Latin manuscripts and texts on his travels. He believed that society needed to rediscover the greatness of classical knowledge and ideals, and to reattain the cultural achievements of earlier times. In his view, it was the only way to reverse the deterioration and decline of the previous centuries (he was the first to use the phrase "Dark Ages"[12]) and to enter a new period of "radiance."[13]

Petrarch's devotion to Greek and Roman literature of antiquity, and his passionate writings about the civilizing power of ancient philosophy, kicked off a trend that eventually became widespread. First in Italy and then abroad, it became increasingly fashionable to study and republish these classical texts. Scholars and secular readers started to create a demand for them, and people began to hunt for old books in Latin and Greek in the courts and monasteries of Europe, often to sell them to collectors. Merchants brought them back from their trading trips to the East—from Christian Constantinople and the Muslim states. New libraries were built to house and facilitate access to them. All of this gave profound momentum to the humanist movement, and eventually inspired the whole wave of revolutionary cultural and intellectual thinking that emerged from the Renaissance.

One thing is certain: If the preceding centuries were a period of stagnation, the Renaissance period was an age of the new. There were new philosophies and ideals; new styles and techniques of art, literature, music, and architecture; new scientific breakthroughs; new industrial methods; new economic models; new forms of commerce; new trading patterns; new influences from the East; new and bigger towns; new kinds of government; new secular education systems; new ways of dressing; new kinds of food; and even new countries and colonies on the map.

Much of the quantum leap in creativity and innovation during this period came from the ability to understand and harness these new trends. Revolutionary breakthroughs are often built on some deep discontinuity—a convergence or systemic cluster of trends—that has the potential to create dramatic change or disruption.

Look at the map of various Renaissance trends on the next pages, and try to figure out how the intersections between these individual trends opened up opportunities for innovators who were paying close attention.

{ Petrarch recognized the revolutionary power of emerging trends—the "varied and confusing storms" of change that would herald a "better age." }

GROWTH OF TRADE IN ITALIAN COASTAL CITIES

- Decline of feudalism
- Shift from land-based to money-based economy
- New trading patterns and routes
- Increasing urbanization
- Booming cities and towns

Expansion of trade with the East

Rise of powerful banking families

INCREASING FOREIGN TRAVEL

- Influence from Islamic and Asian societies
- New foods, fashions, philosophies
- New technological inspiration from other lands

EMERGING MIDDLE CLASS SOCIETY

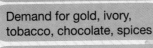

- New urban jobs in banking, commerce, and trades
- More disposable income and leisure time
- Increased literacy
- Mainstream interest in finer food, fashion, art, literature, and music
- Demand for gold, ivory, tobacco, chocolate, spices
- Demand for silk and cotton clothes

SURGE OF INTEREST IN CLASSICAL ANTIQUITY

- Patronage of the arts and sciences
- New painting, sculpture, and decorative arts
- New styles, techniques, and technologies in art
- Growing popularity of theater and opera
- Rebirth of classical art, literature, science, and philosophy

- Increasing use of oil paint
- Use of linear perspective
- Archeology of ancient Rome
- New architectur

RISE OF MECHANIZED INDUSTRIES

- Spinning wheels and horizontal looms
- Growth of cotton industry
- More mining
- Better metallurgy

- Use of blast furnaces
- Increased use of fossil fuels
- Growing iron and steel industry
- Use of rails for underground transport

Rapid spread of clockwork

Improved mechanical engineering

ADVANCES IN MATHEMATICS AND SCIENCE

IMPROVED TRANSPORTATION

Improved ship-building

- Improved cartography and navigation
- Use of telescopes, compasses, astrolabes, quadrants
- Increased naval exploration
- Increased canal and river transportation
- Better boats
- Better canal locks and dikes
- Use of rail
- Start of tourism
- Better horse-drawn carriages
- Discovery and exploitation of new worlds

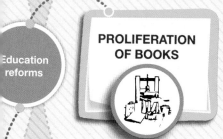

PROLIFERATION OF BOOKS

Education reforms

- Rapid adoption of the printing press
- Wide availability of literature, poetry, technology texts, sheet music, newspapers
- Growth in paper-making industry
- International book trade
- Spread of libraries
- Use of eyeglasses
- Study of art, literature, mathematics, science, and music

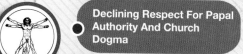

- **Rise And Spread Of Humanism**
- **Declining Respect For Papal Authority And Church Dogma**
- **Emergence Of Protestantism**

- Study of classical mathematics
- Spread of scientific and technical knowledge
- Adoption of the scientific method
- Wide variety of new scientific instruments
- Advances in astronomy
- New theory of heliocentricity
- New financial trading mechanisms
- Introduction of double-entry bookkeeping
- More efficient agricultural techniques
- More varied uses of wind and water power
- Improving chemical technology
- New approaches to medicine and surgery
- Advent of dentistry
- Introduction of patenting
- More invention

The Mind of the Innovator

3

Leveraging Resources

The third thinking pattern we want to examine in our study of the Renaissance mind-set is the ability of innovators to see themselves, and the world around them, as a collection of skills and assets that can be recombined or stretched into new opportunities.

Consider Johannes Gutenberg, whose mechanical, movable type printing press is considered by many to be the most important invention of the modern period. Let's look a little deeper at the various skills and assets Gutenberg leveraged to make this innovation possible.

First, Gutenberg was no dummy. He studied at Germany's University of Erfurt,[14] which had opened its doors only a few decades earlier. He had a smart and entrepreneurial mind that seems to have been busy searching for new business opportunities. Before he became famous for revolutionizing printing, he came up with a scheme to manufacture small "magical" mirrors from polished metal that he claimed could capture holy light from religious relics and impart healing powers to the user. His idea was to sell this little miracle to religious pilgrims at a big event coming up in Aachen[15]—in 1439 the city was planning to display an exhibition of relics from Emperor Charlemagne. However, the event was postponed due to severe flooding, so Gutenberg was forced to put his creative energies into another, much more promising venture—the printing press.

It is important to note that Gutenberg's background was in metalworking (hence the metal mirrors). He came from a long line of goldsmiths. His father, like his ancestors, was employed by the mint in the business of making coins.[16] So it was natural for Gutenberg to take on the same trade, and over the years he acquired extensive knowledge and technical skills, not just in metalworking but also in gem-polishing. More importantly, he is said to have dabbled in the new craft of intaglio printing using copper engravings.[17] This method of printmaking had been invented in Germany just over a decade before Gutenberg developed his movable type technology.

Even more interesting is the fact that movable type had already been invented hundreds of years previously in China,[18] and was already in use there as well as in Korea. So did Gutenberg find out about this existing technique and adapt it to Western needs? We will never know for sure. But we do know that sea trade between Europe and Asia was already well established in Gutenberg's day, and was growing at a steady clip. So it's theoretically possible that he had heard about this Asian printing method from traveling merchants, or had even perhaps seen it for himself, but there is no actual evidence of this. Whatever the case, at some point Gutenberg was inspired to cast individual, reusable metal letters to make printing faster and easier, deploying the skills he had learned as a professional goldsmith.

Thankfully, paper was quite abundantly available in Gutenberg's time. Having spread from China to the Middle East, it was discovered there by the Crusaders and brought back to medieval Europe in the thirteenth century. So paper was easily obtainable for Gutenberg's printing purposes. Indeed, one of his business partners owned a paper mill.[19]

What Gutenberg lacked was an effective way to print his inked types on the paper itself. The old method of wood-block printing relied on putting a piece of paper or cloth on top of inked wooden blocks and then carefully rubbing it by hand to form an impression. But this was too slow and laborious. Gutenberg's radical breakthrough was to design a mechanical press that could stamp inked letters against paper in a fast, durable, and commercially viable way. So where did he get the idea? Apparently, from a device that had been around for thousands of years, and that was commonly used in his day throughout the Rhineland region of Germany: the wooden wine press. Essentially, Gutenberg's invention was based on the same screw-type press mechanism used to squeeze the juice out of grapes during wine making. It was also used in other common devices back then, such as the papermaker's press and the linen press. So it wasn't much of a stretch to adapt it to printing.

But the story doesn't end there, because there was one more problem: the ink. Conventional water-based ink would simply run off Gutenberg's metal types. It also formed halos on the paper, and even penetrated it, making it useless for mechanical printing. So Gutenberg needed to create a whole new kind of ink to use in his press. Luckily, the Flemish painter Jan van Eyck had provided the answer just a few years earlier. Van Eyck was an innovator himself, having revolutionized fifteenth-century art by perfecting oil paint (made by boiling powdered pigments in linseed oil) as an artistic medium. Gutenberg realized that what he needed was not traditional liquid ink, but a sort of thick oil paint like van Eyck's that would stick to the metal type. So, with his knowledge of metals and engraving enamels, he set out to modify van Eyck's boiled-oil paint formula for his own purposes, by mixing carbon with copper, lead, titanium, and sulfur. That's how oil-based printing ink was born.[20]

The printing press, in other words, was an excellent example of recombination. First, Gutenberg leveraged his own skills and assets in a completely different setting, venturing beyond his professional trade as a goldsmith to create a whole new opportunity in mechanical printing. Second, he made use of other, mostly unrelated skills, processes, technologies, and assets available in the world around him to piece together his revolutionary device.

Gutenberg's printing press was an excellent example of recombination

Brunelleschi's Breakthroughs

We find a similar pattern when we examine other Renaissance innovators. Filippo Brunelleschi, for example, who is regarded as one of the seminal figures of the entire period, started out as a master goldsmith just like Gutenberg. But he also studied literature and mathematics, and had a strong artistic leaning. Brunelleschi was able to masterfully leverage his portfolio of skills beyond metalworking into sculpture, clock-making, architecture, archeology, engineering, and even ship design—in many cases achieving what had literally never been done before.

Having learned the skills of mounting, engraving, and embossing as a goldsmith, Brunelleschi turned his hand to sculpture, entering a competition in 1401 to cast new, gilded bronze doors for the Florence Baptistery that depicted the Biblical story of the sacrifice of Isaac. His entry, which survives to this day, lost out to that of Lorenzo Ghiberti, who was awarded the tender. Bitterly disappointed at losing the competition, Brunelleschi looked for some other application of his talents.

At the beginning of the fourteenth century, mechanical clock-making was the cutting-edge trade, representing the most advanced technology of Brunelleschi's day. So he decided to learn all about the precision mechanics of clock-making; the cogs, wheels, gears, and weights. But one thing frustrated him. Back then, if you wanted to know the time you had to go and search for a clock, or wait for its bells to chime. You couldn't carry the time around with you because clocks were too large and heavy, and they had to stay in a fixed position in order to work at all. So Brunelleschi set out to change things, and in 1410 he succeeded in inventing the world's first portable clock.

His breakthrough was to drive the clock's wheels with a spring rather than with a weight on a cord as with conventional clocks. Coiled springs had begun to be used in locks about 10 years earlier, and since many clockmakers were also locksmiths, this is probably how Brunelleschi made the connection. He also incorporated a tiny "fusee"—a conical pulley with a spiral groove wound with a cord—which was attached to the mainspring to compensate for the lessening torque of the unwinding spring. This technique had previously only been used on windlasses, either as a cocking mechanism in military crossbows, or in mechanical lifting machines used to hoist heavy weights such as masonry stones. By borrowing and repurposing technologies from different fields, Brunelleschi was able to make a clock that was not only much smaller and lighter, but, more importantly, portable for the very first time.

However, Brunelleschi is best remembered not for his contribution to clock-making, but for his achievements in architecture. His major work was the huge dome of Florence

Cathedral (known as the Duomo), which is considered one of the greatest engineering accomplishments since antiquity. At the time of its completion it was the tallest building in all history. And almost everything about this remarkable piece of architecture, which spans 144 feet (44 m) and reaches up to 375 feet (114.5 m) above the pavement, required Brunelleschi to innovate.

Nobody had ever built a self-supporting dome before, and none of his contemporary architects had any idea how to do it. It is said that Brunelleschi won the commission by taking out an egg, while meeting with the church building authorities, and standing it upright with a cracked and flattened bottom on a slab of marble.[21] The top part of the egg was his vision for the shape of the dome—tall and pointed rather than hemispherical.

Brunelleschi had just returned from several years in Rome, where he had been studying the architectural forms in the city's ancient ruins. In particular, he had dedicated himself to understanding the construction of the Pantheon and its own colossal dome. While his idea for the Duomo was more Gothic than classical in shape (in keeping with the style of the cathedral itself), he was convinced he could build something to match what only the Ancients had previously achieved. However, the enormous dimensions and actual construction of the Duomo were so challenging that traditional building methods would have been absolutely useless. Therefore, Brunelleschi had to rewrite all the architectural rules, inventing his own mathematical, structural, and building solutions at every step of the project.

The unanimous opinion of the experts was that building a dome that big would be impossible, unless it could be temporarily supported from the inside by a giant wooden frame. However, this would have required all the timber in Tuscany, as well as being far too expensive. Instead, Brunelleschi ingeniously designed a double shell—a massive inner dome with a rib-like skeletal structure, and an outer dome made of interlocking bricks arranged in a herringbone pattern that would support itself against the inner ribs as it was being built. Thus, both shells could be raised simultaneously, dispensing with the need for a supporting wooden frame.

Since nobody knew how to counter the immense outward thrust such a giant dome would create, Brunelleschi borrowed from the design of wooden barrels or casks, with their horizontal metal hoops around the vertical staves. Using the same basic idea, he wrapped the vertical ribs of the inner shell with a girdle of horizontal tension rings made of sandstone and iron chains, which held the whole structure together and stopped it from spreading outward.

To lift the 37,000 tons (33,566 tonnes) of building material, including over 4 million bricks, to his workers several hundred feet above the ground, Brunelleschi invented and patented his own ox-driven hoisting machine. It was able to raise half a ton (453.5 kg) of materials 200 feet (60 m) in the air in just 10 minutes (including attachment and detachment), and is recorded to have carried out 50 loads per day on average (imagine if the workers had to carry all that material up hundreds of stairs instead!). The machine also featured the world's first reversible gear, allowing for a load to be raised or lowered simply by switching gears, instead of unyoking the two oxen and turning them around to pull in the opposite direction. This remarkable new hoisting machine took a lot of unnecessary time, energy, and risk out of the construction process.

Sketches of Brunelleschi's hoist (made later by Leonardo da Vinci) reveal a set of gears and shafts that look remarkably similar to those used in clockwork. Clearly, it was Brunelleschi's earlier training as a clock-maker that enabled him to later imagine and construct such an innovative machine. The ambitious architect had also read in *De Architectura*, by ancient Roman author Vitruvius, about machines the Romans had used to build gigantic structures like the Pantheon. So inspired was he that, in addition to his revolutionary hoist, Brunelleschi also designed and built another monumental machine called the "castello" to move masonry materials (sometimes weighing more than a ton)

> *Renaissance innovators leveraged their own resources—and those they discovered around them—to create solutions the world had never seen before*

horizontally for placement in the dome. It stood 65 feet (19.8 m) tall, and could rotate 360 degrees, very much resembling the tower cranes used in construction today. In fact, the American Institute of Architects states that "the ingenuity and capability of these magnificent machines rivaled the accomplishments of the dome itself."[22]

This wasn't all. Brunelleschi also created movable cantilevered scaffolding that was hung consecutively higher, from each completed section of the dome, giving his builders a platform from which to work on the next section up. He erected a safety net to stop workers from falling to their deaths, and installed a chiming clock to regulate their working hours. He even built a small taverna halfway up the dome so builders didn't have to walk all the way down to the ground to get some lunch. And he made sure they stayed sober on the job by watering down their wine! Yet Brunelleschi managed the whole project with no formal training in architectural engineering, or in the running of an enormous building site, and no precedent to lean on for what he was actually constructing. Everything he did was pure invention.

And there's more. Brunelleschi not only reinvented architecture; he is also credited with developing (or at least rediscovering) the technique of linear perspective, which became one of the defining features of Renaissance art, and which forever changed the way artists and architects approach their work. In addition, he designed military fortifications, theatrical machinery, and even a gigantic cargo barge with hoisting equipment, for which he received the world's first patent in 1421.

Like Gutenberg, Brunelleschi refused to define himself narrowly as a goldsmith. Instead, he was constantly trying to expand his portfolio of skills and assets, and to redeploy them in new ways or new contexts. He proved himself a genius at leveraging his own resources—and those he discovered around him—to transition into different kinds of opportunities. It's a key characteristic of some of the most preeminent figures of the Renaissance—"universal men" like Leonardo da Vinci, Michelangelo, Galileo Galilei, Nicolaus Copernicus, and Francis Bacon—who were able to span a range of different fields, such as painting, sculpting, architecture, music, mathematics, engineering, astronomy, geology, scientific invention, anatomy, geography, cartography, botany, medicine, writing, poetry, and philosophy. They reflected the humanist belief, as expressed by fellow polymath Leon Battista Alberti, that "a man can do all things if he will."

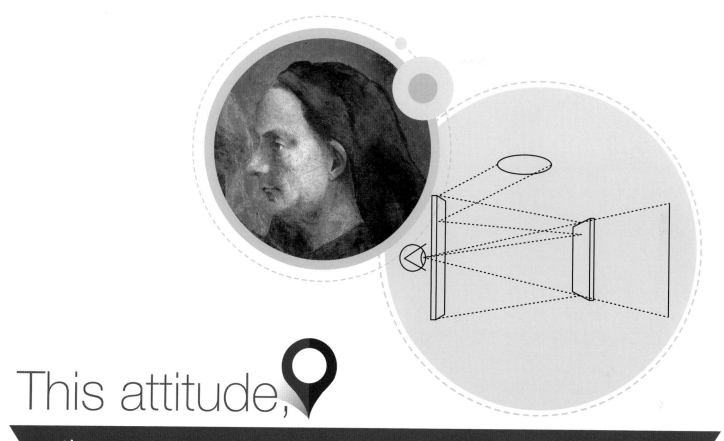

This attitude,

the awareness of our limitless capacity for developing, stretching, and synthesizing resources,

is one of the recurrent thinking patterns we find

when we study the mind of the innovator.

4

Understanding
Needs

The fourth pattern of thinking that was characteristic of Renaissance innovators was their seemingly insatiable curiosity for the world around them, and their unshakeable belief that they could make the world an increasingly better place.

Fundamental to humanist philosophy was the idea of progress—the notion that human beings have the power and the responsibility to continuously improve the quality of their lives through technology and science, individual liberty, and social modernization. Unlike the introspective philosophers of ancient Greece, who held that the way to understand the world was to look inside ourselves, or the priests of the medieval church, for whom questions and curiosity were synonymous with heresy, the Renaissance mind sought to understand *everything*—humanity, nature, and the universe—by intensely observing, investigating, and studying it. The scientific method, which gradually crystallized in those centuries, was a way to not only acquire new knowledge, as well as correct erroneous previous knowledge, but to apply that new knowledge to solving unaddressed problems and unmet needs.

No figure from the period epitomizes this more than Leonardo da Vinci. Helen Gardner, in her book *Art through the Ages*, writes of da Vinci's "unquenchable curiosity," and we see this reflected in the 13,000 pages of his famous journals, in which he made a daily record—in notes, drawings, and scientific diagrams—of his observations and studies.[23] These notebooks cover a wide range of interests and phenomena, from human anatomy and facial expressions to animals, birds, plants, rocks, water, chemistry, optics, painting, astronomy, architecture, and engineering.

Biographer Daniel Arasse recounts just how far da Vinci would go to try to understand everything around him. On one occasion, the great man coated the wings of a fly with honey to find out if this would change the sound of its buzzing noise in flight.[24] Observing that the note produced by the fly was lower than usual, he attributed this to the fact that the ballasted wings were beating the air less rapidly than before. Thus, he concluded that the pitch of a musical note is connected with the speed of the percussive movement of the air.

Da Vinci's acute observations led him to think about and try to solve problems that hadn't been seriously considered before. Nobody, for example, was asking for a parachute, a car, a submarine, a hang glider, a diving suit, a helicopter, a calculator, or floating shoes and stocks for walking on water, but Leonardo da Vinci invented, or at least conceptualized, these things. He also came up with military innovations like the machine gun, the armored tank, the finned mortar shell, a giant crossbow, a triple-barrel cannon, and a mobile bridge. He sketched mechanical breakthroughs such as a steam engine, a hydraulic pump, a reversible crank mechanism, a flywheel system, ball bearings, a hoisting machine, a more accurate clock, an automated bobbin winder, a lens-grinding machine, and a machine for testing the tensile strength of wire. He designed the world's first canal lock system, a method for excavating tunnels through mountains, a 720-foot (220 m) single-span bridge, a new kind of musical instrument, a double hull for ships, an industrial use for solar power, and a fully functional robot (which he built and displayed for his patron, Ludovico Sforza, at a celebration in Milan in 1495).

Most of these inventions were created to address needs that people were not even aware they had, or were not articulating at the time, and they offered solutions people could previously not have imagined.

{ Da Vinci was able to spot unmet needs and innovation opportunities because he was vastly more observant and more engaged with his environment than others. He was focusing his attention on issues and frustrations that most people simply ignored. }

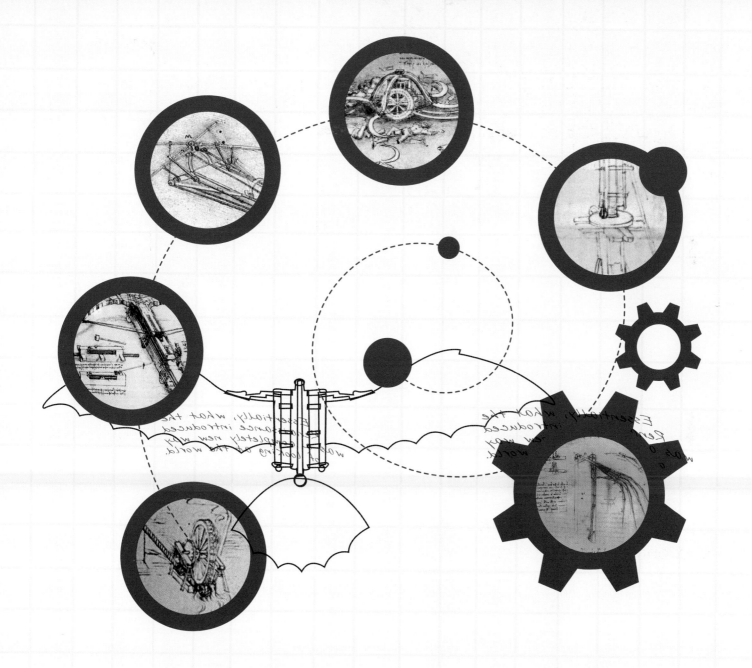

Essentially, what the pen & source introduced was a completely new way of looking at the world.

33

Innovators are the world's *noticers*

Stanford professor Tina Seelig writes in her book *InGenius* that "scientists and artists of all types are the world's 'noticers.'"[25] This pattern truly had its modern foundations in the Renaissance, as exemplified not just by Leonardo da Vinci but by a whole string of innovators from the period. Consider some other "noticers" who used their restless curiosity and their excellent observation skills to identify and solve problems that everyone else had taken for granted, or had traditionally viewed as unsolvable.

Galileo Galilei is perhaps best known for supporting Copernicus's heliocentric view of the universe, and it was his passionate observation of the night sky by telescope that brought him to this controversial conclusion. The refracting telescope he was using at the time was actually of his own design and construction (inspired by the original telescopes invented a few years earlier by Dutch opticians). Galileo's first model was rather simple, and offered only three times magnification. However, as he improved the design over time, even grinding his own lenses for the purpose, he increased magnification to eight or nine times, and later to as much as 30 times. These terrestrial telescopes, or spyglasses as they were commonly known, became a profitable business for Galileo, and he quickly found a growing market with scientists, sailors, merchants, and the military.

It wasn't long before Galileo was using his telescope to observe things a lot closer to home than the moon and the stars. After feeding his feverish curiosity by magnifying insects at very close range, he realized the potential of these lenses for understanding the natural world, and later worked on perfecting another important instrument of discovery—the microscope—for which he saw a clear need in scientific and medical fields.

Galileo's curiosity also inspired him to conduct numerous scientific experiments. Some of them, involving water and other liquids, led him to discover that a liquid's density changes in proportion to its temperature. This inspired him to invent a thermoscope (the predecessor to the thermometer) to measure temperature variations. Prior to this invention, there was simply no way of telling how hot or cold something was.

One day, while Galileo was sitting in the Cathedral of Pisa, his gaze was drawn upward to a bronze chandelier swinging from the ceiling. After a while, he began to time the swings against his heartbeat, and in so doing he was amazed to discover what we now call the law of the pendulum—or "isochronism." What Galileo noticed was that even though the size of the arc was gradually diminishing, the chandelier was swinging back and forth at exactly the same speed. This kicked off a whole series of experiments focused on the steady motion of pendulums, and in 1641, near the end of his life, Galileo designed the first pendulum clock. Unfortunately, he never completed it before his death, and it was Christiaan Huygens, about 100 years later, who used Galileo's principle to create an accurate pendulum-based timepiece.

Renaissance innovators figured out how to connect what was possible with what was needed

Another of Galileo's commercial innovations was created for the military. It was a compass-like tool called a "sector," which was designed to enable gunners to aim their cannons more accurately in battle by quickly determining the necessary elevation, as well as the gunpowder charge, for different sizes of cannonball. Based on the success of this military compass, Galileo subsequently adapted it as an instrument for land surveyors, giving them a quick and easy way to make geometric calculations. In all, Galileo produced and sold over 100 copies of this device, and he made additional money by offering a training course in its use.

Like da Vinci, Galileo was a "noticer." He asked questions about issues nobody else seemed to care about, he spotted phenomena that others had missed, he figured out ways to connect what was possible with what was needed, and he applied himself to addressing these unmet needs before anyone else.

Ambroise Paré was a military doctor in the early part of the sixteenth century who gained extensive experience treating battlefield wounds. He regularly came across horrific gunpowder burns, missing limbs, and all kinds of other severe injuries. In those days, there wasn't a lot of hope for soldiers who were hurt so badly, and many never even made it from the battleground to the medic because their comrades thought it more humane to put them out their misery. That's no surprise when you find out about some of the agonizing treatments practiced at the time. To stop heavy blood loss, for example, especially during amputations, patients were commonly treated with boiling oil and then cauterization—heating a piece of iron over the fire until it was red hot and then pressing it onto the gaping wound. In many cases, this not only failed to stop the bleeding but actually caused death due to shock. In others, it caused excessive tissue damage and led to dangerous bacterial infections.

Paré wondered if he could find a more effective solution. So he began to experiment with different treatments, observing and comparing the effects on his patients, and documenting all the results. This led him to the conclusion that the age-old practice of cauterization was doing his patients a lot more harm than good. As an alternative, he introduced the breakthrough procedure of sealing off arteries with a ligature of thread, especially to prevent hemorrhaging during amputation. He also invented a new surgical instrument, which was the predecessor to the modern hemostat, for clamping bleeding blood vessels. Instead of the boiling oil that was commonly used to treat open wounds, he developed a soothing antiseptic ointment, containing herbs and turpentine, that was much more effective—and a lot less painful!

After taking all this effort to alleviate suffering, Paré was frustrated to find out that some of his patients had later committed suicide because they felt their lives were not worth living after losing a limb. Back then, people that survived an amputation were likely to end up with metal hooks instead of hands, or wooden "peg-legs" for lower limbs—the kind we usually associate with pirates like Captain Hook or Long John Silver. As a solution, Paré began to design revolutionary prosthetic limbs based closely on human anatomy, with joints at the elbow and knee that would allow them to work like real arms and legs, as well as artificial eyes made of porcelain and glass. His masterpiece was a mechanical hand made of iron, with fingers and movable joints that were operated by a series of intricate springs and catches. It was fitted to the lower arm of a French army captain, who wore it into battle on horseback and reported that he was able to use the new hand to effectively grip and release his horse's reins.

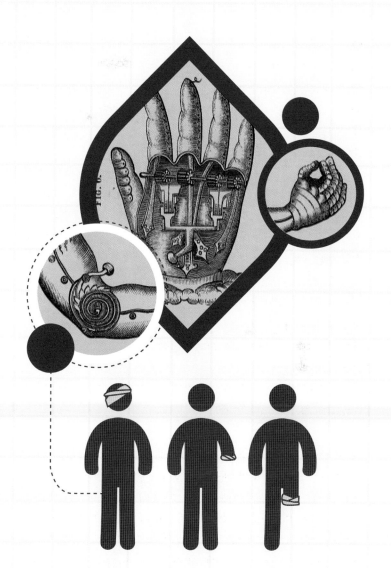

Other "noticers" from the late Renaissance period include Blaise Pascal, who set out to make accounting work easier for his father and in the process created the world's first mechanical calculator, and Pierre Fauchard, who believed there had to be a better way to treat an aching tooth than going to the barber to have it painfully extracted with primitive forceps. Fauchard became known as the "father of modern dentistry" for developing the whole science of dental surgery. He is credited with many innovations, including dental fillings, braces, dentures, the dentist's light, and a range of new surgical instruments. And whereas dental patients had previously been commonly placed on the floor (!), Fauchard treated them with empathy and dignity on a comfortable chair covered with horsehair.

{ *What all of these Renaissance examples teach us is that curiosity, scientific investigation, and observation, as well as deep empathy, led to the discovery of innovative solutions to important human needs and problems—solutions we still benefit from today.* }

The 4 Lenses of Innovation

This, then, is the fourth perspective or

thinking pattern of the innovator

—the desire to develop deep insights

into all kinds of phenomena, and to use new knowledge to solve problems, address needs, and

improve quality of life in completely novel ways.

The Four Lenses
of Innovation

If we could distill from our study of the Renaissance a key principle of creativity and innovation, it would be this: The breakthrough discoveries of that period were made not because people were simply connecting and conversing with a rich network of contemporaries from different fields, but because they were looking at the world from some refreshingly new and very particular angles of view.

The philosophical and cultural movement we now call the Renaissance entirely transformed people's thinking patterns, giving them a whole new set of lenses through which to view themselves and everything around them. These lenses enabled them to see existing concepts, common situations, and natural phenomena in completely new ways, and to spot opportunities for radical change and improvement that their predecessors had overlooked. It was this fundamental shift in mental perspectives that unleashed the unprecedented wave of creativity, curiosity, and inventiveness that came bursting out of that era. After all, people who happened to be born in Europe in, say, the fifteenth century were physiologically no different or more creative than people who were born a thousand years earlier. The only difference was in the attitudes, opportunities, and cultural influences of their day.

As we have learned so far, there were four particular perspectives or patterns of thinking that became prevalent in the Renaissance period:

 **1** ### Challenging Orthodoxies

Questioning deeply entrenched beliefs and assumptions, and exploring new and highly unconventional answers

2 ### Harnessing Trends

Recognizing the future potential of emerging developments, and using these trends to open up new opportunities

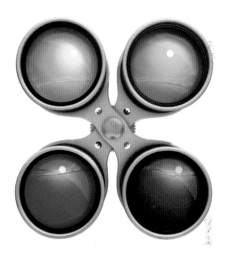

3 ### Leveraging Resources

Understanding our limitless capacity for redeploying skills and assets in new ways, combinations, or contexts

4 ### Understanding Needs

Paying attention to issues and frustrations others have ignored, and experimenting with new solutions to problems

These four perceptual lenses were an important part of **the recipe for Renaissance invention and innovation.** And they can be an equally powerful formula for catalyzing **the innovation efforts of your own organization.**

Stop for a moment and ask yourself: ❓

How often does my company challenge the deep-seated dogmas or orthodoxies it has about how we need to do business? How often do we take a critical look at our industry and ask ourselves how we could completely revolutionize it by overturning conventional thinking?

Do we truly have a deep and clear awareness of all the fundamental changes taking place in the external environment? Are we working hard to harness the power of transformative or potentially disruptive trends in ways that will create exciting new value for our customers, and revitalize or even reinvent our business model?

How many of our people view this organization not as a set of business units but as a portfolio of core competencies and strategic assets that could be leveraged in new ways, new combinations, or new settings to generate future growth? How good are we at connecting the resources of external companies with our own to radically change the way things are done in our industry?

Are we doing everything possible to fully understand and document the existing and emergent needs of our customers (or perhaps our customers' customers)? Are we using these insights to redesign our company's offerings from the customer backward, perhaps using new technological solutions to address these unmet and possibly unarticulated needs?

Think about what would happen if the Four Lenses of Innovation were used every day across your company to drive new thinking, generate novel strategic insights, and produce big, breakthrough ideas for growing and renewing your business. What if you could embed these thinking patterns into your corporate culture, at every level of the hierarchy, in every function and business unit, and in every geography? What impact do you think that would have on your company's capacity for innovation in its products, services, processes, technologies, marketing strategies, cost structures, and business models? What if it's possible to create the same kind of cultural conditions and attitudes inside your company that were so prevalent in Renaissance Europe, and that were so conducive to innovation, economic growth, and progress?

The Mind of the Innovator

Time for an Innovation Renaissance

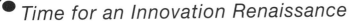

Imagine if you could start an innovation renaissance inside your own organization. Imagine if people came to work each day knowing your company viewed every single employee as a potential innovator. Imagine if everyone, everywhere (not just the folks in R&D or New Product Development) was encouraged to tap into their own inherent creativity—their inner genius—and to get involved in dreaming up and developing exciting new ideas for the company. Imagine if people were free to challenge the status quo and suggest different ways of doing things. Imagine if they were motivated to submit insights on nascent trends and unvoiced customer needs, perhaps based on their own observations or front-line experience. Imagine if they could follow their curiosity, their interests and passions, and spend time experimenting with their own pet projects, or be assigned to pursue emerging

business opportunities which they themselves had identified. Imagine if all the latent brainpower and human potential across your company, and even beyond it—in your value network and with a variety of external constituencies—was unleashed and mobilized to continuously rethink your business for the sake of the customer. Imagine if your firm maintained a rich and vibrant ecosystem of connections—both internal and external—where people could inspire each other and cross-pollinate ideas from different domains. Imagine if yours was a work environment that celebrated independent thinking, inventiveness, originality, individual expression, entrepreneurial spirit, and risk-taking—one where nobody was punished for making mistakes while trying new things. In short, imagine if yours was a corporate culture where innovation could truly flourish—the kind of culture we usually associate with companies like Google, Amazon, Facebook, or Zappos.

Unfortunately, the reality in most organizations is a management culture that more closely resembles the medieval church. What we usually find is a culture that relentlessly enforces standard operating procedures, and that chastises people for questioning them, or for trying to do things differently. A culture that discourages people from thinking independently, from expressing their own opinions, and from making unconventional suggestions. A culture that doesn't tolerate contrarians, and that will fight or even fire anyone who is pushing for ideas that don't fit with the modus operandi, or that lie outside the current core business. A culture where people are afraid to take unnecessary risks on new or untested ideas. A culture where people are expected to just shut up and do as they are told.

Instead of an organization that encourages its people to keep looking outward at the trends that could reshape its industry, and at the emerging needs and deep frustrations of its customers, we often find a self-interested culture where all the eyeballs are focused inward on the company's own management issues. We find a culture where leaders believe in centralization and control. A culture where only a few select executives at the top are empowered to take initiative on new opportunities, and where employees at lower levels or on the front lines have no power or incentive to try to solve customer problems in novel ways, or to create and implement their own visions for improving the business. A culture where people are held back by a hierarchy that believes more in bureaucracy, policies, and rule-making than in progressive thinking and rapid adaptation to developments in the external market. What we find, in other words, is a culture that actually gets in the way of innovation and that strangles it at every opportunity.

Does your organization already have a Renaissance-type corporate culture that functions as a powerful catalyst for continuous innovation? Or does it have more of a medieval management culture that is acting as an innovation anchor by holding people back in their efforts to be creative?

Given that we are now in an economic era in which innovation and value creation have become the central drivers of business growth, competitiveness, and corporate valuation, the issue of organizational culture is not trivial. There is a proven relationship between cultural environment and human behavior, so the group norms, shared values, and leadership style inside your company are going to have a huge effect on its innovation performance. There is also no evidence that the era of innovation economics is going to play itself out any time soon. In fact, we could be in for many more decades—if not the rest of the century—in which the pace and the intensity of innovation will continue to increase around the globe. So the burning strategic issue for today's companies is how to turn corporate cultures that are currently reducing and resisting innovation into cultures that perpetually facilitate and foster it.

"Cradles of Creativity"

We now know that it's possible to create pro-innovation cultural environments. We regularly read about companies, university campuses, technology hubs, certain city neighborhoods, and even governments that have managed to achieve this. But these cases are still the exception rather than the norm. The challenge for your own organization will be to speed up your efforts to achieve innovation excellence before the competition overtakes you. The good news is that this can be done, but only by applying some fundamental principles that have proven to significantly boost innovation performance time and time again, whether we look at a whole period of history like the Renaissance or at business success stories from our own times.

Fundamental to building an "all-the-time, everywhere" capability for innovation is the belief that creativity is not some rare mystical power possessed by only a few specially gifted people who were simply born different from the rest of us. We need to understand that creativity is a skill that is innate in all human beings, and always has been, as the archeological record from our earliest ancestors clearly attests. Of course, some individuals, either thanks to nature or nurture (or the fortunate interaction of both), have managed to develop this skill to a much higher degree than others. But all of us have the mental capacity for idea generation and imaginative problem-solving, and all of us can improve our creative abilities, as Stanford professor Tina Seelig writes in her book *InGenius*:

> Many people question whether creativity can be taught and learned. They believe that creative abilities are fixed, like eye color, and can't be changed. They think that if they aren't currently creative, there is no way to increase their ability to come up with innovative ideas. I couldn't disagree more. There is a concrete set of methods and environmental factors that can be used to enhance your imagination, and by optimizing these variables your creativity naturally increases. Unfortunately, these tools are rarely presented in a formalized way. As a result, creativity appears to most people to be something magical rather than the natural result of a clear set of processes and conditions.[26]

After studying creativity in a wide range of people from Picasso to Disney, British historian Paul Johnson concluded in his book *Creators* that "there is creativity in all of us, and the only problem is how to bring it out."[27] Neuroscientist Nancy Andreasen echoes this conclusion in *The Creating Brain: The Neuroscience of Genius,* when she writes about "the creative nature that we all share" and "the neural basis for ordinary creativity" that is in every human brain.[28]

Is that the way you view creativity in yourself and in the people around you? Is it the way your organization views its employees? Does your management see the potential genius in every single person that works for or interacts with your company? Are you really convinced that literally everyone, everywhere can develop the mind of the innovator? This is the starting point for turning your company into an innovation powerhouse.

How then do we increase everyone's inherent capacity to come up with innovative ideas? How do we "bring out" the creativity that is in all of us? One thing we need to do as leaders is work hard to build the kind of organizational environment that nurtures a person's ability to be creative. We have already learned a thing or two about the cultural conditions that led to the great flowering of invention and innovation we now call the Renaissance. Nancy Andreasen considers this outstanding period of history to be "prototypical as a cradle of creativity" and uses it as her prime example of how "environmental factors may influence the emergence of creative ideas." So what if you made a serious attempt to emulate the Renaissance spirit inside your company by trying to develop a social architecture that encourages people to deploy their creativity? What if you could make yours an exciting place to work where people feel that their energy and their brainpower is being channeled into "putting a dent in the universe" and shaping a new and better era for your organization? A place where there is always a "buzz" in the air—a sense of breaking new ground, of exploring and experimenting with ideas that haven't been seen before, of creating stuff that will have a significant impact on customers' lives, and perhaps even change the world. An adventurous place where there are few bureaucratic boundaries to get in the way of progress; where people have the freedom to stretch their thinking along new lines, suggest radical new solutions, and try "cool" new things. A place that offers employees a rich network of intellectually stimulating connections across and beyond the organization that can inspire them with fresh, combinational thoughts and opportunities. A place, in other words, where innovation is not just management rhetoric but a daily cultural reality.

> *"There is creativity in all of us, and the only problem is how to bring it out."*
>
> *Paul Johnson*

PASSION

CREATIVITY

connections

NEW IDEAS

exciting

INSIGHTS

TRENDS

INSPIRATION

INDEPENDENT THINKING

original

Cool

ENTREPRENEURIAL SPIRIT

RISK

The 4 Lenses of Innovation

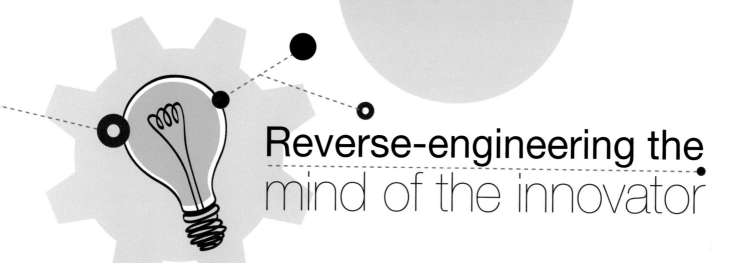

Reverse-engineering the
mind of the innovator

Turning a conventional corporate culture into a "cradle of creativity" is not an easy thing to do. If it were, we would already be inundated with thousands of examples of innovation excellence from all around the world, and you probably wouldn't need to read this book. Clearly we are not, because it seems to be the same small collection of "innovative companies" that is featured in the business media every single month. Building a pro-innovation culture also tends to be easier for a company that is just starting out, or that happens to be in a creative or high-tech industry of some kind. Older, larger organization in traditional industries often find that they have allowed themselves to take on some or a lot of the characteristics of medieval management that actively stunt innovation. In many cases, there is a need for a deep and long-term transformation process to remove these impediments and allow an innovation-friendly culture to develop and perpetuate itself. But whatever your company's own circumstances, there is no alternative to building a sustainable, enterprise-wide capability for innovation if you are going to stand any chance of success and survival in today's economy.

There is, however, something much more immediate we can do to push up the level of creativity and innovation inside our organizations. As I pointed out in the introduction to this book, building a social environment that fosters creativity and risk-taking is only half the story. The other half of the equation has to do with the patterns of thinking inside our minds that unlock our ability to innovate. On the preceding pages, we learned about the Four Lenses of Innovation—the particular mental perspectives that enabled Renaissance thinkers to discover their breakthrough insights, ideas, and solutions. It was by using these "lenses" that they were able to see things which others couldn't see—opportunities for radical invention and innovation that had effectively been "hidden in plain sight." So now that we are closer to understanding the mind of the innovator, the great excitement is that we can actually try to reverse-engineer it by deliberately emulating and employing the same thinking patterns or perspectives that others have used to spot unexploited opportunities and build big, breakthrough ideas.

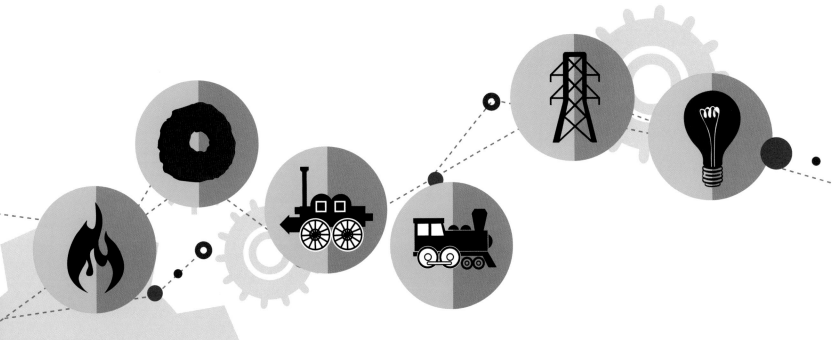

The 4 Lenses of Innovation

CHALLENGING ORTHODOXIES

HARNESSING TRENDS

This is not about adopting a trendy new ideation methodology. It's about developing the same perspectives that have driven creative thinking, technological progress, and innovation throughout human history—from the invention of fire, or the wheel, or cuneiform writing, to the creative achievements of classical antiquity, through to the innovations that ultimately shaped our modern world, such as the steam engine, the railway, electric power, the light bulb, the telephone, the automobile, the airplane, the television, the digital computer,

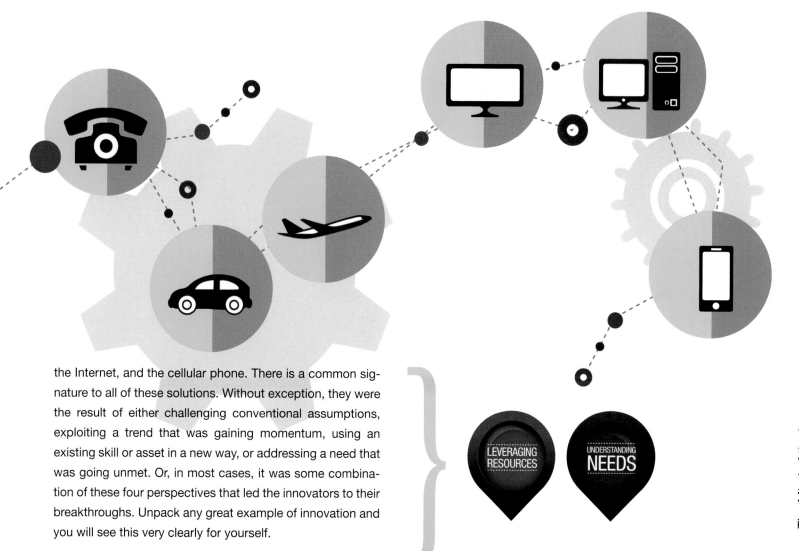

the Internet, and the cellular phone. There is a common signature to all of these solutions. Without exception, they were the result of either challenging conventional assumptions, exploiting a trend that was gaining momentum, using an existing skill or asset in a new way, or addressing a need that was going unmet. Or, in most cases, it was some combination of these four perspectives that led the innovators to their breakthroughs. Unpack any great example of innovation and you will see this very clearly for yourself.

LEVERAGING RESOURCES

UNDERSTANDING NEEDS

The Mind of the Innovator

Over the last two decades, thousands of people around the world have been learning how to develop the mind of the innovator by systematically applying the Four Lenses to their own strategic or creative challenges. You can do it, too. And so can your organization. Like many other successful companies, you can choose to embed the Four Lenses into your insight generation and ideation processes, and then train your employees how to use them effectively. You can optimize these processes by setting up a company-wide IT platform based on the very same innovation principles. And you can even create a three-dimensional center for innovation that is architecturally designed around the Four Lenses, where your people can actively challenge orthodoxies, harness trends, leverage resources in new ways, and understand and address unmet customer needs. All of these are

practical ways to dramatically increase the quantity and the quality of creative ideas inside your organization. This will increase the odds that your innovation pipeline gets filled with compelling new products, services, strategies, and business models that have the potential to create substantial new value for your customers, and in turn substantial new wealth for your company.

On the pages ahead, you will learn exactly how to use the Four Lenses to launch an innovation renaissance inside your own organization. You will find out how others have successfully deployed these Lenses to seize new growth opportunities, create new markets, and even transform entire industries. You will come to understand how the Lenses support the creative process by enabling you to generate superior insights, and then build these strategic insights into more powerful and disruptive ideas. You will receive practical guidelines for improving the effectiveness of your own ideation sessions using the Four Lenses. Simply put, you will find out how literally anyone, anywhere can apply the Four Lenses of Innovation to bring out the genius inside them that is waiting to be unleashed.

LESSONS
TO TAKE AWAY

There is an innovator inside all of us—literally everyone on earth has the potential for creative thinking because it's an innate human capability.
(We have to stop believing that only certain people can come up with big ideas.)

Innovation is stifled in an environment that restricts individual expression, independent thinking, and creative curiosity—an environment that enforces blind adherence to standard operating procedures, and that doesn't allow people to question organizational dogma or suggest new ways of doing things.
(Example: the medieval church—they don't call it the "Dark Ages" for nothing!)

Innovation flourishes in an environment where everyone is encouraged to tap into their own intellectual and creative capacities in an effort to improve existing things, invent novel solutions, and open up new opportunities.
(Example: Renaissance humanism threw open a wide door of discovery and invention.)

Building a "fertile" environment for innovation involves creating a rich ecosystem of connections where people can share and recombine different concepts, capabilities, and domains—from internal and external sources.
(Example: Northern Italy in the fifteenth and sixteenth centuries, where talented people cross-pollinated ideas from many different kinds of fields, disciplines, and cultures.)

Encouraging creativity, maximizing connections, and designing an inspiring work culture are not enough on their own to produce innovation. People also need to develop the right thinking patterns or angles of view. (Breakthrough ideas don't come out of social systems themselves, but out of the brains of people who are connected to those systems.)

There is an underlying signature to innovation in the Renaissance period and throughout human history. In case after case, we find that innovators came to their breakthrough discoveries by subconsciously looking at the world in four particular ways:

1. Challenging Orthodoxies
2. Harnessing Trends
3. Leveraging Resources
4. Understanding Needs

Anyone can learn to use these four perspectives to generate new insights and ideas, unlocking their inherent ability to innovate. (Companies all over the world have used the Four Lenses to catalyze their innovation efforts. Now you and your organization can do the same.)

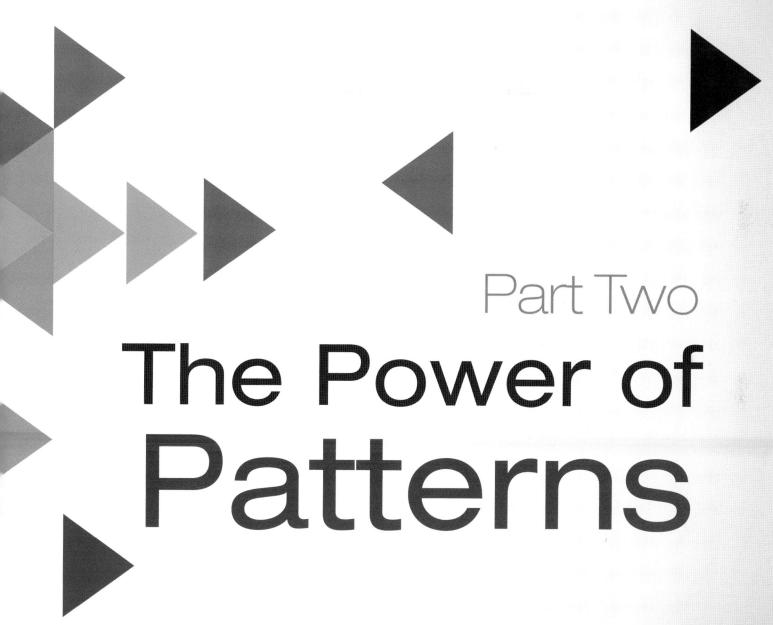

Part Two

The Power of
Patterns

Seeing things from a fresh perspective

A bagless vacuum cleaner. An on-line bookstore (and later megastore). A tiny cable TV channel that transformed itself into a global sports empire. A women-only fitness franchise. How did radical innovators come up with game-changing businesses like Dyson, Amazon, ESPN, and Curves? Why didn't anyone else spot and exploit these opportunities for industry revolution?

Whether or not they were aware of it, the creative visionaries behind these success stories were using the perceptual lenses described in Part One of this book: Challenging Orthodoxies, Harnessing Trends, Leveraging Resources, and Understanding Needs. Either by accident or design, they were looking at the world from the particular angles of view that are common to every case of great innovation. And it was exactly by applying one or more of these lenses—these particular ways of perceiving things—that they were able to discover breakthrough insights and ideas that everyone else seems to have missed. **Here's how they did it.**

Challenging Orthodoxies

Back when vacuum cleaners all looked boringly similar, British engineer James Dyson questioned some common and deeply rooted industry assumptions by asking, "Why does a vacuum cleaner need a vacuum bag? What if there's a much more effective mechanism for sucking up and collecting dust? And why does a vacuum cleaner have to look so ugly and old-fashioned? Why can't we turn it into a cool, 'must-have' design statement?" Dyson's company now sells its popular and fashionable cyclone-technology vacuum cleaners, as well as other innovative appliances, in over 50 countries around the world.

Harnessing Trends

In the early nineties, Jeff Bezos, a young executive at an investment firm in New York City, happened to read in a trend report that Internet usage was projected to grow by 2,300 percent annually. Immediately recognizing the fantastic potential of e-commerce, he decided to give up his job and focus on setting up a web-based book business. After the meteoric early success of Amazon.com, Bezos rapidly diversified beyond books in an effort to create "Earth's biggest anything store," and succeeded in building what is now the world's largest online retail business.

Leveraging Resources

Following a shaky start in the early days, ESPN's leaders masterfully leveraged the cable channel's core competencies in sports coverage, its special relationships with industry associations and franchises, and the equity of its own brand, to stretch the business into all kinds of new growth opportunities. These now include several additional TV channels, America's number one sports radio network, a biweekly magazine with a circulation that exceeds 2 million, video games and mobile apps, innovative TV shows, films and documentaries, fan apparel, competitions, restaurants and clubs, and a hugely popular website. Today, ESPN is the world's most powerful sports media company, with over 50 business assets and an empire that distributes content in 16 languages and more than 200 countries.

Understanding Needs

Gary and Diane Heavin, an entrepreneurial couple from Texas, recognized that traditional fitness clubs were not catering to the needs of women. A glaring problem, it seemed to them, was that gyms tended to be full of men, which could often be intimidating or embarrassing for female customers, especially if they were being stared at or, worse, sexually harassed. So the Heavins decided to open Curves—a fitness franchise exclusively for women and managed by women, where the motto was "no makeup, no men, and no mirrors." It became the fastest-growing franchise in history, and now has over 10,000 locations in more than 85 countries, serving more than 4 million members. That makes Curves the largest fitness chain in the world.

These four examples illustrate how amazing things can happen when you open your eyes. Just as we learned from our study of the Renaissance in Part One, it is only by learning to see things from a fresh perspective that we begin to notice exciting possibilities that were previously hidden from view. That's how innovators manage to peer through the walls of convention and glimpse opportunities that others don't notice.

What the innovators are actually seeing is **patterns**. They recognize some existing configuration of things that doesn't make sense to them (so they want to question it or alter it), or an emerging cluster of trends that has the power to change the game, or a potential recombination of elements that could create significant new value, or a repeated pattern of behavior that reveals a deep customer need. There's a reason the rest of us don't seem to have the same awareness for these patterns. We need to understand what that is, and how we can overcome it, so that we can start to see the world as innovators do.

What's wrong with our brains?

The problem is that most of us are not using our perceptive powers in the way that innovation demands. Although every human mind is equipped with the capacity for creative thought, we tend to stop taking full advantage of this ability long before we even leave school.

Our creativity is usually very evident in kindergarten where we all seem to be natural artists, inventors, explorers, and investigators. It's a glorious time when we let our imaginations run wild without inhibitions, rules, or regulations. We paint the sky green and the grass blue, and everybody thinks we're a genius. We turn empty cardboard boxes into castles, and plastic containers into space rockets. We look at everything from a childlike perspective, full of curiosity and wonder. We ask a lot of questions that begin with "How?," "Why?," or "What if?" and we think that any problem in the world can easily be solved. We dream up all kinds of magical uses for technology because everything seems possible.

But somewhere along the line—generally between the ages of 6 and 12—something changes. We learn at school that there's a right way and a wrong way of doing things. We learn what can and can't be done. We learn to put limits on our imaginations, and not to ask "dumb" questions. We learn to memorize facts, figures, and formulas, and to use books or the Internet to find all the existing answers, because that's the way to get higher grades. We learn, in other words, that creativity is silly and naïve, and that it's not valued or wanted from us anymore. So we gradually leave it behind us, just like the toys we once played with. It becomes nothing more than a cute and even embarrassing characteristic of our early childhood that we have now grown out of. And we start taking on a more rational, structured, and noncreative mindset to prepare ourselves for adulthood.

"Every child is an artist. The problem is how to remain an artist once we grow up."

Pablo Picasso

The pattern-recognition principle

There's another reason why our creative senses tend to become dulled as we get older—this time a neurological one. It has to do with the way we think.

At its very essence, all human thought is based on patterns. Inventor Ray Kurzweil, in his book *How to Create a Mind*, describes the neocortex structure of the brain, which is the area where we do our hierarchical thinking, as "a large pattern recognizer."[1] We use this innate ability of pattern recognition all the time, without even being aware of it, to identify faces, forms, voices, language, words, musical melodies, images, stories, concepts, and so on. All of these things are patterns.

As we grow up, get an education, and gain experience in a particular line of work, the brain organizes whole bundles of information into fixed patterns known as *scripts*, *frames*, or *schemata*, which we store in our memories for rapid access and use. It is these cognitive maps that enable us to make sense of our world every day without too much mental effort, because they allow us to automatically recognize and even predict familiar patterns—in objects or situations—while we concentrate most of our brain's processing capacity on tasks that seem more important.

In effect, this is how the mind saves energy. If it were not the case, we would literally be overwhelmed by everything that is going on around us all the time. Every piece of sensory information would be like a completely new and potentially bewildering experience that we would need to identify, interpret, and analyze in order to understand our environment. We would constantly have to relearn everything, and every single decision, however basic, would be unnecessarily complex. But by storing familiar patterns for spontaneous recall, we don't have to consciously think about these things anymore. Our pattern recognition system simply takes over the job—almost like the automatic pilot on modern airplanes—to reduce the cognitive load and free our minds to focus on other matters.

Our minds save energy by automatically recognizing and using familiar patterns

Do you remember your first driving lesson? Can you recall how mentally tiring it was to try to learn the right sequences of actions, generate and coordinate the appropriate movements of your hands and feet, use your spatial reasoning, pay attention to the road and to other drivers, follow the rules and the road signs, and listen to your driving instructor, all at the same time? Perhaps you wondered if you'd ever get the hang of it. But consider how effortless driving probably seems to you today. Through repetition and practice, all the activities you learned were eventually stored in your memory as an automatic response pattern, so that driving now requires a lot less brain activity. The whole thing has become habitual and reflexive, which means that while you are driving you can simultaneously think about something else, talk to another person, or listen to your favorite music. That's the power of patterns. They help us to form habits and routines, to block out what would otherwise be too much sensory information, and to avoid using up the brain's precious processing capacity on low-level details so that we can think about other stuff. In cognitive psychology, this phenomenon is often referred to as *automaticity*. It's our innate ability to learn, retain, and repeat complex behaviors and scripts which, with time, become almost unconscious to us.

▶ *Why we stop noticing* ◀

Of course, we should be very thankful that the brain works the way it does, otherwise we wouldn't be able to function as normal human beings, and as responsible members of society. But the downside for innovation is that we rarely go back and reexamine the patterns we have already learned, understood, and filed away for future use. Once our cognitive maps have stored a certain concept in a certain way, the reality is that we don't pay much attention to it anymore: a vacuum cleaner is a vacuum cleaner, a store is a store, a TV channel is a TV channel, and a gym is a gym. Our minds are extremely good at recognizing and applying existing patterns, but we are nowhere near as good at critically questioning or creatively rethinking these patterns on a continuous basis. Instead, we simply come to accept them as they are, and that's that. They mentally recede into the background and we happily turn our attention to other, seemingly more important things as we go about our daily activities.

What most of us experience is a cognitive condition called "functional fixedness," a kind of mental block that limits us to understanding and using the things around us only in the traditional ways we have learned. The more fixed our patterns become, the more difficult it is for us to mentally move beyond them—to look at something conventional and reimagine it in unconventional ways. This is why we become blind to new opportunities. We stop noticing or thinking about what has become familiar to us. We take it for granted. We no longer focus intently on some object or situation and wonder how it could be different or better. We simply allow it to become part of the landscape of our lives.

When we are young children, it's the reverse. We notice everything. We question everything. We take things to pieces to find out how they work. We build new things with very few preconceptions about how they are supposed to look. We see objects not as they are but as we imagine they could be. We invent things that don't exist. That's because we have a lot fewer patterns stored in our minds—we have significantly less information that is already bundled in static scripts, frames, or schemata. Our cognitive maps are incomplete. Our worldview is not yet fixed. So our minds are open to all kinds of possibilities. We actually show no signs of functional fixedness until about age seven. But as we grow up, we encounter and memorize more and more patterns. We narrow our perspectives in terms of what is possible and what is not. Our thinking and behavior become more rigid over time. We learn to view things and do things in particular ways, and before we know it our thoughts and actions are habitually following the same old established paths over and over again, just like water running into increasingly deeper gullies every time it rains. Once we have formed and ingrained these powerful neurological routines, it becomes harder and harder to change our recurring thought and behavior patterns, or to replace them with new ones.

Here's a familiar object that you see and use every single day. Did you ever stop to think about how you might make it different or better?

What about a toothbrush you wear on your tongue? Or a solar-powered ionic toothbrush that attracts plaque like a magnet? How about a self-balancing toothbrush? Or an electric toothbrush with silicone bristles? Or an intelligent toothbrush linked to a smartphone app? Or an environmentally-friendly bamboo toothbrush? Or a $4,000 luxury titanium toothbrush? Or a singing toothbrush that plays hits by Lady Gaga? All of these existing innovations were created by looking at something familiar from fresh perspectives.

This tendency to form fixed or habitual thinking patterns also occurs at a group level, in societies, and in corporate cultures. There is a body of received knowledge in every institution—a set of perceived truths about reality—that informs members about what to think, value, and believe. Any information that doesn't fit with this pattern is automatically resisted or rejected by the community. Recall the way Galileo Galilei and other advocates of heliocentrism were suppressed by the medieval church because their view of the universe was out of sync with religious dogma. It isn't much different today for those who are brave enough to publish papers that contradict the prevailing scientific or medical consensus, or for courageous executives inside large organizations who suggest some radical departure from the company's core business or its current economic engine.

Then there are institutional patterns of behavior—explicit rules and regulations, standard operating procedures, codes of conduct, and accepted industry practices, as well as implicit cultural norms and the unwritten rules of organizational politics—which guide, condition or prime members of a given institution in how they should act and interact. These recurring patterns are reinforced across the entire group, so that if one member starts behaving differently the others will reflexively nudge him or her back to the accepted way of doing things. In a recent international survey conducted by learning institute Hyper Island,[2] hundreds of top business leaders were asked about the most desirable qualities they look for when hiring new workers. While only 39 percent of respondents rated "Skill Set" as the most desirable quality, a full 53 percent put "Cultural Alignment" at the top.

We might want think of this as the pattern of the crowd. It's a phenomenon that has been around since people first began to form tribes and create cooperative societies for migration or agricultural purposes. It seems to be a natural human tendency to learn and adopt the attitudes, beliefs, and behaviors of the larger group, or at least of the influencers in a group. Alignment comes to be expected of every member.

Societies form collective patterns that manifest themselves in many ways. For example, we usually find that a large number of people around the world follow the same clothing fashions, watch the same TV shows and movies, listen to the same songs, play the same video games, download the same apps, use the same social media sites, read the same books, and buy the same products from the same brands. Why? Because these things have somehow become socially popular or trendy. People are simply conforming to the pattern of the crowd and subconsciously making impulsive choices based on what others are saying or doing.

In fact, buying decisions are very often *consciously* influenced by the opinions of others. We actively search for online feedback from customers who have already purchased a product or service before we decide to buy it ourselves (even though this feedback may be questionable). In one marketing survey conducted by Dimensional Research in 2013, 90 percent of the respondents said that their purchase decisions were influenced by positive online consumer reviews (and 86 percent by negative reviews).[3] We also see this phenomenon playing out in the herd mentality that sometimes leads to mass hysteria or stock market bubbles. And it's the reason why so many companies in any given industry end up with product and service portfolios, organizational structures, and entire business models that are essentially identical to those of their competitors.

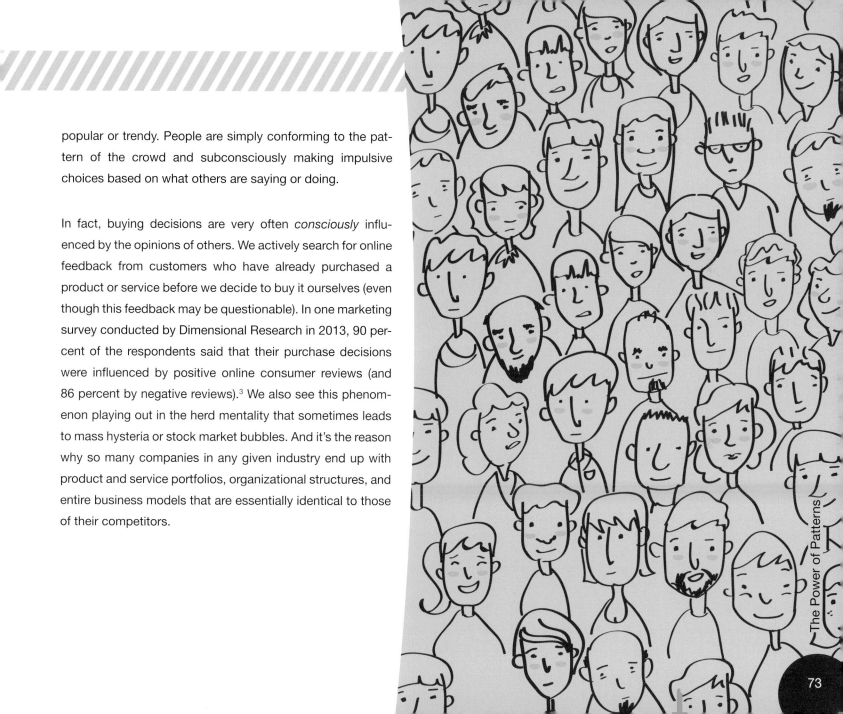

The Power of Patterns

Resistance to change

As human beings, we seem to have an inherent aversion to altering our familiar patterns. Think about how hard it is to break old habits and to form new ones, or to see things from another perspective once we have come to view or understand something in a particular way. Instead of trying to change our own way of thinking, we usually try to make things fit with the way we see them. And the whole reason we sometimes get into arguments is because we want other people to see things the same way we do.

Consider, too, how often we find ourselves regularly repeating behavioral routines. For example, think about the way you travel to work every day; the style of clothes you usually wear; the kinds of newspapers, magazines, and books you read; the websites and social media networks you visit most often; the restaurants you eat at regularly and the menu choices you commonly make; the tasks you perform at work every week, the people you usually associate with; and the way you spend most evenings and weekends. How much variation is there really in all of these activities? Even the way we brush our teeth or tie our shoelaces usually follows the same pattern every time.

It's no different if we look at organizations. Scale up this principle of pattern formation across a large corporation, or even a whole industry, and it's not hard to see why companies tend to develop a more or less fixed way of thinking about their businesses, and a whole set of static operational routines for doing whatever it is they do. Understandably, the more successful they have been in the past, the more fixed their institutional patterns become, and the less motivation they have to alter them. These institutional patterns become embedded in an intricate matrix of business units, functions, processes, management responsibilities, best practices, quarterly goals, KPIs, ERP platforms, supply chain configurations, logistics systems, operating policies, corporate regulations, and countless Excel sheets, and it becomes extremely challenging to change them—even in quite minimal ways—because everything is integrated with everything else, and the whole point of the system is to perpetuate what worked so well in the past.

No wonder managers typically resist new or disruptive ideas that don't fit the company's current operational paradigms. Any deviation from existing plans or procedures would not only jeopardize their own performance metrics, but also potentially put a spoke in the company's wheels that could throw the entire machine out of balance. Who would want to take that risk, or create such havoc?

Perhaps some managers are mindful of avoiding the so-called *centipede effect*. This can occur when a task that is normally performed with automaticity is disrupted by conscious reflection. It is named after a poem in which a centipede is happily walking along and unconsciously moving its many feet until a toad innocently asks it which leg moves after which. Thinking about the toad's question perplexes the centipede so much that it can no longer walk at all, and eventually falls exhausted into a ditch. This syndrome is also known as *hyper-reflection*. It was originally propounded in 1923 by the British psychologist George Humphrey, who referred to the centipede parable in *The Story of Man's Mind*, writing that "no man skilled at a trade needs to put his constant attention on the routine work. If he does, the job is apt to be spoiled."[4]

Many executives are afraid of the kind of reflective thinking that could lead to disruption. They avoid fixing what "ain't broke." They understandably prefer to keep their heads down and work within the system, sticking to the tried and tested, the familiar routines, the agreed-upon organizational patterns, without thinking too much about them. After all, what are managers usually rewarded for? Certainly not for "rocking the boat." In most cases, they are rewarded for making the deadline, making the budget, and not screwing up. So they have no real motivation to "think different," or to act like the proverbial toad in the centipede parable, and certainly no desire to be ostracized as contrarians or nonconformists.

As a result, there are relatively few corporate mavericks. There are few managers who are willing to give up the known and venture into the unknown, or to try innovative things that nobody has tried before. Instead, their objective—reflected in their quarterly goals and KPIs—is generally to do more of what they are already doing, only faster and cheaper.

Of course, on the one hand, institutional patterns are very useful. They enable us to create and maintain standards, to ensure employee safety, and to achieve a consistently high level of quality in our products and services. They also enable increased productivity and operational efficiency. After all, it was organized manufacturing patterns that gave birth to the industrial revolution, eventually leading to Henry Ford's sequential assembly line, which inspired the production model now used by countless industries around the world.

On the other hand, almost by definition, patterns produce sameness. Henry Ford's famous motto was "Any color you like as long as it's black." Most industrial operations, even today, are set up to ensure repetition and standardization rather than variation or customization. Their managers usually try to avoid any deviation from the norm. Patterns—particularly highly successful ones—also produce rigidity in the business model, making it difficult for a company's leaders, managers, and general employees to think outside of the organization's current paradigms and operating procedures.

A successful enterprise usually focuses on becoming increasingly efficient at replicating the same basic things, rather than on becoming equally efficient at doing *different* things. This was a big factor in the demise of once-great companies like Kodak, Blockbuster, and Nokia. They simply got stuck in their ways—imprisoned in the patterns of the past—while new technologies and disruptive competitors came along and shifted the whole game. They didn't realize until it was too late that yesterday's success recipes can turn out to be recipes for disaster tomorrow. In the end, they had simply become incredibly efficient at doing what customers no longer valued.

> *Break* is the important part of *breakthrough.*
>
> *Mathew E. May*

Patterns
and innovation

Here's why we need to understand patterns in order to understand innovation. First, at the basic neurological level, an idea is nothing more than a pattern. It's a pattern of thought elements arranged in a particular configuration.

So when we come up with a new idea, what we are actually doing is generating a new pattern or combination of thoughts—one that suggests to us an original, exciting, or better course of action.

Human creativity is what produces new ideas. Innovation is about successfully introducing those ideas, and thereby giving them commercial or social value. Some innovations introduce ideas for improving patterns that already exist in the world—for example, traditional products, services, processes, technologies, cost structures, or industry business models. Other innovations introduce ideas that break these existing patterns and replace them with radically new ones. This is disruptive innovation—the kind that totally changes the customer's expectations and behaviors, reinvents the economics of an industry (or creates a whole new industry), or establishes a different basis for competitive advantage that favors the revolutionary innovator.

So, at its core, innovation is all about the formation and exploitation of new patterns. To become successful as innovators, we need to be able to step back from the many existing patterns that surround us every day—in our businesses and our personal lives—and start looking at them from completely fresh perspectives. We need to notice the company or industry paradigms and practices that deserve to be challenged. We need to notice the emergence of nascent trends and discontinuities that could dramatically change the competitive rules. We need to notice ways to potentially recombine or stretch resources to open up new business opportunities. We need to notice deep customer needs and frustrations that are currently unaddressed. Simply put, we need to start noticing the patterns to which we may have formerly been blind.

In turn, this requires that we alter the *patterns of thinking* in our minds. Quite obviously, if we keep viewing something the same old way with the same old mind-set, we will never be able to envisage it any differently. Thus, we need to literally change the way we think about all kinds of objects and situations in order to discover opportunities for their evolution or revolution. We need to rethink or reframe these things by looking at them from new angles of view.

Throughout history, the world's most outstanding artists, inventors, and innovators have exhibited the same four thinking patterns or perspectives that consistently lead to great creative achievements and big breakthrough ideas:

Challenging and overturning deep-seated orthodoxies and assumptions

Recognizing and harnessing the power of nascent trends and discontinuities

Leveraging available competencies and assets in new combinations or contexts

Spotting and addressing important human needs that are going unmet

We need to develop these thinking patterns, too, if we are going to unearth the exciting opportunities for innovation that are hidden out there waiting for us to find them.

"Creativity involves breaking out of established patterns in order to look at things in a different way."

Edward De Bono

The Power of Patterns

perceptive powers

Have you ever looked at a brilliantly simple idea and wondered why you didn't think of it yourself? How often do we kick ourselves for missing creative solutions that seem so obvious in retrospect? The only way to overcome the mental blindness that keeps us from seeing these opportunities is to sharpen our perceptive powers.

Rather than racing through life and business without paying much attention to the landscape, we need to train our minds to bring all-too-familiar patterns back into focus. We must learn how to turn off the automatic pilot that so easily blurs our vision, and begin to notice and actively think about objects, situations, and concepts that we may have long taken for granted. We need to stop simply accepting these things as they are and start imagining how they could be or should be. We need to look at existing patterns from alternative perspectives and ask ourselves how we might make them different or better. We need to work at breaking down our preconceptions and opening our minds to all kinds of novel possibilities. Leonardo da Vinci reportedly once scribbled the words, "Stand still and watch the patterns. . . . If you look at them carefully you might discover miraculous inventions."

As we have noted, every human being has the cognitive ability or the capacity for creative thinking. We are actually born with it, and we all demonstrate it in our early childhood, so none of us can claim that creativity doesn't come naturally to us. In fact, you probably use your creative thinking skills on many occasions without being consciously aware of it—for example, when engaging in a hobby, or solving puzzles, or doing some practical tasks around the house or in the garden. It's just that a lot of people long ago lost the inclination to use these innate thinking skills in their daily work. In general, employees don't have the passion, the motivation, or the impulse to engage in creative thinking or behavior during work hours because it is neither expected nor rewarded by the organization, so they can't see the value in it. Instead, the majority simply memorize the patterns they are taught, work within those patterns, and perpetuate them, without giving them too much regard.

Unfortunately, creativity is like a muscle: If you don't use it, you lose it! This is what happens to too many people—they allow their creative thinking skills to become dulled through disuse or neglect. A similar thing happens to other human skills when we stop using them regularly and become overly dependent on established or even automated patterns. In recent years, a U.S. advisory panel, commissioned by the Federal Aviation Administration, has repeatedly warned that airline flight crews are becoming too heavily reliant on auto-pilot systems.[5] In their studies, they found that some pilots in high-tech airplane cockpits now only touch the controls around seven times during the entire length of the flight, and as a result their manual flying skills are becoming rusty.[6] In several fatal air crashes over the past five years, this phenomenon—so-called automation addiction—has been cited as a major contributor to these disasters.[7] Contrast this with what became known as the "Miracle on the Hudson," when Captain Chesley "Sully" Sullenberger expertly hand-maneuvered his US Airways plane without engine power, famously landing it on the Hudson River and saving every passenger on board. That was true airmanship!

If we want to master the art of innovation, we are going to have to reverse the mental laziness that comes from sitting back and letting the systems, patterns, and processes do all the work and the thinking for us. There is no other option but to dust off and hone the powerful creative thinking skills with which nature has endowed us, even if those skills have been underutilized for years or even decades. We need to figuratively put our hands back on the controls and learn to fly our imaginations again. With time and practice, and the right tools, it definitely can be done.

I'm not suggesting that we need to pretend we're still in kindergarten. This is not some crazy appeal for finger painting in the office (although I have seen it used to great effect in a few creative corporate cultures). However, there is certainly a lot to say for trying to rekindle the creativity, curiosity, playfulness, and open-mindedness we once had as kids. Albert Einstein said, "To stimulate creativity, one must develop the childlike inclination for play."[8] Companies like Google, Facebook, Microsoft, Zappos, and others seem to understand this. Their offices are designed to be fun places to work, complete with playrooms, informal spaces, and inspiring breakout areas, where people can regularly relax and spend time thinking creatively together. And if we examine the key thinking dispositions of great innovators, we do find a strong tendency toward intellectual patterns—or habits of mind—that are characteristic of childhood. For example, they usually ask a lot of probing questions to search for reasons, they like to follow their curiosity and investigate things, they courageously venture into unknown territory, they try all kinds of stuff without worrying too much about making mistakes or what others might think of them, they let their imaginations conjure up fantastic possibilities, and they are never willing to accept "no" for an answer! Individuals like Albert Einstein, Thomas Edison, Pablo Picasso, Walt Disney, Steven Spielberg, Sir Richard Branson, Jeff Bezos, and Steve Jobs come immediately to mind.

"But wait," you might be thinking, "that's just not me! I'm never going to be Steven Spielberg or Steve Jobs." That may of course be true, but the reality is that all of us can improve our creative thinking skills and dispositions. Some have suggested that it helps to shake up our traditional patterns of thinking and behavior by altering our habitual routines. For example, by taking a different route to work, wearing a different style of clothing, trying new kinds of food and drink in different kinds of restaurants, going somewhere new on vacation, taking up a creative hobby, reading books and magazines you wouldn't normally read, subscribing to the RSS feeds of some interesting new websites, hanging out more with teenage kids, listening to different music, watching some foreign or indie movies, making time for games, seeing more of the cities that you visit on business trips, losing your inhibitions by singing in a public karaoke bar, or hanging toys or a surfboard above your desk. These techniques may indeed work to some degree by bringing more variety into your life, awakening your curiosity and playfulness, inviting new impressions, and giving you some fresh perspectives. But most people find it difficult to sustain these new behaviors over the longer term, and unless they become firmly embedded in your lifestyle their practical value will be limited.

A Power Tool for
Creative Thinking

What we really need is a simple tool or systematic methodology that we can use every single day to dramatically enhance our brain's natural capacity for creativity and innovation. A tool that will help us apply the exact same patterns of thinking that great innovators throughout history have used instinctively, but that may not be so instinctive for us. A tool that enables us to deliberately look at the world through different perceptual lenses, revealing inspiring insights and exciting opportunities for innovation that we otherwise would never have seen. A tool that is designed to give anyone, anywhere the ability to generate big, breakthrough ideas with the potential for industry revolution.

The Four Lenses of Innovation provide us with precisely this tool. Like many thousands of other people around the world who have learned and deployed the Four Lenses in their companies, you can discover the amazing power of this methodology for supercharging your own innovation performance. It will remove the mental blindness that may in the past have caused you to miss some significant chances for changing the game. It will open your eyes to notice the many fixed patterns, paradigms, and routines in your company and your industry that you have probably been taking for granted, and that may be ripe for rethinking and reinvention. It will equip you to radically remodel or break outdated patterns from the past and replace them with innovative new patterns for the future—before some disruptive rival beats you to it. It will help you to not only innovate within your current core business, but also to see beyond it and spot huge untapped potential for profitable growth. It will allow you to see what is wrong or frustrating about your current offerings from your customer's perspective, and reveal how to solve these issues by thinking from the customer backward. It will free you from the pattern of the crowd—the herd mentality in most industries that forces companies to gravitate toward a common business model—and allow you to differentiate your organization and its offerings in ways that will delight your customers and confound your competitors. In short, the Four Lenses will enable you to think with the mind of the innovator, making you more like Thomas Edison, James Dyson, or Jeff Bezos than you might imagine.

Perhaps you recall that Steve Jobs once referred to the computer as a "bicycle for the mind," in the sense that it acts as an enabling tool that vastly amplifies our natural capabilities. Likewise, I like to think of the Four Lenses as "a power tool for creative thinking" because of the remarkable way these lenses extend our capacity for creativity—either as individuals or as teams—effectively catalyzing our innovation efforts.

In the next part of the book we will look more closely at the four perceptual lenses themselves—Challenging Orthodoxies, Harnessing Trends, Leveraging Resources, and Understanding Needs—and consider some examples that illustrate how these creative thinking patterns have inspired brilliant ideas for break-the-rules innovation.

LESSONS
TO TAKE AWAY

Some time after kindergarten, most of us stop using our creative and perceptive powers in the way that innovation demands.

(Creativity is like a muscle. If you don't use it, you lose it.)

Innovators use the Four Lenses of Innovation to see patterns that the rest of us may not see.

(Amazing things can happen when you open your eyes!)

Our brains save mental energy by learning and storing familiar patterns for automatic recognition and use.

(We tend not to notice or think about the patterns we have already learned. They recede into the landscape of our lives.)

Institutions form fixed patterns of thinking and behavior that become habitual, and are very difficult to change.

(Managers typically resist new or disruptive ideas that don't fit their current operational paradigms.)

An idea is simply a combination of thought elements arranged in a particular pattern.

(Innovation is about introducing ideas that either improve existing patterns or replace them with new ones.)

To spot opportunities for innovation, we need to change our patterns of thinking.

(If we keep viewing something the same old way with the same old mind-set, we will never be able to envisage it any differently.)

The Four Lenses of Innovation give us a perceptual power tool for recognizing, rethinking, and reinventing patterns.

(They amplify and extend our natural creative thinking capabilities—as individuals and as teams—effectively catalyzing our innovation efforts.)

Part Three
Looking through the
Four Lenses

In the previous two parts of the book, we began to unpack the mind of the innovator to try to understand some of the core thinking processes involved in creativity and innovation. Now that we have opened up this mysterious "black box" and begun discover how it works, and we have identified the four main perspectives that seem to be common to creative breakthroughs, it's time we considered some contemporary examples of these four perceptual lenses in action.

On the following pages, we will look through each lens in turn, first digging deeper into the principles behind it, and then reviewing some cases that illustrate how others have successfully used this particular lens to make innovation happen.

THE 4 LENSES OF
INNOVATION

HERE'S TO THE *crazy* ONES

When Steve Jobs launched Apple's iconic "Think Different" marketing campaign in 1997, it was clearly a reflection of his own philosophy and ideals. He praised "the crazy ones. The misfits. The rebels. The troublemakers. The round pegs in the square holes. The ones who see things differently." Nobody would disagree that Jobs himself personified this category, along with the famous individuals who were featured in Apple's ads, such as Albert Einstein, Martin Luther King Jr., Sir Richard Branson, John Lennon, Thomas Edison, Ted Turner, Mahatma Gandhi, Amelia Earhart, Martha Graham, Frank Lloyd Wright, and Pablo Picasso.

By their very nature, radical innovators tend to be contrarians, heretics, revolutionaries. They are forever discontent with the status quo. They are people who challenge conventional thinking, who show no respect for rules, or precedent, or popular opinion, and who never accept "can't be done." They dare to defy the deepest-held dogmas, dispute the most established industry practices, and trash the proudest of institutional legacies. Where everyone else seems content to "zig," they feel compelled to "zag"—to swim against the mainstream, contradict prevailing wisdom, break the accepted patterns, slaughter the sacred cows, question the unquestionable, fix things that "ain't broke," turn the seemingly impossible into the possible, and, well . . . to simply "think different."

Innovators are not satisfied just playing the game. They have an irresistible itch to rethink it, to change it, to improve it. Or to invent an entirely new game. They are, as George Bernard Shaw once explained, unreasonable people. Shaw argued that "the reasonable man adapts himself to the world; the unreasonable one persists in trying to adapt the world to himself. Therefore, all progress depends on the unreasonable man."[1] Rather than conform to the existing patterns of the world, innovators can intuitively see what is wrong with those patterns—where others cannot—and they instinctively want to put them right, or to replace them with their own patterns. They quite literally want to change the world.

In a 1994 interview conducted by the Silicon Valley Historical Association, Steve Jobs said the following:[2]

"When you grow up, you tend to get told the world is the way it is, and your life is just to live your life inside the world. Try not to bash into the walls too much. . . . That's a very limited life. Life can be much broader once you discover one simple fact, and that is—everything around you that you call "life" . . . you can change it, you can influence it . . . you can mold it. That's maybe the most important thing. It's to shake off this erroneous notion that life is there and you're just going to live in it, versus embrace it, change it, improve it, make your mark upon it. . . . Once you learn that, you'll never be the same again."

Jobs summed it up very well. Innovators don't just accept that "the world is the way it is." They are always driven to reshape it into the way they envision it could be. Innovators behave exactly as those "Think Different" ads said they do: "They invent. They imagine. . . . They explore. They create. They inspire. They push the human race forward. Maybe they have to be crazy. . . . Because the people who are crazy enough to think they can change the world, are the ones who do."

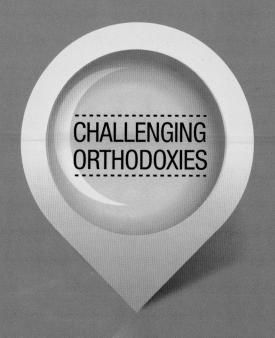

CHALLENGING ORTHODOXIES

Of course, you don't have to be "crazy" to apply this particular thinking disposition of successful innovators. All you have to do is start systematically challenging some of the fixed patterns that exist inside your own company, and across your industry.

For example, when was the last time you sat down with your team and seriously questioned the deep-seated assumptions you have about the "right" way of doing things? How often do you revisit the core beliefs you all share about the customers you serve, the markets you operate in, the products and services you offer, the kind of value you provide, the way you structure your business processes, how you make money, who your competitors are, how you differentiate your offerings, and how you intend to drive growth in the future? What if these beliefs and assumptions are no longer—or never were—valid? Where did they come from

in the first place? What if some of them are only based on common industry patterns, practices, and precedents—or folklore inside your organization about how things have to be done? What if you merely inherited them from your company's past and took them for granted, without ever thinking deeply about them or asking if there is any truth in them? What if these beliefs and assumptions are in fact unfounded, outdated, or obsolete orthodoxies that have long been accepted as gospel, but that now deserve to be challenged and overturned to open up new opportunities for innovation?

" The problem is never
how to get new,

innovative thoughts into your mind,

but how to get the old ones

out. "

Dee Hock, Founder of VISA

What exactly is an orthodoxy?

An orthodoxy is a deeply held belief, a traditional practice, or a conventional way of thinking that is commonly assumed to be true or correct.

The word *orthodox* literally means "right belief." It comes from the Greek words *orthos*, meaning straight, true, or right, and *doxa*, meaning belief or opinion. So orthodoxies are the beliefs or opinions that are commonly held to be true. They are broadly shared patterns of thinking (usually representing the viewpoint of the majority), that determine the way most people perceive certain things. Orthodoxies are the accepted norms or general standards to which a group of people adhere with a sense of certainty, and which they expect new members of the group to embrace without question.

George Orwell dramatically described the way orthodoxies can negatively influence human thinking in his famous dystopian novel *Nineteen Eighty-Four*. In the fictional world of protagonist Winston Smith, everyone mindlessly follows the same mandatory routines for living and working that "Big Brother" dictates and controls. They also unquestioningly accept the official version of reality propagated by the ominous "Ministry of Truth."

Outwardly, Smith may appear to be just as much an obedient drone as anyone else, but he secretly becomes guilty of "thoughtcrime" by harboring doubts about this totalitarian system, and by challenging its fundamental principles. Gradually he begins to think and act more independently, opening his eyes to the mental enslavement that has been inflicted upon himself and his fellow citizens. He realizes that, in the pursuit of a peaceful life, people have allowed themselves to be lulled into a kind of hypnotic state in which automaticity and orthodoxy have replaced conscious thought. According to Smith, "Orthodoxy means not thinking—not needing to think. Orthodoxy is unconsciousness." This is the inherent danger of orthodoxies—they can dull our senses and create complacency in our thinking.[3]

Just as we learned in Part Two of this book, orthodoxies are patterns of thought and behavior that the crowd impulsively or unconsciously follows. They condition us with a shared mindset that automatically determines what we believe, what we value, and how we respond. These habitual patterns or collectively wired norms embed themselves so deeply in our lives and our organizations that they usually become invisible to us, which is why we rarely contest, discuss, or even consider them anymore. They are simply always there in the background guiding us like natural, self-evident laws, while we go about our daily activities and focus our minds on other things.

The term *orthodoxy* was first used to denote conformity to the creeds of the early church—the core beliefs and agreed-upon understandings of doctrine that were shared across the religious community at that time. Today, business institutions similarly develop orthodoxies—established paradigms and patterns that determine the way they develop, price, market, distribute, and deliver their products and services, and how they organize themselves to operate efficiently and compete with rivals. These orthodoxies inevitably come to form the dominant logic about "the way things are done around here" inside a company and within an industry. So when a new recruit starts working at a firm, he or she gets indoctrinated in the beliefs and behaviors that that particular company considers to be "right," and is influenced by the larger group to conform to these organizational patterns. Over time, the employee takes on the collective cultural mind-set—the assumptions, methods, and corporate customs that will henceforth shape the way he or she habitually thinks and acts while working at the firm.

An orthodoxy is a deeply held belief, a traditional practice, or a conventional way of thinking that is commonly assumed to be true or correct.

> *In themselves, orthodoxies are not necessarily bad. Actually, they are an essential part of building a large-scale enterprise.*

They enable companies to create, capture, and mobilize a shared body of knowledge and experience that can guide their future activities and be passed on to successive generations of managers. In a sense, an organization has a collective brain that functions on the same principle as our individual brains— it recognizes the patterns of thinking and behavior that seem to drive success, and organizes them into scripts, frames, or schemata so they can be automatically repeated over and over, without having to reinvent the wheel every time the company does something. It's the corporate form of automatic pilot, necessary for achieving high levels of quality, safety, and operational efficiency. In fact, no large and geographically dispersed organization could function without orthodoxies.

The problem is that, if left unchallenged, orthodoxies can blind organizations to new ways of doing things. We might compare them to the "blinkers" or "blinders" that are commonly put on either side of a horse's eyes during a race. These leather or plastic cups prevent the horse from viewing what is happening at the rear or the side, narrowing its field of vision exclusively to what lies in front. The idea is to reduce distractions from the crowd or from competitors, and thus keep the horse's attention focused on the racetrack (and the finish line!). What often happens inside organizations is that orthodoxies implicitly discourage people from looking backward and questioning things, or from looking around them at what is happening in the external environment. Rather than taking time out to think about alternative business models, or to consider other possible solutions to familiar challenges, employees are incentivized to simply press forward toward their agreed targets, squarely focused on the way things are "supposed to be done."

Orthodoxies create the proverbial "box" within which people come to think, operate, and make decisions on a daily basis, and it becomes difficult for them to see outside of it. Again, what those people—those companies—are actually doing and how they do it might not be wrong. Indeed, it may still be highly successful and profitable. But it is certainly not the *only* way of doing things. And that's the key point: By seriously limiting our field of vision, orthodoxies can blind us to the possibility of radically different ways of doing business that lie outside of our current paradigms.

The problem is that, if left unchallenged, orthodoxies can blind organizations to new ways of doing things.

This is why disruptive industry newcomers often have a big advantage. They come into an existing industry without any of the preconceptions that blind incumbents to revolutionary opportunities. They have no attachment to the established industry molds that have long been producing the same old products and services. Instead, they feel free to break those molds and set up their own unique approach to things. They typically leverage an innovative technology, a fresh product idea, a truly novel service concept, or a game-changing business model to reinvent a stagnant industry and often seize the dominant position away from some sleepy incumbent.

We know this story very well. A long-standing industry leader is blindsided by a small visionary upstart and is toppled from its throne, perhaps to eventually become merely a footnote in the history books. The reason this happens to some large, successful companies is that orthodoxies can lead to what is sometimes referred to as "mental inertia."

The principle of inertia, as defined in Newton's First Law of Physics, states that a physical object will continue to move uniformly forward in a straight line (or stay at rest) unless it is acted upon by an external force. Mental inertia is the tendency of an individual or an organization to get "stuck in a rut"—to maintain a particular mind-set, and to resist any change in thinking and behavior, unless some external force exerts pressure otherwise. In business, that external force might be a discontinuous trend in the market, a sudden change in economic conditions, an aggressive move by an existing competitor, or the contrarian strategy of a new entrant to the market. Suddenly an organization is forced to fundamentally rethink what it is doing and where it is going when there is probably no longer enough time to make the changes necessary for survival. When you're going full speed ahead in what turns out to be the wrong direction, it can be almost impossible to quickly and radically turn a company around without having a fatal or near-fatal crash.

That's why it's so important to regularly shake ourselves loose from this mental inertia and recalibrate our perspectives with the first lens of innovation. We need to learn to actively adopt a different, more contrarian, more provocative stance. We must find ways to surface and overturn the flawed assumptions, the comfortable orthodoxies, the erroneous core beliefs that may be locking us into one way of thinking and blinding us to new possibilities. Every so often, we should try to disrupt our own patterns before a competitor does, by taking the conventional wisdom inside our company and our industry and asking what would happen if we turned it completely on its head. We have to become more like the industry challengers on the following pages, all of whom were able to open significant opportunities for innovation and wealth creation by applying this particular perceptual lens.

"Companies fall apart when their model is so successful that it stifles thinking that challenges it."

Mark Parker, CEO Nike

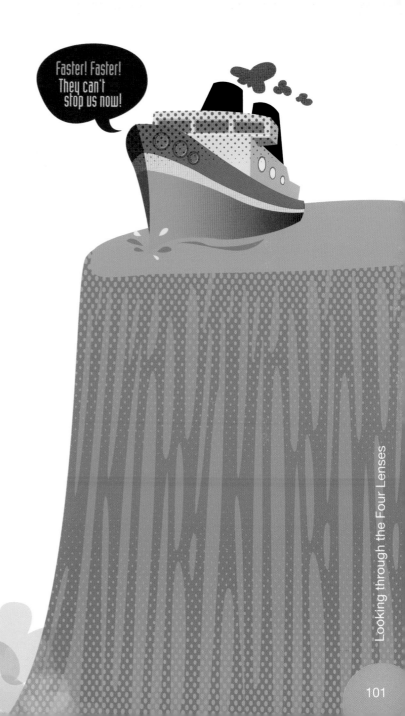

Meet the Challengers

It was by challenging orthodoxies that Nicolas Hayek turned around the entire Swiss watch industry in the early 1980s. Hayek's iconic Swatch brand, based on an inexpensive quartz movement and a colorful plastic case, repositioned the watch as a trendy fashion statement rather than as a timepiece. Three decades later, Swatch Group controls virtually every watch company in Switzerland, generating revenues that now exceed $10 billion annually, and producing well over a billion new watches every year.

Consider how Michael Dell built what is now one of the largest PC and technology corporations in the world. While a student at the University of Texas, Dell started a business in his dorm room, selling IBM PC-compatible computers he assembled from standard components. His big idea came from questioning the prevailing wisdom in the computer industry of his day. He asked himself, "Why does an assembled computer cost five times as much as the parts that went into it? Why do computer manufacturers need indirect retail channels to sell their products? Why can't they be sold directly to consumers over the phone at a much better price, by cutting out the dealer's overheads? Why can't computers be built to order, so that consumers can have the product configured to their own specifications? And why do computer companies manage their own inventory when their suppliers could do it for them?" Today, Dell employs over 108,000 people worldwide and generates around $57 billion annually in global revenues.

Think about the way Southwest Airlines overturned common assumptions in the airline industry. For example, they questioned the need for a "hub and spokes" route system, two segregated seating classes, and a fleet of different types of aircraft. They also asked why the flight crew couldn't have some fun with their passengers, which is why Southwest's pilots and flight attendants are now known for their humorous announcements on board, or for making hilarious preflight safety speeches.

IKEA, the world's largest furniture retailer, asked why home furnishings had to be fully assembled before being sold and delivered. Instead, why not design modular units that customers could simply pick up at the store and assemble themselves?

While every other rent-a-car company assumed that airport locations and travelers should be the primary focus, Enterprise chose instead to open thousands of offices near local auto dealerships and service centers. That way, they could serve customers who needed a replacement car due to an accident or theft, or while their regular vehicle was undergoing mechanical maintenance. Only after several decades did the company finally expand into airport locations. Today, it's the largest rental car company in the United States, reportedly purchasing 7 percent of all new automobiles sold in the country.

The designers of the Nintendo Wii asked why competition in the video games industry was exclusively focused on realistic graphics, fast processing speed, and winning over the hardcore gamers. What if it was possible to simply change the whole experience by putting a motion sensor in the controller and physically integrating players into the game?

Netflix challenged the notion that people have to go to a physical store to rent a video. Why not just order it online and have it delivered to your home? Also, why should people pay per individual rental and have all the hassle of late fees if they return a movie after the due date? Why not introduce a monthly, flat-fee subscription model with unlimited rentals and no extra charge for late returns?

In the mid-1990s, Rolls-Royce recognized a glaring orthodoxy in its civil aerospace business model. The basic attitude was, "We design and sell engines for airplanes. Service and maintenance are an afterthought." This model functioned similarly to the automobile business, where customers have to pay each time an engine needs repairs or routine service. But Rolls-Royce radically changed that by introducing its "TotalCare" long-term service contracts for jet engine customers, covering engine health monitoring and maintenance, with optional extras like technical records management. Today, around 55 percent of the company's revenues come from its aftermarket services, making it a more valuable business than the sale of new engines. And as a side benefit, TotalCare generates important data that Rolls uses to improve its engines and monitoring software.

Lush reconceived the whole concept of cosmetics with its fresh, handmade products presented in colorful, delicatessen-style outlets and fun mail-order catalogs. Rather than following the rest of the beauty industry, founder Mark Constantine asked, "Why can't you order a 'slice' of your favorite soap or shampoo—just like fresh cheese—rather than buying it in a typical bar or bottle?"

Zara asked why a fashion brand needs its own "style." Why not create a broad selection of trendy items so there's something for everyone's taste? What if they could keep their designs fresh (and limited) by replacing them every two weeks, instead of every two months like typical clothing chains? In fact, what if the company could respond to new fashion trends in the same short space of time? And what if most of the items could be produced in the company's home country, Spain, rather than the emerging-economy sweat-shops all the other brands seem to use?

Larry Page and Sergey Brin of `Google` asked themselves if using databases of keywords (or hiring human editors to laboriously categorize web pages) was the best way for an Internet search engine to find results. What if AltaVista, Lycos, and Yahoo! were going about it all wrong? What if the relevancy of a web page could be more effectively evaluated by automatically analyzing the number of hyperlinks embedded in its HTML, and the number of other pages that were linked to it? They also asked why a search engine portal needed to have its user interface cluttered with horoscopes, weather reports, stock quotes, and advertising, when most people were only interested in search? Wouldn't it be better if the homepage only had a simple search box and a logo?

After Steve Jobs returned to `Apple` in 1997, he successfully challenged a whole series of orthodoxies. For example, why does a desktop computer have to look so dull? Why can't we put everything in a candy-colored, translucent case shaped like a gumdrop, and offer it in a range of different "flavors"? Why can't we put "1,000 songs in your pocket" by making a portable music player out of a small digital storage device?

And what if we combined it with a super-simple and *legal* way to purchase and download music tracks online? Who says smartphones have to be so clunky? Why can't we create our own touchscreen phone with almost limitless functions that can be enabled with downloadable "apps"? Who says there's no market for tablet computers just because a few others have tried and failed? Why do we need to leave our consumer sales up to the big-box retailers? What stops us from opening our own stores and directly controlling the Apple brand experience? And who says we have to follow the established rules of designing retail space?

The folks behind `Beats by Dre` asked themselves why every other field of consumer electronics—TVs, laptops, smartphones—was being dramatically improved, while people were still listening to music with cheap, low-performance earbuds. What if there was a market for premium headphones, costing hundreds of dollars, that would reproduce music the way artists wanted their songs to be heard? And what if those headphones could be marketed as a fashion statement, not just as an audio accessory? Luke Wood, CEO of Beats by Dre, recalls that "people thought we were crazy. They said the marketplace would never support a $300 headphone."[4] Well, once again, here's to the crazy ones. Today, premium headphones are one of the fastest-growing categories in the consumer electronics industry, making up over 40 percent of all headphone sales, and Beats owns over 60 percent of that market. In 2014, Apple acquired Beats Electronics for $3 billion.

On a path of
disruption

If we're looking for a contemporary innovator who completely epitomizes the principle of challenging orthodoxies, it would have to be Elon Musk—of Tesla, SpaceX, and SolarCity fame.

His path of disruption began in the days of the Wild Wild Web of the mid- to late-nineties, when it simply wasn't safe or easy to move money around online. Musk refused to accept that it had to be so, or that only giant financial services companies could come up with a solution. So in March 1999 he decided to start his own Internet financial services company, called X.com, which quickly became one of the Web's leading financial institutions. One year later, in March 2000, X.com bought another Internet startup called Confinity and formed PayPal. In 2002, eBay bought PayPal for $1.5 billion. Today, PayPal is the leading global online payment-transfer provider.

So what did Elon Musk do next? Sit back and enjoy his millions? Nope. As Chris Anderson put it in a *Wired* magazine interview, "he decided to disrupt the most difficult-to-master industries in the world."[5] The first of these industries was astronautics—a field that was assumed to be the exclusive territory of large government-funded organizations like NASA. Musk's fundamental question was, "Why do space rockets have to be so expensive?" He took a look at the actual material cost of a rocket—the aluminum alloys, titanium, copper, and carbon fiber—and found that it represented only about 2 percent of the typical price of the rocket itself. The rest of the costs came from bureaucratic industry practices and

outdated technologies. So, having decided this was a crazy and unacceptable ratio, he set out to design and build his own space rockets with the audacious goal of reducing the cost of rocket launches by a factor of 10. In June 2002, Musk founded SpaceX with $100 million of his early fortune, aiming to reinvent rocket technology from scratch, and to challenge a plethora of orthodoxies and assumptions that had been around since the 1960s.

Over the last decade, Musk's SpaceX team has designed, built, and launched a whole series of next-generation rockets that have changed industry economics. Around 70 percent of each rocket is manufactured in-house at the company's complex in Hawthorne, California, providing better control over costs, quality, and delivery schedules.[6] In fact, SpaceX is already the largest producer of rocket engines in the United States. In 2008, NASA awarded the company a $1.6 billion contract for 12 cargo flights to and from the International Space Station,[7] effectively replacing the Space Shuttle. And on May 25, 2012, SpaceX made history when its Dragon spacecraft became the first commercial vehicle to successfully dock with the International Space Station.[8] It is estimated that SpaceX projects like these are saving U.S. taxpayers at least a billion dollars a year. Musk is currently working on his next challenge to conventional wisdom in the industry—a revolutionary reusable rocket called the Grasshopper. And his longer term goal is a manned mission to Mars and back. Meanwhile, SpaceX is reportedly valued at upward of $4 billion.[9]

Then, of course, there is the automobile industry. Elon Musk is also reinventing the way we drive. In 2003, he cofounded Tesla Motors to create affordable mass market all-electric vehicles for mainstream consumers. Ten years later, his "sexy and green" Tesla Model S was the third-best-selling luxury car in California (the biggest economy in America and the 12th largest in the world), after Mercedes and BMW, with a 12.7 percent share of the market.[10] The Model S received the highest ever *Consumer Reports* rating,[11] and has picked up numerous auto awards. Tesla has understandably become a favorite on the NASDAQ, and has dominated the financial headlines with the meteoric rise in its stock price (up 625 percent in a single year). In February 2014, Tesla's market capitalization went above $30 billion for the first time, making it worth over half as much as GM.[12] Not bad for a venture that everyone in the automobile industry predicted would be a disaster.

Again, Musk's whole success story is based on his propensity for challenging industry orthodoxies. In an interview at the 2013 All Things Digital conference, he talked about some of the false assumptions that have dominated the thinking of Detroit's senior executives for decades. One was that "you couldn't make a compelling electric car—one that was aesthetically appealing, long-range, and high performance."[13] The Model S has

definitely put those doubts to rest. Its design is visually stunning, it can drive between 265 and 300 miles (426–480 km) on a single full charge, and it accelerates from 0 to 60 mph (0–97 km/h) in just 4.2 seconds. Another was that "even if you did all those things, people would still not buy it because it was electric."[14] Oh, really? In 2013, Tesla sold 18,000 Model S vehicles in the United States, which is 30 percent more luxury sedans than its nearest competitor, Mercedes, with sales of its S-Class reaching only 13,303 in the same period.[15]

There were also other deeply held and widely shared beliefs that had put the brakes on the electric car opportunity for years. Musk had been told, "You'll never be able to bring it to market, you'll never be able to produce it in volumes, and you'll never be able to make a profit." One assumption was that Tesla would need a global dealer network to actually distribute and sell the cars. Instead, Musk decided to market directly to consumers via the Internet, bypassing franchised dealerships and cutting out all the intermediate costs (which has, of course, upset the big auto dealer associations—so much so that they have lobbied with government officials to force Tesla into using the franchise system). It turns out that Tesla also threatens a dealership's traditional service and maintenance model (which is where most of the profit comes from), because

its electric motor never requires new spark plugs, oil changes, or tune-ups, and there's no exhaust pipe to replace. In terms of producing electric cars in volume, just 18 months after the first Model S rolled off the line, Tesla had already sold 25,000 units.[16] Now the company is gearing up to produce 20,000 cars per month at its factory in Fremont, California (which actually has the scale to build half a million cars annually), with the help of a new Gigafactory in Reno, Nevada, for battery production.[17] And what about the financials? In 2013, Tesla's revenues were in excess of $2 billion, five times higher than the preceding year, and the company had already started turning a profit.

The last piece of the puzzle was infrastructure. That's where Musk was also told his concept would ultimately fail—there simply wouldn't be enough electric charging stations to make the car viable for longer-range travel. But Tesla has solved this problem by building its own network of "Superchargers" that already covers most of North America and parts of Canada, and is now expanding in other major markets around the world.

In another highly unorthodox move, Musk has made all of Tesla's patents open source in order help create a common, rapidly-evolving technology platform for the automotive industry.

It's still relatively early days for Tesla Motors, but one thing is already clear: The auto "experts" who once shook their heads or laughed at Musk's audacity are now sitting up and rethinking their game. One could say the industry has received a major "electric shock."

In addition to disrupting space travel and automobiles, Elon Musk is transforming the energy sector with SolarCity, a startup that leases solar-power systems to homeowners. And he made global headlines again in 2013 with another breakthrough concept called Hyperloop—a hypothetical mode of high-speed transportation.

Like Steve Jobs, to whom Musk has often been compared, it's by successfully delivering on the biggest, most radical ideas that one becomes an innovation icon. Rolfe Winkler of the *Wall Street Journal* wrote, "Each time Mr. Musk delivers a better, less-expensive electric car or launches another rocket successfully, he proves his doubters wrong."[18] In *Time* magazine's "100 Most Influential People in the World," Musk was described as "a Renaissance man in an era that needs them."[19] That's as good a description as any for this serial disruptor, whose net worth is now estimated at over $8 billion.

Innovation
means shifting assumptions

Who says there's only one way to make a sports shoe?

Athletic shoes are typically made by cutting material into appropriately shaped pieces and then stitching them together. With the Flyknit, Nike completely reconceived shoe manufacturing by finding a way to knit the shoe in one piece (it's actually more like a thick, flexible sock) rather than assembling it. This innovation is especially bold, given that Nike owns half the running shoe market and 92 percent of the basketball shoe market.[20]

Who says a candy store is only meant for kids?

At a time when celebrities and officials are campaigning to ban sugar, candy veteran Jeff Rubin is making a fortune with his brainchild, IT'SUGAR—the fastest-growing retail candy chain in the world. As if the name of the store were not contrarian enough, Rubin's concept is aimed at adult customers rather than children, selling everything from pink marshmallow Peeps to edible underwear in a cheeky environment designed to appeal to twenty-somethings.[21]

Looking through the Four Lenses

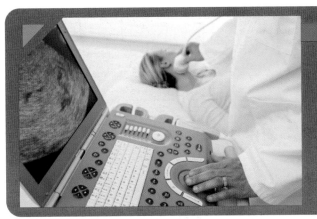

Who says ultrasound equipment is just for hospitals?

The only place to find an ultrasound machine has traditionally been a hospital or clinic. But GE Healthcare challenged that orthodoxy by creating a small, portable ultrasound device called Logiq, which sports doctors can easily carry onto the field and use to examine an athlete's body minutes after an injury.[22] Recently, GE went a radical step further by introducing a pocket-sized, hand-held ultrasound device called Vscan, which is roughly the size of a smartphone and can be taken anywhere.

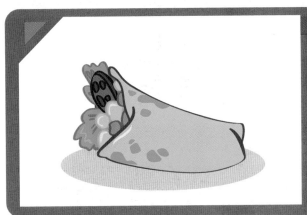

Who says fast food isn't healthy or sustainable?

Chipotle brings fresh produce into its stores every day, sourcing ingredients from sustainable farmers who raise pigs naturally and let chickens roam free rather than penning them up in crates. "Food with Integrity" is the chain's motto.[23] Instead of moving to highly processed foods, the company stands firm on its commitment to healthy ingredients and being able to proudly tell its customers what's actually in their burritos.

Who says you can't watch TV shows on the go?

HBO GO is a comprehensive "TV Everywhere" service that lets subscribers stream any of its 1,600 hours of programming to their mobile devices for free. HBO believes the more content, the better. Rich content helps HBO retain customers and keep them interested. To deepen the engagement factor, HBO provides bonus features for some of its popular features, like *Game of Thrones*, where subscribers can access characters' family trees, maps, and the like.[24]

Who says it takes years to build a skyscraper?

When Dubai's Burj Khalifa tower became the world's tallest building in 2010, it had taken over five years to build. But a company in China called BSB (Broad Sustainable Building) aims to build what will become the world's tallest skyscraper in just 90 days.[25] Sound like a joke? Think again. Using an innovative construction method based on factory-built prefabricated units, BSB has already built a 30-story tower in 15 days, and a 15-story hotel in just 48 hours!

Who says truffles can only be grown in Europe?

Truffles are a pricey delicacy normally only associated with specialist growers in Italy and France. Few have ever questioned that tradition. But that didn't stop Susan Rice Alexander from trying to cultivate truffles on a 200-acre plot in Vass, North Carolina. After learning all she could from the European experts, she has successfully created the second largest truffle orchard in the world, shipping fresh "diamonds of the kitchen" (which retail for $1,500 a pound) to the finest U.S. restaurants, and launching her own products like truffled popcorn.[26]

Who says sports coverage is limited to the season?

Football season is short, with the fewest number of games in sports. That's not great if you only make money on the live games. So the NFL has extended TV coverage across all 12 months of the year by televising draft preparation, league meetings, the scouting combine, the actual player draft, free agency in the summer, preseason, regular season, playoffs, and the Super Bowl, not to mention all the endless analysis, conjecture, and gossip.[27] That means there's no off-season anymore. Sports coverage has become a non-stop, all year round experience.

Looking through the Four Lenses

A doctor's office for healthy people

Imagine visiting a doctor's office that has a modern, friendly interior like an Apple Store, and no waiting room full of sick people—in fact, no sick people or waiting room at all. This is WellnessMart. It's for healthy customers who only need routine stuff like a travel shot, a vaccination, a physical exam, a lab test, or a tattoo removed. Founded by physician Richard McCauley, WellnessMart offers a radically different healthcare experience.[28] It's open seven days a week, with no appointments or insurance necessary.

A battery on a pin head

Researchers at Harvard University and the University of Illinois have found a way to 3D-print a powerful lithium-ion battery that's about the size of a grain of sand.[29] We'll need these tiny energy sources to power the next generation of mobile equipment—imagine them inside minuscule medical devices that are implanted in the human body, or woven into the fabric of a flexible smartphone, or in the myriad of smart sensors required by the Internet of Things.

A restaurant suspended in the sky

Getting bored with the same old dining experience at your favorite restaurant? Just for a change, how about eating a gourmet meal at a table that's dangling from a crane 200 feet (60 m) above the ground? Two Belgian entrepreneurs introduced the

concept as a publicity stunt in 2007. Today "Dinner in the Sky" is a global franchise in 40 countries that serves about 1,000 people a month.[30] Diners get magnificent aerial views of cities like Paris, London, Rome, or Las Vegas, while enjoying great food and wine, and even musicians and dancers. Now that's taking haute cuisine to new heights!

An electric airplane with rotor-blades in its wings

At the Paris Air Show in June 2013, helicopter maker AgustaWestland displayed the world's first all-electric aircraft with tilt-rotors embedded in its wings.[31] Called Project Zero, the rechargeable aircraft takes off vertically like a helicopter, then tilts the rotors 90 degrees so that it can fly at high speed like a plane. It represents a convergence of technologies that opens completely new possibilities for the future of flight.

A virtual supermarket for busy commuters

In 2011, British grocery giant Tesco opened the world's first virtual supermarket as part of its Homeplus business in South Korea.[32] The award-winning concept, which was first used in a subway station in Seoul, is based on interactive panels from which customers select and order products (using a shopping app on their smartphones) that are delivered to their homes the same day.[33] It's so popular with busy commuters that Homeplus has since opened virtual stores in many other locations, including bus stops. Now Tesco has introduced it to the UK, with the first virtual supermarket at London Gatwick Airport.

An apartment building powered by algae

Forget about electricity bills, and solar or wind energy, for that matter. Splitterwerk, the Austrian architecture firm, has created the world's first building that gets all its power from algae.[34] The five-story residential building is in Hamburg, Germany. It has a bioreactor façade made of glass strips containing micro-algae that convert sunlight into energy, generating 34,000 kilowatts of power annually for the apartments inside (that's three times more than the average American home uses yearly).

An optician that sells its glasses online

Warby Parker sells designer-type prescription eyeglasses and sunglasses at a fraction of the price that is common in optical stores and fashion boutiques. How? By selling directly to consumers via their website, thus circumventing traditional retail channels that commonly mark up such products by two or three hundred percent. The company ships up to five frames (no charge for shipping) to customers so they can try them on before buying,[35] and succeeded in selling more than 100,000 pairs of glasses in just its second year.[36]

A "silk" dress made from milk yarn

Most clothes are traditionally made from cotton, hemp, wool, or synthetic polymers. But one microbiology student has found a way to extract protein fibers from milk, which she then spins into yarn.[37] The material is used to make clothes which feel like silk, and which can be washed and laundered just like other garments. The fabric has benefits for both the wearer and the environment. It is antibacterial, non-allergenic, and requires only a half gallon of water to produce two pounds of material, compared to thousands of gallons of water to make the same amount of cotton.

What if you
CHALLENGE
your assumptions?

LESSONS
TO TAKE AWAY

Orthodoxies can easily blind us and our organizations to new ways of doing things. (They create the proverbial "box" within which we come to think and operate, and make it difficult for us to see outside of these fixed boundaries.)

Learn from disruptive industry newcomers. (They have no preconceptions about how an industry is "supposed" to work, so they spot the opportunities for revolution that incumbents either don't see or don't want to accept.)

Innovators tend to be contrarians, heretics, and revolutionaries. (We have to be willing to challenge conventional thinking and to shift our basic assumptions.)

Try to identify and systematically question the fixed patterns that exist inside your own company, and across your industry. (Is there really only one "right" way of doing things? What if you opened your mind to radical alternatives?)

Remember, it's the "crazy" ones who change the world. (Whenever you hear "that's just the way it is," take it as an invitation to imagine how it could be or should be—then go out and make it happen!)

An orthodoxy is a deeply held belief, a traditional practice, or a conventional way of thinking that is commonly assumed to be true or correct. (Orthodoxies form habitual patterns of thought and behavior that are rarely questioned.)

Avoid the inhibiting trap of "mental inertia." (It's the tendency to maintain a particular mind-set, and to stubbornly resist any change in thinking and behavior, unless some external force exerts pressure otherwise.)

SEEING THE
FUTURE
IN THE PRESENT

Innovators understand change. They welcome it rather than trying to resist it. Somehow they know how to make change work for them rather than against them. They have the skills that enable them to turn discontinuity into opportunity.

It's not that innovators are better at trend forecasting or scenario planning. They are not futurists. They don't have any proprietary data about "the next big thing," and they are not very interested in making long-term predictions. It's just that they seem to have a knack for recognizing and harnessing the potential of things that are already changing, where others do not. To paraphrase Martha Graham, "No innovator is ahead of his time. He *is* his time. It is just that others are behind the times."

Did Amazon know something about the future of retail that Walmart didn't? Did Apple know something about the future of mobile telephony that Nokia or Motorola didn't? Did Netflix know something about the future of movie rental that Blockbuster didn't? Everything that needed to be known to revolutionize these industries was already known by both the pioneers and the laggards. All the data was out there in the public domain. The difference is that the industry challengers saw an opportunity to use the power of change to their own advantage, while the incumbents either underestimated or ignored critical trends until it was too late to catch up.

In his book *Mind Set! Reset Your Thinking and See the Future*, John Naisbitt—who has spent decades successfully studying emerging trends—astutely noted that "the future is embedded in the present."[38] Similarly, novelist William Gibson once remarked in a radio interview that "the future is already here—it's just not evenly distributed."[39] Innovators intuitively get this. Their ability to imagine what's next comes from their keen awareness and understanding of what is happening now. They look at the same panorama of information as everyone else, but they see more, and they see things differently. Just as an eagle can reportedly spot a rabbit moving in the grassland 2 miles (3.2 km) away, or spy a fish swimming under the rippling surface of the water from a great height above, radical innovators tend to have a wider field of view and an amazing sharp-sightedness, allowing them to perceive even minimal changes taking place in the landscape. They pay attention to a much broader range of inputs. They show more acute interest in what is going on in the world around them. They are sensitive and alert to the kinds of trends that—if scaled up—could profoundly impact the future, or that could enable them to drive significant industry change.

Innovators are not just better at picking up the signals. They are better at *reading* them. Their accurate powers of observation are matched by exceptional powers of reflection. They have a deep curiosity that makes them wonder where some nascent development might eventually lead, how it could potentially alter the current rules of competition, what kind of new value it might create for customers, or what would possibly happen if this trend intersected with others. They take the same basic information that is openly available to everyone else, but they construct out of it a clear, compelling, and unique vision about how they could use the momentum of change to shape the future. Most importantly, they act on this vision before others do, usually because their rivals are still denying or discounting the importance of these change factors. As Harvard professor and philosopher Willard Van Orman Quine once put it, "One man's observation is another man's closed book or flight of fancy."[40]

"The future will be influenced by trends that are now existent and observable."[41]

Emily Greene Balch

HARNESSING TRENDS

A global "change bomb"

Whether we like it or not, "shift happens." The pace of change has gone hypercritical. Think about how much difference a decade makes. If we turn back the clock to 1997, for instance, most of us were probably just getting our first simple cell phones, Google didn't yet exist, and Apple was so down on its luck that Steve Jobs was begging arch-nemesis Microsoft for a bailout. Ten years later, we had sexy and sophisticated iPhones in our pockets, Google was one of the top 10 biggest companies by market cap, and Apple was the most valuable computer maker in the world.

When Antonio Pérez became CEO of Eastman Kodak in 2005, the company's market cap stood at over $9 billion[42] and its future in a new era of digital photography looked bright. In fact, at the time, Kodak was the best-selling brand of digital cameras in the United States.[43] Over in Finland, Jorma Ollila, chairman and CEO of Nokia, was also looking forward to the years ahead. With a market cap of over $98 billion,[44] a global market share of close to 40 percent, and a brand new range of products ready to launch, Nokia's continued domination of the mobile phone market looked like a no-brainer. Just 10 years later the great Eastman Kodak company was bankrupt, and what was left of Nokia's once-giant phone business was sold to Microsoft for the bargain basement sum of just $7 billion.

Remember the days before social media? Again, let's go back to the beginning of 2003, which wasn't a million years ago. Back then, there was no such thing as Facebook, Twitter, or LinkedIn, and China had never heard of Qzone or Tencent Weibo. Nobody used their mobile phones for social networking activities other than sending friends short messages, or conversing in chat rooms, or of course telephone calls. But how quickly things changed. Ten years later, Facebook had well over a billion users, Twitter nearly 646 million users, LinkedIn 225 million users, Qzone 712 million users, and Weibo 507 million users. And thanks to the advent of 3G, camera phones, mobile data services, apps, widgets, media sharing, location software, and more recently 4G, social media has become by far the main driver of mobile Internet usage all over the world. Hundreds of millions of people can now no longer imagine their lives without their daily dose of information exchange, content sharing, community interaction, and self-expression on their favorite social media sites, either via computer, tablet, or smartphone.

When Apple's App Store officially opened in July 2008, Steve Jobs proudly told *USA Today* that it already offered 500 downloadable applications for the iPhone.[45] Today, there are well over a million apps available on the store. Less than five years after its launch, Apple announced that the App Store had just had its 50 billionth download. At the time, customers were downloading more than 800 apps per second, and over 2 billion apps per month.[46] Nothing has ever accelerated so rapidly in the history of humanity. Think about your own business. How much has it changed over the last decade? How much is it likely to change in the next 10 years? Is there any company or industry on earth today that can realistically expect the future to be a linear extrapolation of the past? The fact is that linearity and predictability no longer exist. These concepts are outdated. They are an artificial and misleading way of viewing the world. Change is increasingly non-linear, discontinuous, and unpredictable, which is why the future is becoming less and less like the past, and less like we expected it to be. Every day we seem to get new surprises, as somebody somewhere adds a little more change to the world, which interacts with all the other changes taking place in countless domains so that the whole effect is cumulative. Think of it as a global "change bomb." The more networked and interconnected we all are, the more each individual change inspires, enables, builds upon, and collides with other changes, so that everything gets multiplied in a giant, self-propagating chain reaction. That's why the rate of change has become exponential, and why the impact of change has become so explosive.

The race for **tomorrow**

Once we accept that the future is going to be a series of discontinuities, some of them with potentially disruptive consequences, it becomes clear that we need to alter our perspective toward the dynamics of whatever business we are in. Instead of viewing change as a constantly irritating and threatening aberration from the way things are supposed to be, we need to start embracing this endless stream of aberrations as the new norm. In fact, we have to realize that the only way to ensure the continuity of a company over time is to make certain it is changing as fast as the world is changing.

Jack Welch, the illustrious ex-CEO of GE, once remarked, "If the rate of change on the outside exceeds the rate of change on the inside, the end is near."[47] This is a message every organization should take to heart. There is a pressing need for acceleration, not just in the pace at which we generally do business, but in the pace at which we develop foresight about the future and then use that foresight to adapt and evolve our corporations. We need to speed up our efforts to understand the portent of discontinuous change, as well as our efforts to harness the power of that change in our products, services, strategies

and business models. One of the fundamental lessons of our times is that business success is increasingly transient; it must be rapidly and incessantly renewed if it is to be sustained.

Many senior executives, if they are honest, would admit that they are currently more concerned with internal organizational issues than they are with the maelstrom of change happening in the external environment. Their eyeballs are predominantly focused inward rather than outward. Of course, there's nothing wrong with trying to optimize a company's operational effectiveness. Indeed, it's an absolute must for staying in the game. The problem starts when leaders are so preoccupied with making improvements to today's business that they fail to notice the discontinuities that could fundamentally reinvent their business tomorrow. They need to make sure they are also devoting enough time, energy, and bandwidth to learning about the evolution of their industry, the rapidly changing competitive landscape, and the emerging needs of their customers. They should be thinking deeply about the implications of incipient trends and technologies, and about how their industry might be fundamentally different 10 years from now

Admittedly, it is not at all easy to keep up with and even ahead of the change curve. For a start, exactly which change curve are we talking about? There is just so much happening simultaneously in so many spheres. In addition to trends specific to any given industry, deep changes are also taking place in technologies, lifestyles, work styles, consumer behavior, demographics, economics, regulation, sustainability, geopolitics, the continuous churning of competitors and collaborators in the market, and a wide range of other fields. Any one of these trends may one day trigger a radical departure from the way things are now, so we need to make sure that all of them are on the management radar screen. But staying abreast of so many changes can make companies feel like they are running full speed ahead in all directions. It's like being stretched apart on a torture rack!

Most businesspeople shy away from the hard intellectual work involved in synthesizing a proprietary vision of the future out of all this disparate data. It can be extremely discomforting and time-consuming to try to make strategic sense out of so much

office door and sit there in denial, immersing yourself in running the business as it is today, and trusting that the future will take care of itself. But we could compare this to having a few glasses of whisky each evening to help you cope with your troubles. You know deep down that those problems are not really solved—in fact they might be getting worse—but you temporarily feel better about them because you have drugged yourself into ignoring them. Likewise, too many organizations have allowed themselves to get addicted to short-term, quarter-to-quarter objectives and internal issues while they ignore the drivers of external change that could potentially reshape their future. It's as if they hope that revolutionary trends—and perhaps any disruptive pioneers that are already harnessing them—will somehow just go away.

> *"Innovation is a continuum. You have to think about how the world is transforming and evolving. Are you part of the continuum?"*[48]
>
> *Marc Benioff, Founder and CEO, Salesforce.com*

> "Lots of companies don't succeed over time. What do they fundamentally do wrong? They usually miss the future."
>
> *Larry Page, CEO Google*

Getting off that drug—tearing down the mental façade that business as usual will be sufficient, and that current priorities are more urgent and important than future ones—is quite a challenge. And often it takes a crisis to produce a change of mind-set. At some point a serious threat comes along that creates a strong sense of urgency inside the company—a sense that future success is no longer inevitable—and people finally begin to sit up and take notice. Sadly, when a company reaches this point it can already be too late for the deep strategic realignment or organizational transformation that may be necessary to avoid disaster.

That's why it's far better to build a system right now for continuously spotting and anticipating the driving forces that are most likely to impact the future of your industry, or which could be harnessed to gain a strategic advantage over your competitors. You need to get busy figuring out how these change factors might be utilized to create new value for your customers and to grow new sources of profit for your company—before your rivals beat you to it. Truly innovative companies are always trying to imagine whether particular trends, or clusters of trends, might open up significant new growth opportunities in the future, and then they move fast to acquire the skills and assets that will enable them to capture the maximum share of those opportunities.

In many ways, innovation is "a race to the future," as C. K. Prahalad, the renowned thought leader on business strategy, once put it.[49] And the only way to get to the future before the competition is by working hard to develop a better understanding about how things are changing, planning the appropriate strategic response, and then doing whatever it takes to quickly close the gap between today and tomorrow.

Artificial intelligence. Augmented reality. Cars and trucks that drive themselves. Wearable computers and embeddable implants. Aerial drones that can deliver things to our doorsteps. For many of us, the future has arrived perhaps earlier than expected. We now have paper-thin, flexible smartphones, 3D printers for the home, "Iron Man"-like exoskeleton suits, high-performance electric cars, virtual super-markets, smart thermostats and smoke detectors that learn our behaviors, speech recognition software for controlling our devices, apps for almost everything, social television, 3D holographic displays, wireless electricity, the "Internet of Things," deep data mining, humanoid robots, engineered stem cells, self-diagnostic medi-cine, biomaterials—and the list gets more astounding every day. This is no longer the stuff of science fiction. It's the shape of things that are already here.

Yet all of these technological breakthroughs started out as small, relatively insignificant developments that few people took seriously and most didn't even notice. For quite some time they remained out there on the fringe, with their propo-nents perhaps viewed as a little wacky, until all of a sudden they hit an inflection point where they began to quickly gain acceptance and momentum, and to have an impact on our collective consciousness. From there, it's usually not much of a leap before something goes completely mainstream.

Learning to ride the
waves

Trends and discontinuities are patterns of change. When they start out, these patterns may be imperceptible to most people. But innovators begin to notice. They have the foresight to see things before the curve. They are somehow able to join the dots before others do. They start to wonder if there is an incipient trend here, where that trend might lead if it were to scale up, and how it might intersect with other trends. Innovators can sense a disruptive discontinuity in the making, and they intuitively know when they are on to something. Just like venture capitalists, analysts, investors, and people who run tech accelerators, these visionary innovators know that success is often a matter of making a bet on the future.

I like to think of innovators as wave riders. They see what others would dismiss as a ripple on the ocean and somehow recognize it as an oncoming tsunami of change. Then, with perfect timing, they find a way to ride that wave before anyone else, attaching their business to the gathering momentum of the change curve, and thus dramatically multiplying their growth potential. By the time competitors finally wake up to what is happening—usually when the water is already flooding into their business model and threatening to sink it—the innovators are already way out in front.

Just as a literal tsunami can cause untold physical damage, these tsunamis of change can be devastating for particular industries and their incumbent players. The tsunami for Kodak, for example, was the lightning-fast adoption by Gen Y of digital photography (ironically, a technology that the company invented itself but failed to harness and monetize in ways that resonated with customers). The tsunami for the music industry was digital distribution, first in the form of illegal file-sharing services like Napster and The Pirate Bay, and later with the winning combination of Apple's iTunes Music Store and the iPod. The tsunami for Nokia and BlackBerry was the touchscreen iPhone, with its instant consumer appeal and almost unlimited ways to add functionality through the App Store. (Of course, the tsunami for the iPhone today is Google Android, which is already running on 80 percent of the world's smartphones. App downloads from Google's Play Store now surpass those for Apple's App Store.) The tsunami for Blockbuster was video streaming, with digital-only services like Amazon Instant, HBO, and Netflix replacing Main Street movie rental stores almost overnight.

In true tsunami style, these giant waves of change hit an industry with incredible speed and destructive force. Consider the disruptive impact of Airbnb on the hospitality industry, or the cataclysmic threat to traditional taxi services that comes from private transportation startups like Uber, Lyft, and Sidecar.

Every company should regularly ask itself, **"What will be the tsunami in our own industry? How can we make sure we ride that wave instead of being washed away by it?"**

Waves of change come in different sizes. Futurist Alvin Toffler famously described three mega waves in human history—first, agricultural society, then the Industrial Age, and finally the Information Age. At an intermediate level, there are tsunamis of change or "tides of history"—major discontinuities that are impossible to suppress or restrain. Consider technological progress. As the nineteenth century gave way to the twentieth, nothing could have realistically stopped electric lighting from replacing gas lighting, or telephony from replacing the telegraph, or the combustion engine from replacing horse-drawn carriages. In more modern times, we have also experienced giant, inexorable waves of change that are still transforming people's lives all around the world—including the Internet, globalization, social media, and mobile communications and computing.

At a lower level, there are waves that represent changes in popular tastes, habits, fashions, and spending priorities. Although these waves are smaller by nature, they can still have a powerful impact on the industry sectors they affect. Think about the general shift in consumer preferences away from carbonated drinks, fast food, white bread, and packaged foods and cereals (full of fat, salt, and sugar), toward healthier, freshly prepared, low-carbohydrate or organic alternatives. How does this influence the business of companies like Coca-Cola, PepsiCo, McDonald's, General Mills, Kellogg's, Nestle, or Kraft Foods? And what about the trend away from expensive, physical toys and board games toward cheap or even free digital games on mobile devices? How do you think that touches companies like LEGO, Mattel, Hasbro, or Playmobil? What if you are a razor blade manufacturer like Gillette, Schick, or Wilkinson Sword and you find out that more and more men are choosing to stop shaving daily and grow fashionable facial hair? And what happens to the world's great detergent makers—like Procter & Gamble, Colgate-Palmolive, Unilever, and Henkel—as washing machines become increasingly efficient and require less and less detergent? No doubt for all of these companies such shifts are seismic.

As King Canute once demonstrated in the famous legend by placing his throne on the seashore and making a futile effort to halt the incoming tide, we cannot hope to hold back these unstoppable waves. They are going to happen no matter what we think or do. So our choice is either to harness them, respond to them, or be overwhelmed by them. As Professor Jon Kabat-Zinn once put it, "You can't stop the waves, but you can learn to surf."[50]

If we are going to learn to ride the waves of change, we first need to develop the ability to spot and recognize emerging patterns that can reveal where the world—and our business—might be or should be going in the future. We need to immerse ourselves in what is happening right now by making sure we stay closely connected with our customers, society, and the rest of the world, and by keeping our eyes and ears open at all times. This is not just about reading newspapers, magazines, and blogs from diverse fields, commissioning market research companies or trend forecasters, and attending industry conferences, all which of course have value. It's also about going out and personally experiencing things for yourself—getting a visceral sense of what is going on, rather than merely an intellectual one.

That means regularly engaging in activities that awaken your curiosity by exposing yourself to new trends, impressions, and perspectives. For example, conversing with people from different industries, demographic groups, geographies, and levels of the organization. Or visiting new and out of-the-ordinary places; eating in new restaurants; following new fashions in clothing, music, sport, movies, and theater; getting a close-up view of new technologies; and spending more time hanging out with teenagers and other people who seem to have their finger on the pulse of change. Why do so many innovations seem to come out of the world's coolest cities, busiest university campuses, most widely connected online networks, and most cutting-edge technology hubs and industry clusters? It's because those are the perfect places for people with "one foot in the future" to get together, mix and match ideas and domains, and learn about what's new and what's next.

"There is a tide in the affairs of men, which taken at the flood, leads on to fortune. . . . We must take the current when it serves, or lose our ventures."
William Shakespeare

Meet the trend surfers

It could be argued that Bill Gates built Microsoft's entire software empire on his ability to repeatedly see the next wave coming and then quickly mobilize his resources to capitalize on it. Right at the very beginning, Gates and his friend Paul Allen founded the company on the notion that computer software was going to be the industry of the future. In 1978, just three years later, Microsoft's revenues had already hit $2.5 million (Gates was only 23 at the time).[51] Gates imagined that one day there would be a computer on every desk, and he wanted it to be running on Microsoft software. As the personal computer industry began to take off, Gates made contact with IBM's CEO, and in 1980 he was asked to develop the operating system for the company's new range of PCs. Turning down IBM's offer of a flat $50,000 development fee in favor of a licensing agreement, Gates showed that he had a better understanding of where the computer industry was going than its mightiest player at the time. That legendary deal meant that Microsoft retained ownership of what became MS-DOS and could license it to other computer manufacturers. As companies around the world started producing IBM-compatible PCs and licensing Gates's OS, Microsoft's revenues went into an exponential curve, rising from $7.5 million in 1980 to $140 million by 1985.[52]

When Steve Jobs visited Microsoft in 1981 and demonstrated an early prototype of the Macintosh computer to persuade the company to develop software for it, Bill Gates saw the next wave coming—the graphical user interface and mouse. This represented a huge threat to his business because the user experience on the Mac was obviously so superior to working with MS-DOS, which displayed complicated codes on screen and required laborious text and keyboard commands. In 1983, Gates sent an internal memo to all Microsoft staffers stating that "Microsoft believes in mouse and graphics as invaluable to the man-machine interface," and publicly announced the development of Windows, which would be compatible with MS-DOS–based software.[53] In 1985, Microsoft launched Windows, and one year later Gates took the company public. By 1987, the rise in the value of his stock had made him a billionaire.

> *"We always overestimate the change that will occur in the next two years and underestimate the change that will occur in the next ten."*
>
> Bill Gates

In 1995, Bill Gates sent out another famous internal memo, this one titled "The Internet Tidal Wave," in which he recognized the Internet as "the most important single development to come along since the IBM PC was introduced in 1981."[54] He wrote that this growing phenomenon would be "crucial to every part of our business" and would "set the course of our industry for a long time to come."[55] Having recognized the potential threat from Netscape's Mosaic Internet browser (launched two years earlier), which worked independently of Windows, Gates mobilized his now-giant company to rapidly redefine its offerings for the Web. Just a few months later, Microsoft released Windows 95, bundled with MSN, The Microsoft Network online service, as well as the company's own web browser, Internet Explorer (initially a Plus! pack add-on). Having almost missed the Internet curve, Microsoft made an amazing turnaround. In fact, the company came back with such force that the U.S. Justice Department and several competitors were soon accusing Microsoft of trying to dominate the Internet. When Bill Gates handed the position of CEO to Steve Ballmer in January 2000, Microsoft's annual revenues were close to $20 billion and Gates had long since become the richest man in the world.[56]

Health food is not a new concept. The idea goes all the way back to antiquity. From Hippocrates to Galen to Vesalius, our understanding of nutrition has evolved through the ages. In the nineteenth century, there were many prominent advocates of healthy diets and vegetarianism such as the Kellogg brothers, who became best-known as the inventors of flaked breakfast cereals. The first health food store in the United States opened in 1869 (Martindale's Natural Market is still around today!), and by the 1930s there were a few other stores in the United States and England dedicated to selling vitamin and mineral supplements, as well as natural and organic foods. As agriculture became more industrialized between the 1940s and the late 1960s, in what is known as the "Green Revolution" (during which many new chemicals began to be used in farming), concern grew among the public about foods that were chemically treated, heavily processed, or grown using dangerous pesticides. By the 1960s and early 1970s, organic farming was gaining momentum as part of a larger social trend—a growing environmental awareness. This was the era that gave birth to "green" political parties, activist groups like Greenpeace, and, most influentially, a massive wave of Western youth counterculture, characterized by the hippie movement. That's when health food stores, vegetarian restaurants, and interest in herbal remedies began to be much more common, if not yet mainstream. But bigger things were to come.

In 1978, a 25-year-old college dropout and vegetarian by the name of John Mackey recognized an emerging opportunity in the health food business. A student of Eastern philosophy and religion, yoga, meditation, and ecology, Mackey had been a hippie in the counterculture heyday, and still in many ways epitomized the libertarian attitudes and lifestyle of his generation. Borrowing $45,000 from family and friends, he cofounded a small health food store in Austin, Texas, with his girlfriend Renee Lawson, and had the nerve to call it SaferWay (a spoof of the popular supermarket chain Safeway). With larger ambitions in mind, he and Renee merged their business two years later with Clarksville Natural Grocery, owned by Craig Weller and Mark Skiles, and opened a brand new store with 19 employees and a much larger format—making it more of a natural food *supermarket*. The four partners named the new store Whole Foods Market, which was a success right from the start. Back then, there were only a handful of other health food supermarkets in America, so the competition was limited, but demand was on the rise.

In 1984, Mackey began to expand outside Austin by opening new stores across the country and aggressively acquiring other natural food chains. This strategy fueled rapid growth over the next three decades, at exactly the same time as consumer health awareness was on the increase, and organic food, beverages, and other goods became more mainstream—even trendy. In 2012, the global market for these products was valued at nearly $80 billion, and it is estimated to reach almost $188 billion by 2019, at a growth rate of 15.5 percent. Whole Foods Market is poised to grab a substantial share of that business. Today, John Mackey (together with co-CEO Walter Robb) presides over an organic empire with several hundred stores in multiple countries, employing over 58,000 people, and generating $13 billion in annual revenues.

"Entrepreneurs are the true heroes. . . . They solve problems by creatively envisioning different ways the world could and should be."[57]

John Mackey, cofounder and co-CEO, Whole Foods Market

In the 1980s and early 1990s, decades of research and development in the scientific community, mostly funded by the U.S. government, evolved into the Internet we recognize today. In 1990, when the very first website appeared, only 3 million people were using the Internet worldwide. By 1994, that number had risen to over 25 million. At that point, there were already 2,738 websites, Mark Andreessen's Mosaic web browser had made it amazingly easy to navigate online, and venture capitalists were starting a gold rush by racing to fund new Internet startups. That was the year Jeff Bezos got his wake-up call. After reading a report about the hyper-accelerating growth of Internet usage, he wondered, "What kind of business plan might make sense in the context of that growth?" Settling on the idea of an online bookstore, he famously gave up his job on Wall Street to start Amazon.com. In 2000, at the time of the dot-com crash, the number of worldwide Internet users had risen to over 400 million, there were more than 17 billion websites, and Amazon had emerged as the major force in online retail. By then, the company had millions of regular customers and had expanded beyond books into many other categories. After just five years in business, with a market cap ranging from $24 billion to $28 billion, Amazon was worth more than Kmart and JCPenney combined. And Jeff Bezos, *Time* magazine's "Person of the Year" in 1999, had a personal net worth of over $10 billion.[58]

What's impressive about Bezos is that, since founding Amazon.com, he has continued to ride successive waves of change. For example, after eBay took off in the late 1990s, it became apparent that there was also a global and increasingly popular market for secondhand goods. To tap into this market, Amazon launched what would eventually become Amazon Marketplace to let third parties sell new and used items on the company's platform, with Amazon taking a commission for every sale. The marketplace now generates 9 percent to 12 percent of Amazon's total annual revenues. It has also been an unexpected boon in some geographies. For example, India forbids foreign retailers to sell directly to customers online, but Amazon Seller Services (the local name for the third-party marketplace) now has over 6,000 Indian merchants offering 15 million products in 28 different categories.

Another example is the Kindle. As CEO of "the world's largest bookstore," Bezos was watching the slow, uncertain rise of electronic books since the late 1990s. Like many trends, e-book readers started out on the fringe, with just one or two pioneers—notably the Softbook and the Gemstar Rocket, which were later merged. These eventually proved unsuccessful and had disappeared by 2003, the same year Barnes & Noble decided to stop selling e-books online. But, by then, what iPod and iTunes were doing for music seemed like an obvious precursor for what would soon happen to books. In 2004, Sony released the LIBRIé—featuring the first-ever electronic ink display, making the words on screen significantly easier to read—along with an iTunes-like online library for purchasing and downloading books.

Seeing an oncoming wave, Bezos took the brave decision to go into the hardware business and launch his own e-book reader. The Kindle went on sale in November 2007, just five months after the birth of the iPhone, offering customers a simple and instant way to purchase, download, and save books to the device straight from Amazon.com. The first batch of Kindles was sold out in just five and a half hours. Subsequent versions introduced superior displays for dramatically improved readability, along with touchscreen functionality. In July 2010, Amazon announced that sales of e-books for Kindle had exceeded its sales of hardcover books for the first time. A report published in June 2014 by PricewaterhouseCoopers estimated that the consumer e-book market would triple by 2018, while sales of printed books would decline. Today, the Kindle, backed by Amazon's comprehensive and robust e-book ecosystem, is the most popular e-book reader in the world.

> "What we need to do is always lean into the future; when the world changes around you and when it changes against you . . . you have to lean into that and figure out what to do."[59]
>
> *Jeff Bezos, CEO Amazon.com*

In many other ways, too, Jeff Bezos has shown that he knows how to harness trends that have the potential to reshape the world—and the retail industry. When Apple unveiled the iPad in 2010 and its sales subsequently went through the roof, Bezos immediately got to work on the Kindle Fire—a low-cost, mini tablet computer based on a custom version of Android, which gives customers a direct link to Amazon.com for easy online shopping.

As the battle to control digital media streaming has heated up between players like Apple, Google, Netflix, TiVo, Hulu, and Roku, Jeff Bezos has also entered the fray with the Amazon Fire TV set-top box, and has added a music streaming service, as well movies, games, popular TV shows, and even original TV programming, to his Amazon Prime subscription-based membership service (which is an attempt to lock customers into Amazon's ecosystem rather than, for example, Apple iTunes). And with the launch of the Fire Phone, Amazon's first smartphone, in June 2014, Bezos introduced a game-changing function called Firefly that scans and recognizes products, songs, movies, and TV episodes, and lets users instantly shop for these items (or simply check their prices) in the Amazon ecosystem. A few months later Amazon unveiled Echo, a screen-less, cylindrical computer that combines a virtual assistant (like Apple's Siri) with a far-field microphone and a music speaker. Echo is another example of Amazon's continuous efforts to lean into the future by harnessing tech trends—it's a smart, voice-controlled device for the home or office that is connected to the cloud, enabling it to answer your questions, tell you the news, take notes, or simply stream your favorite music from Amazon Prime. As online grocery sales continue to surge, Amazon has introduced AmazonFresh, Grocery & Gourmet Food Store, and more recently Prime Pantry to cater to customers looking for home-delivery convenience. And Bezos made news all around the world with his radical plans for Amazon Prime Air, a system for rapidly delivering packages via autonomous octocopter drones. The idea is currently banned by the Federal Aviation Administration, but it has generated excellent global publicity for Amazon Prime, and Bezos remains committed to the concept (the FAA has said it will revisit its ruling in future). As another alternative to delivery via courier services, Amazon has also been testing package delivery via taxi using the Flywheel cab-hailing mobile app. For years, Amazon has also been riding the self-publishing wave, providing would-be authors and best-selling writers with a powerful sales platform and a suite of tools for getting their books out into the world. And in July 2014, Bezos added a new retail section to Amazon.com dedicated to the world of 3D printing, where shoppers can browse and buy 3D printed products like toys, jewelry, or home goods (some of them customizable), along with 3D printing machines and materials. Bezos, the trend surfer, now has a personal net worth of around $30 billion, making him the world's twentieth-richest person.

THE MAN FROM THE
FUTURE

Steve Jobs perfectly exemplifies the principle of foreseeing the future and then making it happen. He had an uncanny ability to figure out where things were going long before others. Back in the mid-1970s, when mainframe computers and even minicomputers were still big and rather ominous machines, he somehow intuitively knew that everyone would one day want a personal computer—an absolutely audacious notion at the time. The Apple II, which launched the mass market for personal computers, went on to sell over 5 million units and became a common fixture in offices, schools, and homes—places nobody previously would have expected to see a computer. And of course that was just the beginning. With the introduction of the Macintosh in 1984, Jobs demonstrated his belief that technology in the future would be more "human" and less like a machine. He envisioned the computer as an appliance that was elegantly designed, friendly (it started up with a smiling face), intuitively easy to use (with a graphical user interface and mouse), and democratized ("the computer for the rest of us.")[60] This vision was in many ways decades ahead of its time.

During his "wilderness" years in exile from Apple, from the mid-1980s to the mid-1990s, Jobs continued to invest in technologies that he believed represented the future of computing. Although his company NeXT was not really a commercial success in terms of hardware sales, the technologies on which its products were based—such as object-oriented programming—went on to influence the rest of the computer industry. And when Apple decided to buy the company from Jobs in 1996, NeXT's software platform became the core for what would become Apple OS X and eventually iOS— still considered the industry benchmarks for computer and mobile operating systems.

Along the way, Jobs had also invested in a little spinout company from Lucasfilm's Computer Graphics Division called Pixar, which nobody else was interested in. Seeing a big future opportunity in 3D computer rendering, his original plan was to further develop Pixar's high-end computer hardware for professional use, as well as the company's 3D animation software (called Typestry) for home PCs. But before long, Jobs came to share the real dream of Pixar's principals: creating digitally animated TV commercials and even movies, at a time when computers didn't have enough processing power or memory to make that idea very practical or affordable. Over the next few years, while waiting for Moore's Law to catch up with their ambitions, the Pixar team produced the first version of RenderMan—a revolutionary

software program that went on to become the industry standard for CGI rendering—and made several computer-animated short films and commercials. After winning numerous awards and nominations for this work, including an Oscar, Pixar teamed up with Disney to create *Toy Story*—the world's first computer-animated feature-length film, which became the highest-grossing movie of 1995. The rest is history: the Pixar IPO that made Steve Jobs a billionaire for the first time, the string of hit movies, and the sale to Disney for $7.4 billion.

On his return to Apple in 1997, Jobs was pushing an updated version of his original vision for the future of computing. First and foremost, it was going to be about cool consumer products, not boring business tools. The candy-colored, translucent iMac, Jobs's initial collaboration with Apple Design Chief Jonathan Ive, was the first manifestation of this vision under the "Think Different" banner. It ushered in a new era of industrial design, not just in the computer industry, but in countless other industries, too. Second, computers were going to be digital hubs for storing and sharing personal media—such as music, photos, videos, movies, and games. With this strategy in mind, Jobs and his team decided to focus first on introducing a portable MP3 music player, based on an ultra-thin 5-gigabyte hard drive. Why choose music? Because, as Jobs explained in his introduction of the iPod, "Music's a part of everyone's life. Everyone. Music's been around forever. It will always be around. This is not a speculative market. And, because it's a part of everyone's life, it's a very large target market. All around the world. It knows no boundaries." Within six years, the iPod accounted for half of Apple's revenues.

Steve Jobs could see where the music industry was headed, even if most music executives refused to accept it. As Napster's pirate platform had powerfully demonstrated, it was going to be impossible to hold back the tide of digital music downloads. The only real solution was to find a way to make it legal—to create an easy-to-use music download platform that would work for both the music industry and the consumer. That platform was the iTunes Music Store—which was an amazing achievement for Jobs to pull off, given the competitive nature of the music industry and its intense aversion to digital distribution. Launched in 2003, iTunes sold 70 million songs in just its first year, and in three years that figure had risen to 1 billion. The success of iTunes also had a knock-on effect for sales of the iPod, which rose from less than 1 million in 2003 to nearly 23 million in 2005. In just five years, iTunes was already selling more music than Best Buy in the United States, and by 2010 it had become the largest music retailer on earth. Today, the iTunes Store—which has long since expanded into music videos, TV shows, movies, books, and apps—is at the core of Apple's strategy to dominate the home and mobile entertainment markets.

Another excellent case study of Steve Jobs's foresight is the iPhone. This is an instance where he saw future developments not as an opportunity but as a threat. In 2005, despite the phenomenal sales success of the iPod, Jobs saw a tsunami looming on the horizon that had the potential to completely destroy his star product. That tsunami was the cell phone. He reasoned that if mobile phone companies could turn their devices into easy-to-use music players, the iPod would be obsolete. Having watched the cell phone replace digital cameras, alarm clocks, personal digital assistants, and other dedicated devices, it seemed only a matter of time before the iPod would go the same way. Why would anyone want to carry around two devices when they could combine both functions in one? And while millions of people had an iPod, "everyone carries a phone," Jobs explained to Apple's board. So instead of trying to circle the wagons around his current business, Jobs set out to mercilessly cannibalize the iPod before anyone else could do it, by developing Apple's own cell phone. In the process, he and his team totally revolutionized the concept of the smartphone and shaped the whole future of mobile devices. Just four years after launching the iPhone, Apple surpassed Nokia as the largest mobile handset company in the world by revenue.

The story of the iPad is different, but in some ways it gives us an even more profound display of Steve Jobs's vision.

A secret team at Apple had been working on a touchscreen tablet as early as 2003, long before Jobs started thinking about developing a mobile phone. But when work started on the iPhone (codenamed "Project Purple"), he realized the multitouch finger-sensitive screen would be the optimum interface for the new phone—allowing for brilliant multimedia display as well as simplifying all of the device's control and typing functions. Thus, the tablet project was temporarily postponed and its technology was incorporated into the iPhone. Following the phenomenal success of the iPhone and especially of the App Store platform, Jobs felt the time was right for the launch of a tablet computer (essentially a scaled-up iPhone) based on exactly the same technological model. Once again, he was right on the money. The Apple iPad became the fastest-selling consumer electronics device in history.

In previous years other companies, notably Microsoft, had introduced tablet computers that failed to catch on, and had therefore given up on the opportunity. But Jobs was intent on fulfilling a prophetic vision of the future that he had articulated over 20 years earlier in a speech at the International Design Conference in Aspen in 1983:

"Apple's strategy is really simple. What we want to do is we want to put an incredibly great computer in a book that you can carry around with you and learn how to use in 20 minutes . . . and we really want to do it with a radio link in it so you don't have to hook up to anything and you're in communication with all of these larger databases and other computers."

This statement was made when the PC industry was still in its early infancy, and computers were still relatively big and clunky. In that same speech, Jobs described the computer as a mobile communications device with which one would be able pick up or send e-mail (long before the Internet went mainstream). He also explained that the concept of buying computer software in a bricks-and-mortar store made no sense, since software is digital and could therefore be distributed and paid for electronically via the telephone line (remind anyone of the App Store?). These uncannily accurate predictions have prompted some people to suggest that Steve Jobs might actually have been a time traveler from the future!

Despite Jobs's deep belief in digital retail (as exemplified by the iTunes Music Store and the App Store), he also had a powerful vision for the future of *physical* retail, as the amazing success of the Apple Store testifies. What began as a "store within in a store" concept to ensure the integrity of the Apple brand image, has since grown into one of the world's leading retail chains, with an approach that has forever changed the way companies showcase and sell their products and services. The store's counterintuitive strategy—focused more on the customer experience than on shifting products—was predicted to fail by several retail industry "experts" because its lavish interior layout, as well as space-eating features like the Genius Bar, would result in very low sales per square foot.

How wrong they were. In 2011, 10 years after its launch, the Apple Store was number one among U.S. retailers based on exactly this metric, generating double the sales per square foot of Tiffany & Co., and three times more than that of Best Buy. Visit any shopping mall or Main Street today, and it's impossible to miss the influence that Apple Stores have had on a multitude of other retail outlets, whether we look at fashion companies, sports brands, home furnishing stores, or even banks and health clinics. Somehow Steve Jobs intuitively saw the future of retail—both digital and physical—and by implementing his revolutionary strategies he radically and irreversibly changed customer expectations and buying behaviors across the globe.

"These waves of technology, you can see them way before they happen, and you just have to choose wisely which ones you're going to surf."[61]

Steve Jobs

Fast Forward Companies

To remain the world's largest sports company, **Nike** realized years ago that great shoes, great apparel, and a powerful brand image were not enough. The company would also have to catch the digital and social media wave. One result was the creation of Nike Digital Sport in 2010. This division launched the Nike+ ecosystem of digital products and experiences—Nike+ iPod nano, the Nike+ SportWatch GPS, running and training apps, Nike+ Fuelband, Nike+ Basketball, and the Nike+ online community—for tracking athletic performance and then storing, analyzing, and sharing the data socially. With sales of fitness wearables increasing 700 percent in 2013, and the industry gearing up for fivefold growth in the next three years, the company is now integrating its Nike+ API fitness software and Nike Fuel measurement system into wearable devices from a host of other manufacturers, making Nike's digital fitness apps ubiquitous.

As soon as Internet video streaming technology became mature enough for it to go mainstream, Reed Hastings, CEO of **Netflix**, realized it represented not just the future of the video rental business but the future of TV. Shifting its whole business model from home DVD delivery to video on demand, Netflix went through a tough time but emerged as a winner. While Blockbuster Video has disappeared from the scene, Netflix now has more than 33 million paid subscribers (that's more than HBO), has its own original TV shows (which have received numerous Emmy nominations and the first ever Emmy award for an Internet-only TV series), and has redefined video distribution and consumption for a new era.

Although **Starbucks** has an enviable physical presence with its 18,000 stores, much of the company's innovation takes place in the digital arena. To keep up with what's next, Starbucks has launched a slew of technology initiatives—including flirtations with Groupon, Square, and the Apple Passbook digital wallet service—knowing that some new ideas may fail but others will create enduring value for customers. The Starbucks card, for example, which can be reloaded with cash online, today accounts for 30 percent of in-store revenues. And the company's mobile payments app, which enables customers to make purchases simply by scanning their smartphones, generates over 7 million mobile transactions every week. In fact, there are now 35 million monthly visitors to Starbucks websites and mobile apps, proving that digital tools are just as important to people as their lattes.

 As online content consumption continues to shift from text to video, social media sites are getting the picture. In October 2012, **Twitter** acquired Vine, a service for making and posting six-second looping video clips (described as "the Instagram of video"), which became the fastest growing app of 2013. Five months later, **Facebook** unveiled a similar service on Instagram (15-second videos) with additional editing tools. With strategies like these, both companies made a strong push into the social video space, which could be a potential advertising goldmine.

 In recent years, manufacturers have begun to talk about the "Industrial Internet"—a phrase first coined by **GE**. It refers to the integration of industrial machines with smart networks of sensors and software. Indeed, GE has pioneered the concept in its own high-tech battery plant in Schenectady, New York, where the production process "merges big iron with big data" to create one of the world's most intelligent production facilities. Now the company is not only bringing this know-how to its clients via the GE Global Software Center in San Ramon, California, but it has also launched an incubator to invest in and grow a community of Industrial Internet startups.

 Mapping service **Waze** combined a regular GPS car navigation system with four major trends: social media, location-based networking, online gaming, and mobile. Most navigation software only provides maps, real-time positioning data, directions to desired destinations, and journey timing estimates. Waze goes much further by giving its users avatars that appear on the map, so drivers can see not only their own location but also the location of other Waze community members. Using gaming conventions, Waze engages users by offering them points for reporting traffic conditions and police speed traps, for "driving over" on-screen icons of cupcakes and other items, and for updating its online maps with new info. These points increase a member's status in the community. The service, which is available as a free app for smartphones, has tens of millions of users around the world. It was acquired by Google in 2013 for $1 billion.

It's happening **now!**

Automobile manufacturers are reframing the car as a smart mobile device that learns our driving behaviors, monitors our health and alertness, helps us to park, communicates with other vehicles to avoid accidents, and eventually will drive itself. Think of it as an iPhone on wheels, with downloadable apps, infotainment interfaces, augmented reality displays, and artificial intelligence, that's connected to an "information everywhere" infrastructure—the Internet of cars. Brands like Tesla, BMW, Nissan, and Toyota anticipate an increasingly electric future, based on advanced batteries, hybrid motors, or perhaps even energy-storing body panels. Others are placing bets on biofuels and hydrogen fuel cells to drive tomorrow's transportation. And passenger vehicles are only part of the story. For example, the biggest impact of self-driving technology will be on commercial fleets—millions of trucks and delivery vans are expected to become autonomous in the next one or two decades, saving industries billions of dollars on the compensation, payroll taxes, and health-care of professional drivers, not to mention the benefits of safer roads (robots don't fall asleep at the wheel!). But it also means the trucker's roadside diner will be a thing of the past.

Marketers in every industry are rethinking their strategies for a completely new media landscape, shaped by social networks, smartphones, tablets, and online video. Big brands are creating their own content on YouTube, while YouTube now lets Nielsen measure online audiences just it has traditionally done with television. Twitter offers brands the chance to post promoted tweets at the same time as they run their TV ads, reaching people at the very moment they are tweeting about a show. Google's mobile ads are tailored to a person's location, displaying nearby stores, hotels, and other businesses, and offering a one-click phone icon for instant calls to local advertisers. Facebook provides advertisers with segmented targeting and helps them build loyalty by encouraging a community of customers to engage with the brand. It's all about going where today's audiences are, and where they'll be tomorrow.

Video game companies are reinventing their industry as consumer preference shifts from expensive, CD-ROM–based games on PCs and consoles to cheap or free apps on tablets and smartphones. It's not just the console makers (Sony, Microsoft, and Nintendo) who need to change their game, it's also the design studios like Electronic Arts and Zynga. In recent years, masses of players—and profits—have been going to companies like Rovio (Angry Birds), King (Candy Crush Saga), Supercell (Clash of Clans and Hay Day), GungHo (Puzzle & Dragons), and Ustwo (Monument Valley), because these developers understand that mobile is the new name of the game. As the industry transitions to mobile platforms, the processors inside handheld devices are becoming more powerful, so even hardcore gamers can now enjoy playing on smaller, portable screens. Why sit at home with a joystick or controller when you can play your favorite game on the go with just a tap and a finger swipe?

Banks are being transformed by powerful forces that are challenging the whole notion of what a bank is and what it does. Sure, some banks are redesigning their branches to look more like Apple Stores, with touchscreen info displays, relaxing lounge areas, and espresso machines, and all banks have shifted a lot of their focus to online and mobile banking. But the industry changes go much deeper than that. In the old days, a bank was essentially the only place you could go to get reliable financial services. However, if you look in your wallet today, chances are you have a credit card from an airline, an auto manufacturer, a large retailer (like Amazon, Walmart, or Target in the United States, or Tesco in the UK), or perhaps a major coffeehouse chain like Starbucks. Some of these institutions (Walmart and Tesco are good examples) already also offer bank accounts, debit cards, loans, mortgages, and insurance products, too. Online payments are dominated not by banks but by digital players like Google Wallet, PayPal, Amazon Payments, Dwolla, and now Apple Pay. In Kenya,

it was a mobile phone provider, Safaricom, rather than a bank, that introduced M-Pesa—the revolutionary mobile money transfer service that now has over 18 million active users in Kenya and is rapidly expanding around the world[62] (many African countries now have more mobile money accounts than bank accounts). Peer-to-peer lending companies like Zopa (who needs a bank?) are now entering the financial mainstream, and crowdfunding platforms like Kickstarter, Indiegogo, and FundingKnight are taking over the job of financing small businesses in their efforts to expand.

Then there's the "Gang of Four"—Amazon, Apple, Facebook, and Google. Amazon has been in financial services and online payments for years, and could decide at any moment to take a more serious stab at the banking business. With Apple Pay, Apple is making a big move into mobile payments (with 800 million iTunes accounts,[63] each with a credit card attached to it, this could potentially turn Apple into the world's number one mobile money-account provider). Facebook has applied for a banking license, too, allowing the company to issue its own digital currency (similar to Bitcoin) and to offer e-money transfer and other financial services to its 1 billion active users. And what is to stop Google from making a killer combination of Google Wallet and Google Glass, enabling the instant purchase of anything you are currently looking at? Any one of these developments could change the whole face of online payment, and of the banking industry itself, virtually overnight.

{ What are the forces that will fundamentally transform your own industry? Are you ready to reimagine your business from the ground up? }

The next big thing for
your business

The billion-dollar question is this: Which wave (or waves) are you and your company riding? What are you actually *doing* about the disruptive trends and discontinuities that have the potential to reshape your industry? Are you already harnessing the power of change to create exciting new value for customers, refresh or replace your current business model, stay relevant in a hyper-accelerating world, open up completely new growth opportunities, and reinvent the competitive rules before somebody else does? Are you figuratively up there on the surfboard, with the wind in your hair and the salt water spraying all around you, on the crest of the next big wave? Or are you lying on the beach in the sunshine while, out on the ocean, a monstrous, 100-foot-high tsunami is thundering toward you at 500 mph?

Let's consider one of today's hottest trends—wearable technology—which is projected to be worth at least $70 billion globally by 2024.[64] In just the next four years alone, analysts expect sales growth of around 500 percent.[65] Major tech companies like Google, Samsung, Sony, and more recently, Apple, are putting a lot of focus on this emerging opportunity arena. But what implications does this trend have for your own business? How might you take advantage of the increasing momentum—and the new technical possibilities—to drive radical innovation in your industry?

The potential applications of smart watches, smart glasses, smart wristbands, wearable cameras, and other devices are almost endless across many different fields—from health care and fitness (which is where a lot of the focus has been so far) to law enforcement, security, education and training, transportation, construction, engineering, repair and inspection, retail, factory and warehouse management, real estate, travel and tourism, gaming, sports, entertainment—and the list goes on.

At its developer conference in March 2014, Google announced Android Wear—a version of the company's ubiquitous OS specifically designed for wearables (and oriented toward smart watches)—with the killer app being Google Now, which brings notifications straight to whichever device you are wearing at exactly the moment you need them. The Google Play Store allows you to download a range of different apps to your Android-powered wearable, just as you do with your smartphone. People are already using Google Glass, for example, to navigate in the city, improve their golf swing, perform tasks with their hands while receiving live text or video instructions, keep an eye on their heart rate during exercise sessions, enhance TV viewing by calling up extra info while watching a show, take POV pictures and video, livestream what they are seeing to the rest of the world, keep up to date with the *New York Times* and CNN, and stay in touch socially on Facebook and Twitter. Virgin Airlines has tested Google Glass with its airport concierge agents, who are able to see a person's name, flight number, destination, and loyalty program details when they greet and converse with a traveler. And GE has equipped technicians with Google Glass to carry out hands-free jet engine inspections, verbally instructing the device to check engine status, recognize parts, and deliver data straight to the display, thus alleviating the need to hold a mobile device.

Amazon has a dedicated online store for wearable technology that displays hundreds of different products, along with blog articles, news, buying guides, and a video library. And advertising agencies are already experimenting with ways to deliver advertising and promotional messages directly to wearables, particularly in combination with location-based data (e.g., when you are standing near a certain aisle in the grocery store).

Over the last few years, it has become increasingly common to see people wearing smart wristbands, mostly for fitness tracking—think Fitbit, Nike+ FuelBand, Jawbone, and the like. Disney has taken the concept one step further with its RFID/Bluetooth-enabled MagicBand, introduced in 2013 at the company's Walt Disney World in Florida. The rubberized digital bracelet replaces park entrance tickets, FASTPASSES for rides, hotel room keys at Disney resorts, and even your credit card for making purchases in the park's stores and restaurants. It also enables Disney to enhance the entertainment experience by creating interactive elements, such as Mickey or Goofy welcoming a child by name, or wishing somebody a happy birthday. At the same time, MagicBand feeds back tons of digital data to the park management team to help them improve operations.

Smart glasses, watches, wristbands, and wearable cameras may be grabbing most of the headlines, but wearable technology goes way beyond these kinds of devices. Every day seems to bring a new idea to the wearable world, like connected jewelry, wearable SIM cards, a smart bike helmet, virtual reality headsets, smart clothing, and even sensor-embedded boxing gloves. British Airways has been testing a "Happiness Blanket" for its business class passengers, which connects via Bluetooth to a brain-scanning headset to measure whether a passenger is feeling tense or relaxed. LEDs woven into the blanket change color accordingly. If the blanket is glowing in blue, it indicates that the passenger is peacefully enjoying the flight. If it is red, it signals to the cabin attendants that something might be amiss, or that the passenger is in need of refreshment.

Where do wearables fit into *your* company's future? And what about other potentially game-changing developments? Which trends are currently driving your innovation strategy? What will be the next big thing for your business?

{ "The future is about 'Wearables, Drivables, Flyables, Scannables.'"[66] }

Mary Meeker, Internet analyst

149

WHICH WAVE ARE YOU RIDING?

GPS-enabled drones

AUGMENTED REALITY

Artificial intelligence

Smart Home Networks

Downloadable Apps

Big Data

Streaming Media

HEALTH, FITNESS, NUTRITION

China!

SPEECH RECOGNITION

Electric Cars

Sustainability

Biomaterials

Internet Of Things

Genetics

Nanotech

Social Television

RFID

Mobile Gaming

Robotics

Code Scanning

Cloud

Wearable Computers

3D Printing

VIRTUAL RETAIL

Wireless Electrici

Social Media

Autonomous vehicles

LESSONS
TO TAKE AWAY

Innovators can see the future in the present. (Their ability to imagine what's next comes from their keen awareness and understanding of what is happening now.)

Think about how much difference a decade will make to your business. (No company or industry on earth can expect the future to be a linear extrapolation of the past.)

Is your company changing as fast as the world is changing? (Business success is increasingly transient; it must be rapidly and incessantly renewed if it is to be sustained.)

Innovation is a race for tomorrow. (You need to work hard to recognize emerging opportunities, then move fast to capture the maximum share of those opportunities.)

Trends and discontinuities are patterns of change. (They may be almost imperceptible at first, but if you begin to join the dots and scale things up, you might be able to sense a disruptive development in the making.)

Innovators are wave riders. (At the right time, they attach their business to the gathering momentum of the change curve, thus multiplying their chances for growth and for industry disruption.)

Try to understand and harness the forces that could fundamentally transform your industry. (Make sure you are always learning about what's new and what's next. Don't let internal issues blind you to what is happening in the external environment.)

What will be the next big thing for your business? (Is your company up there riding the waves of change, or is it lying on the beach waiting for the tsunami to strike?)

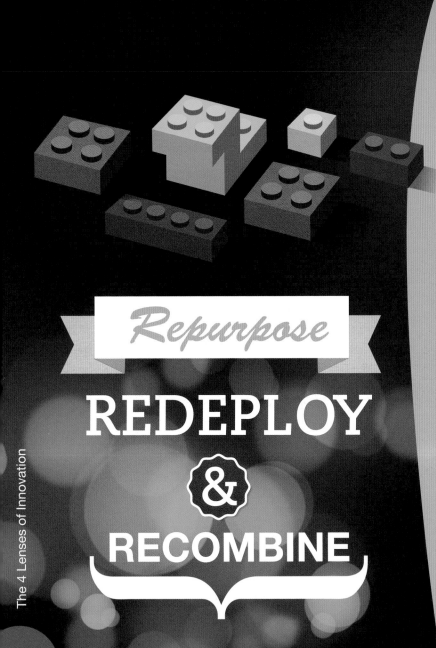

Repurpose
REDEPLOY
&
RECOMBINE

Every company utilizes a specific set of resources (e.g., competencies and assets) to turn some form of input (e.g., raw materials, semifinished goods, information, ideas) into some form of output (e.g., a product or service) of value to others. Many of those resources are embedded in an organization's own business model (e.g., knowledge, skills, experience, infrastructure, facilities, financial capacity, brands). Others are possessed by external companies (e.g., suppliers, partners, distributors) that work with the firm at various points in the value chain as part of a larger business ecosystem.

For most of the industrial era, companies have predominantly asked themselves how to use the resources available to them more *efficiently*—in other words, how do we produce basically the same kinds of goods and services only faster, better, and cheaper? But in today's value-based economy, companies increasingly need to ask themselves how to use the resources available to them more *innovatively*—"How do we leverage existing skills and assets in different ways, different contexts, or different combinations, in order to create new opportunities for value creation and growth?"

Consider some of world's leading companies. Certainly, firms like Apple or Amazon are brutally efficient in their operations—think about the thousands of iPhones and iPads produced by Chinese assembly lines every single day, or take a peek inside one of Amazon's giant, high-tech "Fulfillment Centers." But is it the ability to continually squeeze more and more efficiency from their business processes that has made these companies so successful? Or is it rather their ability to use available resources in a much more innovative way than others, resulting in products and services that deliver unprecedented value to customers?

Right now, the burning issue for a company like McDonald's, for example, is not, "How do we serve up burgers and fries more efficiently around the world?" The issue is, "How do we use our already efficient fast-food retailing platform to deliver offerings tailored to different (and changing) customer preferences?" It's a similar story at Coca-Cola. Nobody on earth knows how to produce and distribute carbonated soft drinks more efficiently than Coke. But the fact of the matter is that soda sales in the United States have been declining for the past 10 years[67] (and are now falling globally), as people in general become more concerned about health, wellness, and obesity issues. So the focus at Coca-Cola is not on how to produce greater quantities of soda at lower cost, but on how to use all available resources to offer customers

{ "Innovation is . . . the act that endows resources with a new capacity to create wealth." }
Peter Drucker

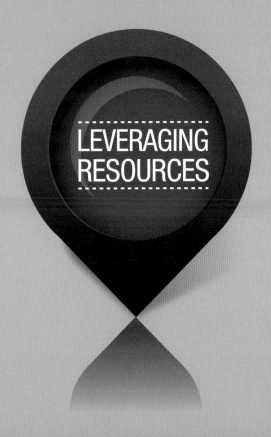

LEVERAGING RESOURCES

healthier or trendier alternatives, such as fruit juices, water, and energy drinks, not to forget Coke's new "healthier" soda, Coca-Cola Life. If a company is not capable of doing this—of using resources not just *efficiently* (for optimized production) but also *innovatively* (for new value creation)—it runs the risk of one day becoming incredibly efficient at producing what customers no longer want. Nokia and Kodak are sad example of this phenomenon.

Over a century ago, in his highly influential book *The Theory of Economic Development*, renowned economist Joseph Schumpeter was one of the first to draw a distinction between the act of production and the act of innovation. "To produce," he wrote, "means to combine materials and forces within our reach. To produce other things, or the same things by a different method, means to combine these materials and forces differently."[68] Andrew Hargadon, in *How Breakthroughs Happen*, puts it similarly: "Innovation is a process of taking apart and reassembling these elements in new combinations."[69] Business history teaches us that innovators often come to their breakthroughs by decoupling, remixing, and stretching existing resources. They view a company not as a set of business units but as a portfolio of distinct, stand-alone skills and assets that can potentially be repurposed, redeployed, or recombined in different ways to create new opportunities for value creation. In fact, they look at the whole world as a rich reservoir of resources that may be leveraged to make innovation happen.

How would you
define Google?

If somebody asked you to define your own company, you would probably respond by describing what it *is* or what it *does*. For example, you might say, "We're a bank," or "We make office furniture," or "We're in the pharmaceutical business." This is quite understandable. It's the most simple and straightforward reply to the question. But that's not the way radical innovators envisage their organizations, or the way they see the world around them.

For example, if you asked Larry Page to define Google, do you think his answer would be, "We're a search engine"? Not very likely. He may have stated that one of his primary goals is still to create "the search engine of my dreams," but judging from his company's diverse and rapidly widening portfolio of products, services, and interests, Page would appear to view Google a little more broadly. For a start, the company has given itself an extremely elastic definition for the word *search*. What began as a friendly software system for quickly finding accurate information on the Internet has been transformed over the years into myriad value-added search services. Think Google Images, Books, Movies, News, Finance, Alerts, Product Search (formerly Boutiques.com), Groups, Hotel Finder, Language Tools, Patent Search, Life Search, Blog Search, Scholar, Shopping, Accessible Search (for the blind and visually impaired), Custom Search, Knowledge Graph, Trader, and Zagat (the restaurant, nightlife, and hotel guide). It's easy to forget that Google also owns YouTube, the world's largest video platform and second largest search engine. Then there are the company's mapping and navigation tools, such as Google Maps; Street View; Google Earth, Mars, Moon, and Sky; Google Transit; Zygote Body (3D anatomy of the human body); plus Waze—the popular community-based traffic and navigation app.

While it remains undeniably central to Google's business model, search was in many ways just the beginning. Consider all of Google's additional online tools for communication, personal organization, and publishing, like Gmail, Calendar, Contacts, Translate, Drive (online backup service and storage space), Hangouts, Google+, Picasa, Profile, Speak To Tweet, and Voice. In addition, there are services designed specifically for mobile devices, such as Google Wallet, Offers, Mobilizer, Goggles (image recognition), Music, Shopper, Sync, Listen (for podcasts and Web audio), Field Trip (for discovering new nearby places and events), and Google Now (a personal assistant app based on voice-command reminders).

If you are an advertiser or business user, you will no doubt be familiar with Google AdWords, AdSense, and Ad Manager, along with FeedBurner, DoubleClick, Analytics, Enterprise Search solutions, Local Business Center, Wildfire, and Maps Solutions, not to mention Google Cloud Platform, the company's infrastructure-as-a-service cloud computing business. Other enterprise tools include Google Consumer Surveys, Public Data Explorer, Trendalyzer, Zeitgeist, and Google Activity Report.

Somewhere along the line, Google obviously realized it had a set of core competencies and valuable strategic assets in the field of software development that would allow it to stretch into new spaces previously dominated by rivals like Microsoft and Apple. First came the company's own web browser. In 2008 Google released Chrome, which is now the world's most widely used browser across the board, beating out Microsoft's Internet Explorer and Apple's Safari. Next up was operating systems. Google introduced Chrome OS for netbooks (aimed at users who spend most of their time on the Web), and then Google Android for mobile devices, which now has the largest installed base of any mobile OS and runs on 80 percent of the world's smartphones. Google has since expanded into Android Wear, a version of the Android OS for wearable computers; Android Auto, to create connected cars; and Google TV, a smart TV system. Google Play, the company's Android-based digital distribution platform, is now bigger than Apple's App Store in terms of the number

of downloadable apps, and also offers music, books, magazines, movies, TV shows, and tech products.

But why stop at software? With its brainpower, financial might, and engineering resources, nothing was hindering Google from producing innovative hardware to run on its own software platforms. After all, the device market seems to be where huge potential profits are, as Apple has demonstrated with iPod, iPhone, and iPad, whereas Google gives its software and operating systems away for free. Thus, the company now offers Nexus smartphones and tablets, Chromebook laptops, Chromebox desktop PCs, the Chromecast media streaming adapter, Google TV (a smart TV interface), and of course Google Glass—the headgear with optical display and integrated camera. Sergey Brin's Google X research group is also currently testing a "smart contact lens," designed to help diabetes patients by monitoring the glucose level in their tears. And with the acquisition of Nest Labs, the startup company that gave us learning thermostats and smoke detectors, Google has moved into the market for home automation appliances and the Internet of Things. All of this Google high-tech hardware is available for purchase on Google Play.

Diversifying even further from its core search business, the company has created Google Fiber to bring high-speed broadband and video services to the home; and Google Energy, which is dedicated to generating, distributing, and managing clean energy. Google has also invested in a mobile gaming app company and an online credit service, and in a bid to rival Amazon, the company is pumping hundreds of millions of dollars into its Shopping Express program, which allows customers to buy products from local retail stores through Google, and have them delivered to their door on the same or next day. Perhaps most interestingly, Google is currently working at the cutting edge of a whole array of science and technology fields, from its famous self-driving cars to airborne wind turbines, artificial intelligence, advanced robotics, high-altitude balloons for broadcasting Internet service to remote or impoverished areas of the world, and even research into the biological causes of aging and its associated diseases.

So how would you define Google? If you try to describe the company in terms of what it *is* or what it *does*, you would have to resort to terms like "Internet search," "online advertising," "Web-based technology," "computer software," or "tech devices," all of which are clearly inadequate or incomplete. Innovators like Larry Page don't even try to compartmentalize things. They think of a company not in terms of what it *is* or what it *does*, but in terms of what it *knows*—its skills and unique capabilities—and what it *owns*—such as infrastructure, proprietary technologies, standards, patents, brands, customer data, and so on. Rather than developing a narrow self-image that pigeonholes a firm in a particular market sector, or locks it up in a certain product or service category, radical innovators are able to stretch the way they define their business based on its collection of core competencies and strategic assets. In other words, Larry Page sees Google as a broad portfolio of science, technology, and Internet-related resources that can be leveraged into almost any meaningful new venture. As he put it in an interview in 2014, "I always thought it was kind of stupid if you have this big company, and you can only do, like, five things."[70]

Of course, Google doesn't always have everything it needs in house to do all the things it wants to. If there is a capability or an asset that the company deems to be important to its future plans but that it currently does not possess, Google will do its best to go out and either buy it (as a long string of acquisitions since 2001 goes to prove) or find a strategic partner to work with. Innovators like Larry Page and Sergey Brin have the ability to picture a new, recombinant pattern of resources—pieced together like building blocks from various places—that will allow them to gear up for some important new growth opportunity, and they work hard to find and orchestrate all of these strategic elements as they pursue their vision.

{ "I don't think we're going to run out of important things to do, compared with the resources that we have."[71] }

Larry Page, CEO Google

LEVERAGING **RESOURCES** IN NEW WAYS

 Competencies

What special skills, know-how, and experience does your company (or your value network) possess?

How could you deploy these competencies in completely new ways or new contexts to expand the boundaries of your business model?

What competencies from outside the company (or value network) could be combined with your own resources to create new opportunities for growth?

 Assets

What strategic assets—i.e., technology, infrastructure, data—does your company (or your value network) currently own?

Can you imagine alternative uses or industry settings for these assets that would create significant new value for customers?

What opportunities might arise if you could leverage certain assets from other companies and add them to your own business model?

Looking through the Four Lenses

159

Extending the boundaries
of the business

In January 2007, at the annual Macworld Expo in San Francisco, Steve Jobs announced that "Apple Computer" was a thing of the past. Henceforth, the company would simply be known as "Apple, Inc." Why? Here's how he put it: "The Mac, iPod, Apple TV, and iPhone. Only one of those is a computer. So we're changing the name."[72] If Apple had continued to think of itself solely as a computer company, it would never have considered stretching into seemingly "out of scope" domains like consumer electronics, online digital media distribution, mobile telephony, home entertainment, downloadable software apps, consumer retail stores, and so forth. But the ability to define Apple based on its competencies (creating user joy through cool, hyper-friendly design) and its assets (cutting-edge technologies and a cult-status brand), rather than on its "core business," allowed the company to expand into wider arenas and build enormous new sources of profit.

Pixar's original business was making computer hardware and software for 3D rendering, but it turned out the company was also uniquely skilled at using its own technology to make computer-animated films. If Pixar had not freed itself from a narrow self-conception based on its legacy business, it would never have been able to leverage its true core competency and transform itself into an animation studio that would revolutionize the movie industry.

Amazon could have stuck to its roots and simply focused on being the "the world's largest bookstore." Instead, Jeff Bezos and his team exploited the company's unique strengths (comprehensive and customer-obsessed online retail) and its valuable assets (infrastructure, logistics, and an Internet brand people trusted) to relentlessly stretch Amazon's offerings into almost every conceivable product category—from CDs and DVDs to electronics, computers, toys, games, clothes, shoes, beauty products, jewelry, groceries, wine, sportswear, garden tools, pet supplies, 3D Printing, and even automotive parts. If you want it, *whatever* it is, chances are you'll find it in the "Everything Store." A Nicolas Cage pillowcase? Barack

Obama toilet paper? A Lady Gaga dog costume? Roswell UFO crash site soil? A Sigmund Freud action figure? A DVD for cats? It's all there, at the lowest price, and with just a couple of simple clicks it will be on its way to your address. Or consider Amazon's decision to launch its own products—book readers, tablets, mobile phones, and the Echo—along with its move into digital media streaming and original TV programming, all of which is a far cry from the company's original core business. Amazon's cloud computing services are another good example (more about that in a few pages). Amazon clearly believes in the principle of leveraging its own resources—and those of others—to open up diversified opportunities for growth and innovation.

Out of a humble cartoon studio in the 1920s, Walt Disney built what is today a global empire with $45 billion in annual revenues.[73] His simple goal was to create exceptional family entertainment that would make people happy, and it would have been quite understandable for him to insist on anima-

tion as the only way for Walt Disney Studios to deliver that experience. After all, he was a cartoonist and animator himself—that's how the studio had started—and for the first two decades its entire business model had been based on animated shorts and feature-length movies with a signature Disney style.

But Walt Disney never developed a myopic point of view about how to create and spread Disney's magic. He saw his company as a collection of deep competencies (exceptional storytelling and entertainment skills, and the ability to connect with the child in all of us) and powerful assets (world-class studio facilities, beloved characters, and the Disney brand name) that could provide a broad platform for future growth. Thus, by the 1930s, Disney was already producing syndicated comic strips and licensing a wide variety of merchandise to complement its popular cartoon films. In the 1940s and 1950s, the studio began to produce pioneering live-action films—such as *Treasure Island* and *20,000*

Leagues under the Sea—along with award-winning family documentaries. By the mid-1960s, when Walt passed away, Disney had also established itself as an innovator in television, and his brainchild, Disneyland, had totally revolutionized the amusement park industry.

Over the last few decades, the Walt Disney Company has continued to leverage its formidable skills and assets to open up new avenues for value creation. Some of these businesses, like video games and Disney retail stores, have had their ups and downs. Others have been wildly successful. For example, Disney's core competency in lavish, three-dimensional family entertainment (learned in the theme parks) became the basis for its theatrical production company, which has delivered a string of Broadway hits, and is also the power behind the highly popular *Disney on Ice* touring shows. Hospitality experience gained from the company's resorts and hotels was redeployed in Disney's cruise line business, which now boasts four huge, purpose-built ships, as well as other vacation services such as Adventures by Disney, which has been named both "North America's Leading Tour Operator" and "World's Leading Luxury Tour Operator" by World Travel Awards.[74] In China, Disney operates Disney English, a language training school for children, based on Disney's immersive storytelling approach, which incorporates Disney characters in the education experience. There are already dozens of Disney English Learning Centers in multiple cities across China and the business is growing at a fast clip. It's also worth remembering that the blockbuster movie series *Pirates of the Caribbean* had its genesis as a theme park attraction at Disneyland back in 1967. This asset was repurposed as a feature film in 2003 and went on to become a major franchise, encompassing several more movies as well as novels, video games, media publications, and additional theme park attractions. The films alone have grossed well over $3.7 billion worldwide.[75]

STRETCHING
into new spaces

Netherlands-based multinational DSM started out in 1902 as a state-owned coal-mining business. Indeed, the company's name stands for "Dutch State Mines." But over the decades, the organization began to stretch away from mining into fertilizers and other businesses, and by the early 1970s DSM had completely transformed itself into a chemicals company. Then, in the 1990s, DSM reinvented itself again, this time selling off almost all of its commodity chemicals activities and moving into material sciences (particularly engineering plastics)[76] and life sciences (biotech products). Today, the company is a global leader in the field of health, nutrition, and materials, with annual revenues of $12 billion,[77] serving a diverse range of markets from food flavors and fragrances to furniture, pharmaceuticals, automotive, and construction.

Or consider Tesco, the UK retail titan. Founder Jack Cohen started out in 1919 with a simple barrow selling fish paste in the streets of London. The first Tesco grocery store opened in 1929, and by the 1950s and 1960s it had established itself as one of Britain's leading self-service supermarket chains. But unlike some rivals, which focused almost exclusively on their core business of selling groceries, Tesco began to stretch into new opportunities by diversifying into all kinds of different Tesco-branded goods and services—from clothes and consumer electronics to fuel, financial services, telecom and broadband Internet, DVD rental, music downloads, online shopping, digital entertainment streaming, beauty salon services, and even its own Android tablets and smartphones (called Hudl). Today, Tesco is the largest retailer in the UK by sales, and the second-largest retailer in the world after Walmart.[78]

Does this mean that a company needs to look far outside its core business to create profitable new opportunities for growth and innovation? Absolutely not. There are always closer adjacencies that represent a logical extension of a company's competencies and strategic assets. Canon, for example, began life in 1937 as a Tokyo-based optical instruments company, and quickly built a reputation for its innovative cameras—a reputation the company still enjoys today. But over the decades Canon has also been able to stretch its core competency in imaging and optical technology into important adjacent opportunities. One of these is photocopiers (now the company's largest division in terms of revenue). Others include printers and scanners. Each of these adjacent moves has been built solidly on Canon's existing expertise and assets, increasing the potential for its success.

Corning Inc. is another good example of adjacency-based innovation. The U.S. manufacturer of glass, ceramics, and related materials traces its corporate history all the way back to 1851. In the early years, the company made a wide range of specialty glass products, including signal lenses for the railroads and glass tubing for scientific and industrial uses. A few decades later, when Thomas Edison needed a process for the mass production of electric light bulbs, it was Corning that made it possible. And when the automobile industry started to take off in the early twentieth century, Corning designed and delivered specialty solutions such as innovative lenses for headlamps. In the Roaring Twenties, the company made a fortune on glass tubing as the demand for neon skyrocketed, and when radio began to become more popular, Corning redeployed its revolutionary Ribbon Machine process (invented for producing light bulbs) to manufacture radio vacuum tubes. The advent of television presented another great opportunity, and the company became one of the first producers of glass panels and funnels for television tubes. In the 1960s and 1970s, Corning began to expand into glass fiber optics for telecommunications, and today is the global market leader in the industry, supplying 40 percent of the world's optical fiber.[79] Corning also invented and successfully marketed several glass ceramic products for the consumer market, including Pyrex, Pyroceram glass-ceramic cookware, and Corelle durable glass dinnerware. The processes involved in manufacturing some of these toughened-glass products later became the basis for developing Corning's now ubiquitous Gorilla Glass—which is used for the screens of millions of smartphones and tablets, as well as some laptop computers and LCD televisions. Again and again, Corning has leveraged its core competencies and strategic assets in alternative ways to build innovative new sources of profit.

Many other companies have also exploited adjacent innovation opportunities. For example, with its McCafé strategy, McDonald's was able to stretch beyond fast food into premium coffee to compete with Starbucks, which was stealing its customers. P&G has stretched its Mr. Clean brand from cleaning liquids into Magic Erasers, mops, kitchen scrubbers, and a nationwide car wash franchise, and has extended its Tide brand from laundry detergent into fabric care products, clothes hangers, stain removers, and a chain of dry cleaners. Nestlé has stretched its Nespresso concept, the popular capsule-based coffee machine, not just into its own branded boutique coffee bars and stores, but also into similar machines with single-use pods for other segments—Special.T for tea-lovers, and BabyNes for baby milk formula. Beiersdorf, the German personal care company, has stretched its star product, Nivea cream, into what is now a full range of over 300 skin and beauty care products in 19 different categories. And as mentioned earlier, Safaricom, Kenya's leading mobile network operator, has successfully stretched beyond telephony into financial services with M-Pesa, its mobile phone–based money transfer service, and M-Shwari for loans and savings.

Which new spaces will your company be stretching into next?

Unlimited potential for growth

How does a London record store transform itself into an international airline, and then into a leading mobile phone company, and then into a pioneer in space tourism? Indeed, how does a single UK firm morph into a global conglomerate with over 400 different companies in a multitude of diverse market sectors, yet retain exactly the same brand image in each and every one of them? How is it possible to build not one but a total of eight billion-dollar companies from the ground up in several different industries and countries? The answer in three words is Sir Richard Branson.

As a business innovator, Branson is clearly extraordinary. Since the 1970s he has flatly contradicted conventional wisdom on the dangers of brand extension by stretching his Virgin brand into a wide and perhaps odd range of business activities—music and retail, several airlines, mobile telephony, trains, vacations, hotels, spas, media, video games, financial services, health care, balloon flights, books, comics, a bridal emporium, music festivals, cars, motorbikes, cinemas, drinks, cosmetics, energy, digital radio, fitness clubs, limousines, broadband Internet services—and even space travel.

What unites this disparate collection of ventures is Branson's own personal philosophy and Virgin Group's unique set of brand values. At the very core, it's all about being the people's champion—delivering more than competitors while charging customers less, and throwing in some cheeky irreverence and fun for good measure. Branson's most powerful asset—the Virgin brand—communicates identical values whether it is on a credit card, an airline ticket, an insurance policy, the start-up screen of a cell phone, or the front door of a hotel. It guarantees the same consistent experience that people have come to expect from Virgin in every other sector.

Branson's extreme diversification is a direct result of the way he has always seen Virgin—not as a particular kind of business but as a platform for unlimited business opportunities. Instead of following the popular advice to "stick to what you know," Branson has chosen for decades to leverage what he knows and what he owns into whatever interests him next. As he puts it, "My driving force, I realize now, was finding new ways to help people have a good time—ideally, in places where they were least expecting it."[80]

This strategy has not only created a group with $25 billion in annual revenues, but has also spread the risk of failure across many companies, allowing Virgin to weather economic downturns and to pick itself up when, at times, a seemingly promising opportunity didn't pan out as Branson and his team had hoped. Indeed, it has allowed Virgin to continuously expand into fresh territory with an ever-widening portfolio of businesses ventures—some of which have been spectacular successes (to the tune of billions), while a few others have turned out to be duds.

Where would Branson and Virgin be today if he had decided not to diversify, but rather to focus his efforts solely on running the world's best record stores? He recognizes better than anyone else that he would no longer be in business at all, because the music retail industry was eventually upended by the rapid and relentless rise of digital distribution. "It is easy to think there will be record shops forever," says Branson about the company he originally started, "but if we hadn't moved on we would have been dead as a business, because music retailing was our principal business." His advice to other companies? "You shouldn't be afraid to diversify if you are in a position to do so, especially because nothing ever stays exactly the same.[81] . . . Whenever Virgin has money I always renew my search for new opportunities."[82]

> "I believe there is almost no limit to what a brand can do, but only if used properly."[83]
>
> *Richard Branson*

EXPLOITING UNDERUTILIZED ASSETS

After the dot-com crash in 2000, Amazon.com—like many other Internet companies—was left with a lot of excess IT infrastructure. In fact, Jeff Bezos and his team discovered that the company was using only around 10 percent of the available capacity in its data centers. In an effort to leverage these underutilized resources, Amazon launched its web services platform in 2002 to give external users the ability to store and access data on its servers. By 2006, Amazon Web Services had become the first true cloud hosting service, allowing companies and individuals to rent server space for running their own computer applications, and defining the now-standard "pay-as-you-use" pricing model. Today, Amazon Web Services is the uncontested ruler of the cloud. In May 2014, a Gartner report estimated that Amazon now offers five times more cloud computing capacity than all of its 14 major competitors (including Microsoft, Google, IBM, and HP) combined.[84] One year earlier, Amazon Web Services beat IBM in their bid for a 10-year, $600 million contract to build a massive cloud computing infrastructure for the CIA.[85]

In 2002, McDonald's recognized that one of the underutilized assets of its franchisees was the parking space around the restaurants, which was generally empty after 10 PM when the restaurants were closed. In an effort to find new ways to exploit this asset, the company experimented with placing automated kiosks in some of the restaurant parking lots for late-night convenience shopping. What they found was that customers were not very interested in buying grocery items (such as eggs or milk) from these kiosks, but they loved using them to rent DVDs. This was the birth of Redbox—the automated retail-kiosk business for movie and video game rentals—which started at 140 McDonald's restaurants[86] and eventually grew to over 40,000 kiosks in grocery stores, pharmacies, Walmarts, and 7-Elevens, surpassing Blockbuster's retail stores to grab almost 50 percent of the physical DVD rental market.[87]

Sometimes assets are underutilized because they are not being viewed as assets, but instead as waste. For decades, Spanish winemaker Grupo Matarromera had been throwing away the grape skins left over in the process of producing its award-winning wines. Taking a second look at those grape skins, Carlos Moro, the highly innovative founder and president of the group, wondered if it were possible to extract and somehow use the polyphenols and antioxidants (reputed to have various health and anti-aging benefits) contained in the skins. After four years of research, his now patented technique became the basis for a whole new business called Esdor, which markets a high-end range of cosmetics made from these natural extracts. Esdor's skin-care and anti-aging products were an immediate success in its native Spain, and the brand is now sold internationally.

Imperial Billiards is a small New Jersey company that has been building and selling high-quality gaming tables across the United States for 40 years. The Great Recession of 2008 hit the company hard, with sales of its pool tables dropping by 50 percent in a single year. Quickly looking for new sources of profit, Imperial began to expand into kitchen and bathroom cabinetry, but sales remained slow. Then one day a customer came into the warehouse and casually said, "With all that sawdust on the floor, why don't you make wood pellets for burning in stoves and fireplaces?" Six months later Imperial had started selling wood pellets, and within a year they accounted for 40 percent of the company's revenues. It turns out that the wood pellet business is less time consuming and more profitable than the intensive work of making pool tables and other carpentry products. It also creates repeat customers—people come back for more pellets every month, whereas a pool table is for life. Today, Imperial sells thousands of tons of pellets a year, and its pool table and carpentry businesses are once again thriving. Sometimes a company's whole future can depend on its ability to view waste as an asset and then find ways to turn it into value.

At other times, we have assets right under our noses that we fail to recognize, perhaps because they don't fit with the traditional way we view our business. Kengen, the leading electric power generation company in Kenya, taps geothermal energy to run Africa's largest power plant in Olkaria, near the Hell's Gate National Park, which is just an hour's drive from Nairobi. In 2011, the company saw the opportunity to diversify into the leisure and tourism industry by opening a geothermal spa on their property adjoining the national park, with several open-air "lagoons" offering the healing properties of naturally heated brine water, along with steam and sauna rooms, a restaurant, and a visitors' center and museum that focus on Kenya's involvement in geothermal energy.

Duncan McFie was working as a school teacher on remote King Island, in the state of Tasmania, just south of Australia. He began to notice that other islanders would come to collect rain water from his tank because it tasted better than the bore water in town. After a little research, he found out that King Island actually had the cleanest air in the world, and he wondered if clean air translates into clean rain water. As it happens, it does. So McFie decided to see if he could find a way to capture and bottle pure rainwater on a large scale and make a business out of selling it. His venture, called King Island Cloud Juice, now produces about 80,000 bottles a year and markets it as the most pristine water in the world. These days you will find it on sale (for the stunning price of $24 a bottle) at some of the world's finest dining establishments and luxury hotels, such as Claridge's in London and the Ritz-Carlton, Four Seasons, and Mandarin Oriental properties.

What about your own company's underutilized assets? Customer data. Brands. Patents. Infrastructure. Or something you currently don't even consider as an asset. What if you could leverage these resources in profitable new ways?

What else could we do with this?

There are times when innovation comes about by accident. Somebody tries to invent something to solve a particular problem, but afterward either the inventor or another person stumbles upon an exciting alternative use for it. Although there is a great deal of serendipity involved in these cases, they still reveal a lot about how innovation works, and especially about a certain thinking pattern or perspective that often leads to unexpected breakthroughs—namely, the ability to look at an existing idea or asset and figure out how it might be radically repurposed or redeployed to create value in a new context.

John Pemberton was a pharmacist and a Confederate veteran of the American Civil War.[88] In the Battle of Columbus, Georgia, in 1865, Pemberton had been wounded in the chest by a saber and subsequently became addicted to morphine, then commonly used as a painkiller. When the war ended, he used his knowledge of pharmacy to try to create an alternative, opium-free painkiller in an attempt to cure his own addiction. After a few concoctions, what he finally invented was "Pemberton's French Wine Coca," a medicinal remedy for headaches, which contained red wine, coca leaves, and kola nuts.[89] The very same year, Atlanta passed legislation prohibiting the sale of alcohol, so Pemberton was forced to change the recipe for his beverage. What he came up with instead was a base syrup that he eventually mixed with carbonated water, calling the new drink "Coca-Cola." It started life as a health elixir for curing headaches and relieving exhaustion, but soon became a popular soft drink in its own right. Today, The Coca-Cola Company runs the world's largest beverage business, with annual global revenues of close to $47 billion.

In 1945, an engineer by the name of Percy Spencer was conducting research for the Raytheon Corporation on a high-powered vacuum tube called a cavity magnetron.[90] It was principally designed as radar equipment for use by the air force and the navy. What Spencer noticed was that, while standing next to the radar set, a chocolate bar in his pocket had mysteriously melted. Intrigued by the heating effect of microwave beams from the device, he began to experiment with other foods such as popcorn, and soon realized he had discovered a totally new way to heat things up. Raytheon patented the idea, and in 1947 introduced the Radarange—the world's first commercial microwave oven. Today, the microwave is a common appliance in kitchens all over the world.

Kutol is a manufacturer of soap and industrial cleaning products based in Cincinnati, Ohio. Founded in 1912, the company was asked by the Kroger grocery chain to develop a product able to remove coal residue from wallpaper.[91] The company's putty-based solution was at first quite successful, but after World War II most homes began to switch from burning coal to natural gas, so the problem with internal soot effectively disappeared. People also began to use new, vinyl-based wallpaper that was washable, so there was little or no need for Kutol's cleaning putty. In 1955, Joe McVicker, who headed the firm, happened to discover that nursery school kids liked to use the pliable clay product for modeling in the classroom.[92] One year later, he relaunched it as a children's toy called Play-Doh, and set up a new business called the Rainbow Crafts Company to manufacture and sell it. Less than a decade later, General Mills purchased the Rainbow Crafts Company, along with all rights to Play-Doh. It became one of the most widely used toys of the twentieth century, with billions of cans of the colorful putty being sold internationally.

In 1942, during World War II, a chemist at Eastman Kodak named Harry Coover was trying to develop a transparent

plastic material to make gunsights. In the process, he created cyanoacrylate, which proved to be too sticky for the purpose and ended up being used instead[93] as an alternative to stitches on battle wounds.[94] Coover kept the material's formulation in mind, and years later came up with the idea of a "super adhesive." In 1958, Kodak introduced Super Glue, which became an instant hit. 3M's Post-it notes, by contrast, had their genesis with a glue that was so weak it almost didn't work. The reusable adhesive—which was once described as "a solution without a problem"—sat around for five years at 3M without anyone taking a commercial interest in it. Then one day, a 3M product development researcher named Arthur Fry had the idea of developing small strips of paper layered on the back with a thin coating of the glue (initially just to mark the pages in his church choir hymnbook). Post-It notes, which were formally launched in 1980, went on to become a billion-dollar annual business for 3M.

In 1914 Kimberly-Clark developed a material called cellucotton, which during World War I served as a substitute for cotton in gas masks, and was used by army nurses to dress soldiers' wounds. It turned out that many nurses also used the cellucotton surgical pads as sanitary napkins, so in 1920, following the war, Kimberly-Clark decided to introduce Kotex, the world's first disposable feminine hygiene product. Four years later, the company launched another cellucotton

product, Kleenex, which was originally marketed to women as a makeup remover but quickly established itself as a disposable handkerchief.

There are dozens more examples just like these. Bubble wrap was originally invented in 1957 as a new kind of wallpaper, but turned out to be much more practical as a wrapping material. And researchers at Pfizer were testing sildenafil citrate as a possible medicine for angina, not as a treatment for erectile dysfunction, when they noticed the drug's famous side effect. Viagra is now one of the world's best-selling drugs.

We don't have to wait for serendipity to happen. Many innovators seize the opportunity to proactively find new uses for existing ideas and resources.

The inspiration for Listerine PocketPaks Breath Freshening Strips came from ultrathin, paperlike candy products in Japan, which were manufactured using an edible, mostly tasteless polymer called pullulan that dissolves on the tongue. Pfizer used the same concept to create their immensely successful mouth freshening strips, which first appeared on supermarket shelves in 2001 and quickly created a whole new product category. It wasn't long before other innovators followed suit with their own variations on dissolving-film technology—including multivitamin supplements for children, cold and flu medication, soap strips that melt in the hands, dissolving blotters for minor cuts and shaving nicks, and even fresh breath strips for dogs.

For decades, Germany's BASF has been manufacturing melamine foam, which is sold as an insulation material for pipes and ductwork, as well as for soundproofing studios, soundstages, and auditoriums. Around 15 years ago, the company discovered that moistened melamine foam could also be used as an effective abrasive cleaner—acting like extremely fine sandpaper that rubs away difficult stains from surfaces. When P&G saw how well it worked, they decided to use BASF's melamine foam to create a revolutionary new cleaning product—the Mr. Clean Magic Eraser, which has gone on to sell well over a billion units since its introduction in 2003.

For years, miniature digital cameras—for both still and video pictures—have been a standard feature in mobile phones, desktop PCs, laptops, and tablets. But what about applications beyond computing and telecommunications? GoPro is one company that recognized an opportunity for wearable and mountable personal cameras, which are used today by surfers, skiers, skateboarders, cyclists, skydivers, hobby aircraft owners, and many others to capture experiences in unusual places in previously impossible ways. Other innovators have embedded digital cameras directly into their products, such as ski goggles or diving goggles. Some motorcycle helmet manufacturers, such as Reevu and Skully, install a camera in the back of the helmet to provide bikers with an integrated rear-vision system that helps prevent accidents.

The USB flash drive (or "memory stick") has become ubiquitous as a storage medium. But what if it could be put to other interesting uses? Maxell, the Japanese consumer electronics company, found a way to add different scents to its flash drives, introducing a special USB Aroma range in six scents: Apple, Strawberry, Chocolate, Lemon, Orange, and Mint. When Jean Paul Gaultier's Le Male fragrance first went on sale in some markets, it came with a free USB stick (in the same shape as the iconic bottle) that emitted the fragrance when plugged into a computer.

Leveraging resources
from others

More often than not, successful innovations are recombinations of some kind. They take existing ideas, resources, and domains, and bring them together in a whole new mix, or in a new market context. It might be popular to think of innovators as lone inventors sitting there staring out of the window waiting for a light bulb to appear above their heads, but the reality is that most truly innovative people are synthesizers who are very well connected with the world around them, and who find ways to join the dots between what is already out there. In many cases, that means borrowing or buying competencies and assets from other firms to produce novel solutions.

When Steve Jobs led the team at Apple that developed the original Macintosh computer in the early 1980s, he famously exploited revolutionary ideas he had seen at Xerox PARC (Palo Alto Research Center)—the graphical user interface and mouse, along with pop-up menus, icons, and windows—which the Macintosh group then recombined with its own concepts. Apple was thus able to profitably leverage assets that Xerox was underutilizing and failed to commercialize. Years later, when Jobs returned to Apple, it was initially to integrate technology assets from his NeXT computer and its UNIX-based operating system into Apple's products,

with Mac OS X being one direct result. Many assume that the iPod was developed exclusively at Apple, but in fact the reference platform for the device was designed by a company called PortalPlayer Inc., and another firm, Pixo, was called in to help Apple design the user interface. Apple's iPod was also based on an existing idea—after all, other MP3 players were already around at the time. The same is true of iTunes, which borrowed and legalized an idea first launched by Napster, and which was built on a platform called SoundJam MP that Apple had purchased in 2000. The iconic iPhone was not exclusively an Apple project either. In fact, it was designed in collaboration with Cingular Wireless (now AT&T Mobility), and of course its touchscreen display came from Corning. And what about the App Store? How many of those 1 million available apps were ever made by Apple? It's a great example of leveraging the resources of others—in this case third-party software developers—to create incredible new value for Apple's smartphone and tablet platforms.

A few pages earlier, we learned that Disney has proven to be masterful at leveraging its own competencies and assets in important new ways. However, Disney also recognizes the value of resources it can bring in from the outside. The decision to buy Pixar in 2006, for example, has already rebooted

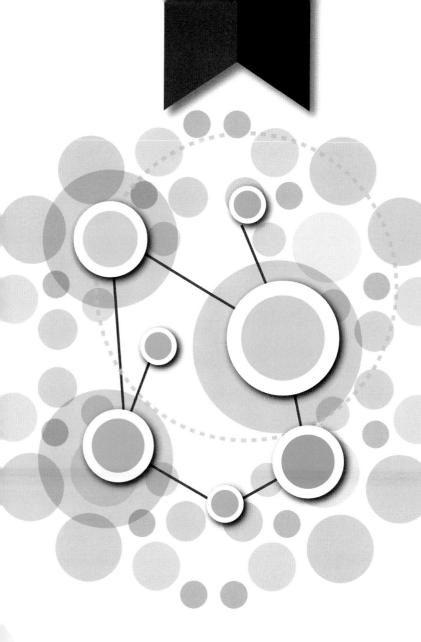

Disney's animation division, as movie hits like *Tangled*, *Wreck-It Ralph*, *Frozen*, and *Big Hero 6* have clearly shown. Then there are Disney's purchases of the Muppets, Marvel superheroes, and *Star Wars* franchises. The revenues from blockbuster movies based on these franchises would probably be enough to justify the purchase prices. But there is more to the company's strategy. Disney knows it needs a fresh stable of instantly and globally recognizable characters to continuously drive its magical marketing machine. After all, how long can the company depend on icons from the 1920s and 1930s, such as Mickey Mouse, Donald Duck, Goofy, and Snow White, to keep drawing crowds? Now that Disney owns Kermit and Miss Piggy, Iron Man and the Avengers, along with R2-D2, Han Solo, and Darth Vader, think about all the new theme park attractions, licensing and merchandising deals, original TV series, live shows, comic books, and other commercial opportunities it can generate.

Other companies have long created value by licensing properties owned by others. Lego, for example, used to simply sell colorful interlocking plastic bricks along with generic figures. That was fine for decades, but around the turn of the millennium the company's revenues began to stagnate. That's when Lego decided to start signing licensing deals for movie franchises like *Star Wars* and *Harry Potter*, as well as comic-book figures such as Spider-Man and Batman. Since then many similar deals have followed, for other franchises including *Indiana Jones, Pirates of the Caribbean,* and *The Lord of the Rings*. Today, partly thanks to these licensed themes, Lego has pushed past Mattel and Hasbro to become the world's most profitable toymaker. In *The Lego Movie*, released in February 2014, many of the characters that Lego has licensed over the years were brought together for the very first time on theater screens. The movie eventually grossed $468 million internationally, making it one of the most successful films of the year, and a sequel was soon in the works.[95]

TomTom was just like any other GPS automotive navigation system until the company hit on the idea of adding somebody else's assets to their business model—in this case, celebrity voices from movie and TV characters, including Homer Simpson, Bugs Bunny, Bert and Ernie from Sesame Street, Darth Vader, Yoda, C-3PO, the Terminator, and James Bond. The voices are available for purchase and easy download at TomTom's online store. Another breakthrough was TomTom's amusing online promotion campaign, based around YouTube videos that are supposed to be from these famous characters' voiceover recording sessions. The company's marketing innovations have helped to make TomTom one of the world's leading suppliers of in-car location and navigation products.

Some of the biggest opportunities for innovation can come from combining your organization's own resources with the competencies and assets of other companies to produce radical new solutions for customers.

LESSONS
TO TAKE AWAY

Develop an elastic view of your company. (Instead of defining it in terms of what it *is* or what it *does*, try to think of your company in terms of what it *knows*—its unique set of skills—and what it *owns*—its valuable assets.)

Identify and leverage underutilized resources. (Imagine your organization, your value network, and the world around you as a rich reservoir of skills and assets that could be exploited differently or recombined in profitable new ways.)

Extend the boundaries of your business. (Don't get locked into a particular market sector, or a single product or service category. Imagine ways to stretch beyond your current business into new spaces and domains—either adjacent to your core or perhaps far outside it.)

Innovators repurpose, redeploy, and recombine resources. (They leverage existing competencies and assets in new ways, new contexts, and new combinations to open up fresh opportunities for value creation.)

Leverage resources from others. (Look for ways to combine your organization's own resources with the competencies and assets of other companies to produce innovative new solutions for customers.)

Try to find new uses for existing ideas. (Something that has been invented for one thing may have an exciting alternative use. Ask yourself how it might be radically repurposed or redeployed to create value in a new setting.)

INNOVATING FROM THE customer BACKWARD

A few years ago, IBM ran a great series of ads, one of which featured the striking headline, "Stop selling what you have. Start selling what they need." Another was directed at the banking industry: "Stop thinking like a bank. Start thinking like a customer." This is precisely the spirit of the fourth lens of innovation. It's all about making the customer a critical starting point for idea generation.

Right up until the 1990s, P&G had a quite different approach to innovation—one that started not with the customer but in the science lab. Thousands of the company's R&D people and engineers would work hard to develop promising new product and marketing ideas, which were then rigorously tested with market research, and finally introduced to customers with convincing arguments to persuade them to buy something they didn't know they needed. On average, the commercial success rate of this approach was just 15 to 20 percent, meaning that only one in six new brand or product introductions would hit a home run while the rest were flops. This was actually quite a typical ratio for the consumer packaged-goods industry at the time.

Starting in 2000, when A. G. Lafley took over as CEO, things began to change. One of the first things Lafley did was to create a simple but powerful new mantra that fundamentally shifted the focus of the organization: "The Consumer Is Boss."[96] In a series of town hall meetings across the organization, Lafley repeatedly emphasized that the consumer had to be "at the heart of all we do" at P&G. Here's how he expressed it:

> "The people who buy and use P&G products are valued not just for their money, but as a rich source of information and direction. If we can develop better ways of learning from them—by listening to them, observing them in their daily lives, and even living with them—then our mission is more likely to succeed."[97]

This concept had a huge effect on P&G's previously insular culture. Suddenly employees were encouraged to get out of their labs and offices and into the homes of consumers and the stores selling P&G products. One program, called "Living It," gave P&G's researchers the opportunity to go and live with consumers in their houses or apartments for several days, eating meals with them and joining them on shopping trips.[98] Ethnographers armed with video cameras were sent out to households all around the world to film the way people wash their clothes, clean their bathrooms, feed their kids, and so on. The objective was to get a more visceral understanding about consumers' lives, their everyday routines and personal care experiences, their needs, aspirations, and emotions, and about how family budget, store layout, product packaging, and marketing strategy influence purchasing decisions. It was also a way for P&G to gain important insights into the lifestyles and local habits of people in many different countries and cultures.

Employees literally everywhere at P&G (not just in R&D or New Product Development) were given the mandate to stay externally focused on the men, women, children, babies, and pets that their business was serving, and to always try to see things through the eyes of the "boss."

How much do you really know about your customers' unsolved problems, unmet needs, and wants?

UNDERSTANDING
NEEDS

P&G's new approach was not purely about acutely observing, listening to, and understanding the customer in the search for inspiring new insights. It was also about involving consumers in the innovation process itself. As A. G. Lafley explains in his book *The Game Changer*, consumers now work directly with the company to "cocreate and codesign new brands and new products."[99] P&G brings them in at the very earliest stages of ideation, and then stays in touch with them at every consecutive step—prototyping, development, qualification, and commercialization—to make sure they are fully integrated into the company's whole product-launch model.

Another important tool for building strong interactive relationships with consumers, and for better understanding their needs, has been digital media. Unlike P&G's first websites in the 1990s, which were mostly static information pages with a strong brand and product focus, later sites and digital marketing activities have been more about engaging customers around the world with tips, advice, and everyday solutions, offering people the chance to post comments and articles of their own. A lot of P&G's product testing is now done virtually through the use of online simulation and computational modeling. Consumers are shown digital prototypes of new ideas and invited to give their opinions and suggest improvements. Alternative designs incorporating these comments can be made right away and then displayed onscreen for further feedback, enabling P&G to test

and refine ideas very quickly while simultaneously reinforcing its connection with consumers.

The results of P&G's cultural transformation have been profound. By putting the customer at the center of the company's innovation efforts, A. G. Lafley was able to unleash a torrent of new value-creating products that not only reshaped entire categories but also allowed the company to more than double its global sales—as well as its market capitalization—in less than a decade. Over the same period, the number of billion-dollar brands in P&G's portfolio increased from 10 to 24, and the number of brands with sales between $500 million and $1 billion grew fivefold. What about the company's commercial success rate for

new product launches? Lafley's customer-centric approach to innovation helped P&G raise this ratio from the previous 15 to 20 percent to a staggering 50 to 60 percent, meaning that when Lafley retired in 2009 roughly one in every two launches was delivering a significant return on investment. Now that he is back from retirement and running the company once again, nothing has changed in his attitude toward innovation. On August 1, 2014, P&G tweeted a statement from its CEO made during the company's earnings conference call: "Everything needs to begin with consumer value creation—and end with consumer satisfaction and loyalty."

Lafley is not unique in his successful approach to innovation. At Amazon.com, the very first of the company's core values is "Customer Obsession." As Jeff Bezos famously likes to put it, "We start with the customer and work backward." Steve Jobs expressed a similar view. Back in 1997, speaking at the Apple Worldwide Developers Conference in San Jose, California, he said, "One of the things I've always found is that you've got to start with the customer experience and work backward to the technology. You can't start with the technology and try to figure out where you're going to try and sell it."[100]

Radical innovators just seem to be naturally skilled at spotting deep, unmet customer needs and then building them into new business opportunities. They are somehow more empathetic than others—they are able to put themselves in the customer's shoes, to feel what the customer feels, to see things from the customer's perspective. This enables them to identify unsolved problems, common frustrations, and market inefficiencies to which competitors may be oblivious. They recognize needs that customers perhaps didn't even know they had, and they set out to address those needs by designing solutions from the customer backward.

{ "Everything needs to begin with consumer value creation."

A.G. Lafley, CEO Procter & Gamble }

Do customers **really** KNOW WHAT **THEY WANT?**

More and more companies are learning to engage their customers in the innovation process. Pulte Homes, for example, the largest homebuilding company in the United States, has spent thousands of hours talking to homeowners about the kind of floorplan that best suits the way they live. Working with focus groups who were invited to walk through and comment on a number of physical prototypes, Pulte was able to use all the feedback to create new, consumer-inspired designs. These include completely novel solutions for various areas of the home, such as a dedicated drop-off point at the entrance for bags and shoes, and a special space for kids to do their homework right next to the kitchen. Pulte likes to say that its homes are "Built from the idea up."

However, innovating from the customer backward doesn't just mean "listening to the voice of the customer." Of course it can be helpful to conduct market research, get customers to fill in a questionnaire, or run focus-group sessions. But merely asking customers what they want or need doesn't always yield the most inspiring or unique customer insights. Why not? In an interview with *BusinessWeek* in May 1998, Steve Jobs remarked: "It's really hard to design products by focus groups. A lot of times, people don't know what they want until you show it to them."[101]

As we learned earlier in this book, all of us have a set of established patterns in our minds that give us a preconceived and very narrow understanding about what a particular product or service is, what it is meant to do, how exactly it does it, what it is supposed to look like, where its limitations are, and so on. Most people find it extremely difficult to see outside of these patterns and to imagine how things could be or should be different. The great American journalist Edward R. Murrow once said, "Everyone is a prisoner of his own experiences."[102] Management consultant Mohanbir Sawhney echoes these words when he writes, "to gain customer insights, we must understand that we are prisoners of what we know and what we believe."[103]

We have probably all heard the famous quote attributed to Henry Ford: "If I had asked people what they wanted, they would have said faster horses." Actually, research reveals no evidence that Ford ever uttered or wrote these words, but although this adage may be apocryphal it nonetheless makes a good point, and if Ford had asked such a question he probably would have received a very similar answer. That's because people tend to respond this way when asked about what they want or what they need. They can quite easily tell you why they like or don't like some existing thing, but they can rarely imagine or articulate a radically alternative solution. So customers usually say things like, "Make it faster," "Make it cheaper," or "Make it easier to buy or use," rather than, "What I want is something that solves my problem in a completely different way."

Nobody, for example, told Apple they wanted a translucent desktop computer, a cool MP3 player, an online music store, a revolutionary smartphone, an App Store, or a tablet computer, but once Steve Jobs showed us these amazing things we realized we definitely wanted them—and needed them. Likewise, nobody was begging Google for a digital mapping service that would enable us to instantly find any spot on the planet, and then fly down to an address virtually and view it from the street. Nobody was asking P&G for a Swiffer mop, a Mr. Clean Magic Eraser, or a Febreze air freshener. Nobody was crying out for free video conferencing via mobile devices, or for a global microblogging network based on 140-character text messages. But obviously people must have needed these things because today they can't live without them.

Did you know you needed TiVo, Netflix, or YouTube? Do you remember wishing somebody would invent Amazon.com, eBay, or PayPal? Were you dying for a social media platform like Facebook, or for Spotify's streaming music service, or for Pandora's personalized Internet radio? When did you tell yourself you needed a mobile phone app for connecting with taxis, private cars, and ride-sharing services (Uber)? Or a home thermostat that learns your behaviors (Nest)? Or a cool set of DJ headphones for listening to your iPod (Beats by Dre)? All of these innovations were designed to address needs that most of us were not even aware of, which is why we were not articulating them. Or they gave us solutions we could never have imagined because we didn't even know they were possible.

> "If you don't listen to your customers you will fail. But if you only listen to your customers you will also fail."
>
> *One of Amazon.com's corporate slogans*

So the challenge is to try to understand the latent needs, wants, and frustrations that customers can't always articulate. Many successful entrepreneurs and innovative companies have developed a flair for uncovering and even anticipating these needs. They look for ways to bring unexpected new benefits to customers' lives, or to solve problems people didn't even know they had, or were not yet expressing. The way they get to these answers is not simply by asking customers what they want, or by reading a market research report, but by trying to look at the world—and at their own brands, products, and services—through the customer's eyes (the fourth lens of innovation). They immerse themselves in the customers' environment and observe how they behave and what they experience. This can uncover recurrent and perhaps unconscious or reflexive behavior patterns that point to unmet needs. At times, it can also lead to surprising discoveries. Tom Kelley, of the award-winning design firm IDEO, says that "a big part of an Anthropologist's discoveries is the departure between what people should do, or even what people say they do, and what they actually do."[104] Whether through direct observation of the customer in his or her natural settings (perhaps making photo or video diaries), or mapping the customer experience at every stage of the demand chain, or trying to viscerally share that experience by using your company's products and services yourself, the goal is to make the customer's needs, problems, frustrations, and feelings your own. This is how you generate the kind of deep customer insights that may trigger big new innovation opportunities. Your next step will be to start thinking creatively about how to address these issues before the competition does.

A great way to discover
new opportunities for innovation is to

"get into the customer's skin"

and start looking at your brands, products, and services
from the customer's perspective

❯ What's **wrong** with it? ❮

One excellent method for identifying unmet needs is to ask yourself what's *wrong* with your product or service from the customer's perspective. Most of the time we tend to focus on all the good things about our company's offerings. We are biased toward the positives, rather than the negatives. Marketing and salespeople in particular are usually well versed in all the relevant features, benefits, and unique selling propositions that add up to make your widgets the very best choice for the customer. But just for a change, try thinking about the annoyances, frustrations, or inconveniences your customers might be experiencing when dealing with your company, or when buying or using your products and services. Where are the customer "pain points"—in your business model, and across your industry? What if you could solve these irritations in a way that would significantly improve the customer experience, making

life easier, more convenient, and more enjoyable for the people you are serving?

For example, what's wrong with carbonated soda, potato chips, ice cream, chocolate, and beer? Most of us love to consume these popular products, but on the other hand we probably don't want to get fat. That's why smart manufacturers gave us diet soda, low-fat chips and ice cream, sugar-free chocolate, and lite beer. These innovators were simply taking the negative out of the equation.

What else is wrong with beer? Let's say you want to go out for a meal with family or friends, but you are concerned about drinking alcohol because you are a responsible driver. No problem. You can still enjoy your favorite ice-cold beverage, because these days most restaurants stock alcohol-free beer. What if you prefer wine? That's shouldn't be a problem, either. Today there are quite a number of decent alcohol-free wines to choose from—perhaps a ruby-red Cabernet Sauvignon or a chilled Chardonnay. Other people have religious reasons for abstaining from alcohol. They might be glad to know that in addition to the drinks just mentioned, there are now also alcohol-free ciders, sparkling wines, and even an alcohol-free whiskey. In 2006, one enterprising couple in the UK saw an opportunity to address this unmet need by founding The Alcohol Free Shop—an entire retail business dedicated exclusively to *nonalcoholic* adult drinks.

What about coffee? Billions of cups of it are drunk every day, so a lot of people around the world must like it, and extensive scientific research suggests various health benefits. But what's *wrong* with coffee? Well, certain folks—including people with hypertension—don't react well to caffeine. That's why decaffeinated coffee was invented at the beginning of the last century. What else is wrong with it? Well, drip-brew coffee takes time to prepare, which is one of the reasons for the success of instant coffees like Maxwell House, Nescafé, and more recently Starbucks VIA. Making a decent cup of espresso or cappuccino can also be a little complicated and messy (not to mention expensive, depending on the method and the machine involved). This prompted Nestlé to develop Nespresso—the capsule-based coffee system.

What's wrong with a power drill? Several things might come to mind. For about half a century following its invention, one of the device's main restrictions was the length of the electric cord and the need to find a nearby outlet. This was solved in 1961, when Black & Decker came up with the first cordless electric drill. What are some of the other negatives? Noise is an issue. Weight is another. And what about the dust that drilling always produces? To solve this particular problem, Bosch created a dust extraction unit that attaches straight to the drill, sucking up all the dust while you work. What else is wrong with a drill? Sometimes it's necessary to drill in a dark area, such as inside a cupboard or in a poorly lit basement, and it's difficult to see exactly where to point the drill bit. Here, too, Bosch came up with a solution—an integrated LED "PowerLight" at the front of the appliance (or on the handle attachment) that illuminates the area for precise drilling in all light conditions.

What's wrong with the air conditioner in your car? Probably not much at all. We're all very grateful for some refreshing climate control on a hot day. But how does it feel when you get into the car after it has been parked in the blazing sun for hours? It might take several minutes before the temperature can be reduced to a semi-bearable level. That's why Audi designed a sunroof with integrated solar panels that powers your AC's fan when the ignition is switched off. Now you can leave the car at the beach all day, and when you return the interior temperature will still be pleasantly cool.

What's wrong with paint cans? Pretty much everything! When you pick one up and carry it, the handle slices into your hand. When you are ready to start painting, it's difficult to pry the lid off—you need to use a screwdriver as a lever (which also isn't very good for the screwdriver). Then you try to pour the paint into a painting tray and much of it spills down the side of the can and around the rim. That makes it tough to get the lid back on (for which a rubber hammer is often required) without it sticking like glue. Metal cans also rust over time, and they frequently get dented and damaged. In fact, the whole packaging concept is terrible, yet it hasn't fundamentally changed for 200 years (since the Napoleonic era). Looking at this long list of negatives, the Sherwin-Williams paint brand Dutch Boy, based in Cleveland, Ohio, decided to reinvent paint packaging from the customer backward. Talking to consumers around the country, Dutch Boy gathered a rich portfolio of insights into the most important customer pain points, and then used these insights to create and test a revolutionary new packaging concept. The result, called "Twist & Pour," was introduced in 2002 and immediately made the rest of the paint industry look archaic. First, it is all plastic rather than steel, making it lighter and more durable. Its ergonomic design features an injection-molded handle on the side, offering a comfortable grip for carrying and pouring, and an easy twist-off lid that doubles as a paint cup and twists back on with a tight seal to maximize the shelf life of any leftover paint. Under the lid there is a convenient pour spout and brush wipe to reduce the normal mess from spilling and dripping. In the first six months alone, the award-winning new package tripled Dutch Boy sales, and also tripled the number of retail outlets stocking the product.

> **Innovators try to solve common problems and frustrations in ways that make life easier, more convenient, and more enjoyable for the customer.**

Since 1890, Heinz tomato ketchup has been sold in those iconic glass bottles, millions of which can still be found on restaurant tables and in kitchen refrigerators all over the world. But it took the company over a century to start thinking about how to address the frustrations consumers had long been experiencing with this traditional bottle design. Let's face it, as delicious as Heinz ketchup might be, it just doesn't move out of the bottle very easily. People would typically shake the bottle, rap it with their knuckles, pound it with the palm of the hand, bang it on the table, stick a knife in the bottle's neck, or smack it repeatedly from the bottom—anything to get the ketchup flowing. And often, after a few attempts, they would finally get a lot more ketchup on their food than they were hoping for, perhaps with a few red stains on the tablecloth and their clothes for good measure. Heinz found out that quite a large number of consumers were already storing the ketchup bottle upside down in an effort to solve this problem, so in 2002 they at last decided to make life easier by introducing their own pour-from-the-bottom bottle. Today, the plastic, upside-down packaging is so popular that Heinz is phasing out the old glass bottles from supermarket shelves, and that epic mealtime struggle is becoming a thing of the past.

Often, innovators come up with a game-changing new idea by trying to solve a problem they have personally experienced. Reed Hastings, founder of Netflix, was frustrated with the late return fees he had to pay to a local video store after misplacing a movie cassette for several weeks. On the way to the gym, he started to think about an alternative business model. Fitness clubs, for example, simply charged a flat monthly membership fee, and people could then work out as much or as little as they wanted to. This was the inspiration for Netflix and its monthly subscription concept back in the late 1990s, making the company the first to offer customers unlimited video rentals for a flat fee, without due dates or overdue fines.

Malcolm McLean, who is known as "the father of containerization," recalled that the seed for his idea of shipping containers was sown one day in 1937 while waiting for the cargo from his truck to be unloaded onto a ship in Hoboken, New Jersey. Sitting in the truck for most of the day while the stevedores laboriously loaded other cargo—lifting each individual crate off the trucks and hoisting them one by one into the ship's hold—it struck him that there had to be a better way of doing things, one that would save all that wasted time and money. His answer was standardized containers for intermodal transport (ship, truck, and rail), which went on to revolutionize global cargo shipping and trade.

Understanding
particular customer groups

One of the most powerful strategies is to ask yourself "What's wrong with it?" from the perspective of a particular customer segment or demographic. For example, we learned in Part Two that the women-only fitness chain Curves was founded on the insight that most gyms were not very female-friendly. Many companies today—from banks to appliance manufacturers to DIY retailers—are now trying to redesign their products or services to make them more tailored to women's needs and tastes.

Take something like the medical thermometer—a device that has been around for hundreds of years, and which seems perfectly designed for its purpose. Start thinking about specific types of patients for whom it may in fact be difficult or impractical to use. For example, what's wrong with a thermometer when trying to take a crying baby's temperature? What if the baby is in a high degree of distress, and won't lie still long enough for a thermometer reading, either orally, rectally, in the armpit, or in the ear? One company—Summer Infant—has come up with the ideal solution: a pacifier thermometer. Pop it in the infant's mouth and it works just like a regular pacifier, but on the outside is a small digital screen that clearly displays the baby's body temperature. This simple innovation allows parents to comfort their baby while simultaneously taking its temperature. It's also

a great way to monitor the infant's temperature while asleep, as the unit will begin to glow red if it detects a fever.

To try to better understand the special requirements of elderly citizens, ergonomics researchers at Loughborough University in the UK developed a "third age suit" that simulates the restricted mobility faced by people when they reach older age. Wearing this suit, researchers can experience firsthand what it is like to face typical age-related challenges when performing everyday tasks. This kind of research has been used by a wide range of companies—including Ford, Boeing, Barclays, and Tesco (the UK-based retail giant)—to help them identify and understand problems their older customers might face, and to find solutions for these unmet and unvoiced needs.

> Ask yourself "What's wrong with it?" from the perspective of a particular customer segment or demographic.

What's wrong with a refrigerator from the perspective of poor rural people living in India? First, it's a luxury appliance that remains unaffordable for 80 percent of Indian families (who earn less than $5 a day). Second, even if villagers had the money to buy a refrigerator, it wouldn't be much use without reliable electricity. Local Indian appliance manufacturer Godrej & Boyce wondered if there was a way to tackle this problem for the sake of so many Indian households that have no way of keeping food from spoiling within a day or two in the country's relentless heat. Their innovative answer was the inexpensive Chotukool—a compact, plastic, portable cooling unit that stores food at temperatures 80 degrees Fahrenheit (28 degrees Celsius) cooler than its surroundings. Instead of using a conventional refrigerator compressor, Chotukool employs a solid state thermoelectric cooling chip, which requires very little power and runs on a 12-volt battery. This radical solution—together with a convenient financing plan and a low-cost distribution system—created an entirely new product category that has changed the lives of rural consumers. It is now becoming increasingly popular as a trendy cool box for higher-income Indian customers, too.

What's wrong with a pizza? It might be one of the world's favorite foods, but it's not very easy to eat while driving a car, or riding a moped through the streets of Naples. For a centuries-old street food, pizza is also not entirely practical to eat while strolling around the city. Enter Rossano Boscolo, the Italian master of culinary art. His brilliant idea was the Kono Pizza—the pizza in a cone. By folding the traditional pizza dough into a conical shape, much like an ice cream cone, and then filling it with the "topping," Boscolo created a way for pizza lovers to enjoy a delicious Margherita or Pepperoni on the go, without the usual mess. And because all the topping ingredients are inside the cone, those great Italian flavors stay hot to the very last bite. Today, Kono Pizza is a rapidly growing fast-food franchise with locations in 20 countries.

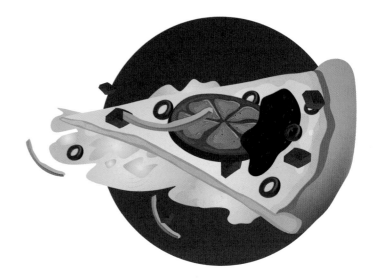

Where are the customer pain points? Try to search for them in your products and services, throughout your business model and across your industry.

INNOVATING FOR LOCAL NEEDS AND TASTES

Over the last two decades, many global brands have also discovered the critical importance of innovating for local needs, tastes, and values. For example, when P&G initially tested its Febreze air freshener in Japan, most consumers rejected the product. Rather than give up on it, P&G's team decided to rethink almost everything about Febreze except its core technology—including the bottle design, the fragrance profile, the viscosity of the product, and the spray pattern—in order to match Japanese preferences. Following these changes, Febreze went on to be phenomenally successful in Japan.

McDonald's has also become extremely good at adapting and redesigning its offerings to local cultures, culinary tastes, and religious customs. In India, for instance, the fast-food chain does not sell any beef products because Hindus, of course, venerate the cow. Instead, McDonald's has spiced up its menu with local products like Chicken McCurry, fiery Paneer Wraps, McAloo Tikki burgers, Masala Grill Veg, and the chicken Maharaja-Mac. In Israel, McDonald's operates kosher restaurants where all burgers are charcoal-grilled instead of fried, and meat and dairy products are never mixed (so you won't find a cheeseburger, and the milkshakes and ice cream are sold in the booth next door). Local favorites include the McShawarma and McKebab, both served on flatbread. In Muslim countries, the company serves only certified halal food at all locations, and several of these markets have their own special menu items, such as the McFalafel and the McArabia grilled chicken flatbread sandwich, which are very popular in Egypt and across the Middle East. During the Islamic holy month of Ramadan, McDonald's restaurants in Morocco offer dates, milk, and cookies for the breaking of the fast. In various Latin American markets there are also local adaptations—McBurritos, McNifica, McPalta, Cheddar McMelt, and banana-flavored pies. In China, Hong Kong, and Taiwan, you will find exotic McDonald's items like the Shogun Burger,

Seaweed Shaker Fries, kao fan ("baked rice"), and the Green Tea & Red Bean Ice Cream Sundae. Other Asian specials include McRice, McSoup, and McSatay (Indonesia); Bubur Ayam McD, Ayam Goreng McD, and Bubur Ikan McD (Malaysia); the Samurai Pork Burger (Thailand); the Kaisu Burger, Kampung Burger, and mango and durian milkshakes (Singapore); and the Mega Teriyaki burger, Filet-O-Shrimp, Chicken Katsu, Gratin Korokke Burger, Yassai Seikatsu vegetable juice, and green tea–flavored milkshakes (Japan). Australia has its McOz burger, Big Kahuna Burger, and Chive Omelette Roll, while New Zealanders can enjoy the Kiwiburger, the El Maco, and Georgie Pie.

A tour of Europe reveals additional local variations—the "Belgo" burger and Croque McDo (Belgium); the McCountry sandwich and the McToast (Croatia); the Greek Mac, Greek Chicken, and McFarm (Greece and Cyprus); the McSmažák (Czech Republic), Chicken Salsa Cheese and Daim McFlurry (Denmark); the McRuis (Finland); McCurrywurst (Germany); the McKroket, ChickenSaté burger, Joppie Burger, and Stroopwaffle McFlurries (Netherlands); Laksewrap (Norway); the WieśMac, Pikantny Kurczakburger, and Kanapka Drwala (Poland); the McBifana (Portugal); the McSy and McDonuts (Slovakia); the McTurco, Kofteburger, and ayran drink (Turkey); the Chicken Legend (UK and Ireland); and the McBaguette (Serbia).

Finally, let's not forget Canada, where you will find McLobster, the McMini, and Poutine, and last but not least the United States, where there are regional favorites like lobster rolls in New England, crab cakes in the Mid-Atlantic states, Johnsonville Brats in parts of the Upper Midwest, the Texas Homestyle Burger in Texas, traditional local breakfast items in the Southern states, and saimin, along with haupia pies, in Hawaii. This astounding list of products demonstrates just how far McDonald's is willing to go to adapt to the taste buds and local customs of its customers all over the world.

Oreos, which have been around for over 100 years, have long been the world's bestselling cookies. But when Kraft Foods introduced the Oreo brand to China in 1996, the company was in for a disappointment. Even after almost 10 years in the market, Oreo sales remained so low that Kraft was seriously thinking about pulling the brand out of China. Instead, the company decided to dig deeper into what might be going wrong. What they found was that historically the Chinese have not been very fond of cookies. Moreover, consumers found the Oreo both a little too sweet and a little too bitter for their taste. The cream was also a bit too gooey, and there was not enough chocolate in the cookie. Oh, and the price was too high. With this feedback as a starting point, Kraft's Chinese division set out to reinvent the Oreo from scratch. After testing 20 prototypes of alternative recipes with Chinese consumers, they finally found a formula that seemed to work. But it was quite different from the original product. Instead of the familiar round sandwich, it had four layers of crispy wafer sticks filled with reduced-sugar chocolate and vanilla cream, and the whole thing was coated with chocolate. Kraft introduced the new Oreo in smaller, less expensive package sizes to match Chinese purchasing behavior, and sales began to take off. Later, new flavors followed, inspired by popular Asian desserts: Green Tea Ice Cream, Raspberry-and-Blueberry, and Mango-and-Orange. Today, Oreo is the top-selling packaged cookie in China, where sales are second only to the United States.

Like P&G, McDonald's, and Kraft Foods, many other multinational corporations are decentralizing their innovation efforts in an effort to focus on the specific needs of local markets. Companies like Coca-Cola, PepsiCo, Nestlé, L'Oréal, 3M, and DuPont all operate global networks of regional R&D centers to support their various geographies around the world. PepsiCo's Chinese innovation team has come up with popular local flavors for its Lay's potato chips, like "Cucumber," "Iced Lemon Tea," and "Numb & Spicy Hot Pot," while the Russian team developed "Crab," "Red Caviar," and "Pickled Cucumber" flavors to boost sales in the Russian market. L'Oréal's Shanghai-based Global Innovation Center has developed beauty products incorporating traditional Chinese medicinal remedies, such as white fungus and ginseng. And at its Indian center in Mumbai, the company is busy creating new products especially for Indian hair and complexions, as well as smaller package sizes for price-conscious consumers, many of whom get paid weekly rather than monthly.

{ "Stop selling what you have. Start selling what they need."

IBM advertisement }

Matching what is *possible* with what is *needed*

For most of the last century, corporate innovation was driven primarily from the technology side rather than the customer side. That is to say, in most large organizations it tended to start with technical R&D and engineering rather than with deep insights into customer needs. This approach worked well in an economic era when there was more demand than supply, when consumers had few options and were happy to stand in line for whatever products and services they could get. But in today's value-based economy, where global competition and overcapacity have given the consumer more choices and more power than ever before, a large number of companies from all over the world are now competing for the same customer's money. Success has therefore come to depend on an organization's ability to bring exciting and compelling new benefits to customers—or address their unmet needs—before the competition.

Nobody of course would argue against the need for cutting-edge technological research, and thankfully scientists in every corner of the globe continue to amaze us with new breakthrough discoveries. But what makes the difference today is how quickly, effectively, and differently companies can leverage these technologies to radically improve the customer experience. In many cases, it's still the technology that comes first and the consumer application second, which can nevertheless work out just fine. But increasingly companies are starting from the other end, by first identifying an important customer need and then working backward to find a technical solution. The key point here is that both sides of the equation are vital, so the real challenge for organizations is how to get better at bringing the two together.

Consumer products giant Procter & Gamble provides a powerful lesson in how to break out of a purely technology-centric mindset. Back in the 1990s, a group of P&G's senior managers woke up and realized the company had missed a series of big commercial opportunities by encouraging innovation solely from the R&D department—by historically being too technology-driven.

For example, P&G's Oral Care division had looked into the idea of adding baking soda to toothpaste as a way of reducing plaque-related periodontal diseases. The R&D people tested it and concluded that, from a technology perspective, there was no merit in the idea. There was absolutely no way they could clinically demonstrate any benefits. So they said, "OK. It's just smoke and mirrors. We're not interested in it." But then some of P&G's competitors added baking soda to their toothpaste—along with a premium price tag—and made a huge business

The 4 Lenses of Innovation

success out of it. How was that possible? It was because, even though the idea didn't work as a piece of technology, it worked in the consumer's mind. It leveraged the fact that generations of dentists had told people they should use baking soda under certain circumstances for oral-care-related problems. So rather than being a technology-based innovation, this opportunity was based on a deep consumer need that looked, at least psychologically, as if it was being met.

This, and a few similar experiences, began to hammer the message home to Procter & Gamble that innovation is not just an R&D game. Of course, technology remains critically important to the company, and P&G still invests heavily in technical research, but what senior management finally understood back then was that it's only half of the loaf. That was what prompted them to develop an internal strategy aimed at bringing both the technology side and the consumer side together. It was called "Matching What Is Possible with What Is Needed."

It was a pivotal moment for P&G—the moment when its marketing people made the fundamental switch from managing brands to managing consumers' needs. For example, when they talked to consumers they found out that many of them assumed soap was not good for their skin (P&G had been making and selling soap since 1837!). So they went back to R&D and combined the cleansing action of a soap bar with the moisturizing effect of a lotion to create Olay Body Wash, which was a huge commercial success.

When P&G listened to consumers talk about hair care, they found that people thought shampoo would make their hair shiny but that it wouldn't actually make it very healthy. So they asked the scientists in R&D to add some vitamin technology to the shampoo, which was the birth of Pantene Pro-V (pro-vitamin) products. Today, they are among the best-selling hair care products in the world. The range includes products designed exclusively to meet specific consumer needs: from the hair textures of different ethnic groups, to color-treated hair, to hair that needs

> The challenge for today's organizations is how to get better at innovating from both the *technology* side and the *customer* side.

protection from urban pollutants. And when consumers said they would like a hairspray to provide hold but without the gluey stiffness that makes hair impossible to comb, P&G responded with Pantene Pro-V Flexible Hold Hairspray, which was an instant hit.

This is not to say that innovation at P&G can no longer originate on the technology side. Far from it. But the company has managed to strike the right balance between technical R&D and customer-centric marketing so that the two sides work symbiotically to create new value. That means the correlation between P&G's innovation investments and commercial outcomes is now much stronger than ever before.

Sadly, in many other companies we still find a great divide between these two sides of the business when it comes to innovation. We find engineers and scientists locked away in isolated research labs, assuming that marketing's job is simply to advertise and sell their finished inventions. We find R&D people protecting their turf rather than embrace new concepts like co-creation, crowdsourcing, and open innovation—where customers and other external constituencies become integral partners in the innovation process. On the other hand, we find marketing and sales managers who are far more focused on the technical features of their offerings than on the unmet needs of their customers. And when R&D comes up with a truly disruptive innovation, we often find the marketing department arguing vehemently against it on the basis that it would cannibalize their existing business.

How do things work inside your own organization? Have you achieved a high level of synchronicity between engineering and marketing? Are your marketing people generating a constant stream of quality customer insights to guide your engineers on where to innovate? And are your engineers producing a slew of new technical possibilities that your marketing people can leverage to address unmet customer needs?

In short, is your company already adept at matching what is possible with what is needed, and vice versa? Or will it have to get a whole lot better?

How could we apply this new technology?

How could we address this unmet need?

For a great example of matching what is technically possible with what is needed, take a good look at Apple's App Store or Google Play. Before 2007 or 2008, almost nobody was thinking about mobile apps, or "application software" for smartphones. But soon developers were using simple tools to create mobile apps for almost every conceivable human need—from general productivity and information tools to banking, cooking, gaming, fitness and medical monitoring, flight tracking, navigation, social media, and all kinds of other stuff—some of it useful, some of it weird.

Amazon.com has taken great efforts to apply technology in highly innovative ways to create a better and more convenient customer experience—from its original 1-Click shopping system to its automated recommendations for related products, all the way through to its Firefly app for instant object recognition and shopping using Amazon's Fire phone.

Google is another company that knows how to connect cutting-edge technology with latent and unarticulated customer needs. Over the years, it has given us all kinds of friendly search and mapping services we never requested but that are now essential to our daily lives. With Google Now, the company has gone one step further by transforming any Android smartphone into a proactive personal assistant. Google Now knows you so well—based on your personal search habits, e-mail, calendar, and current location—that it tells you what you need to know before you even ask for it. In 2012 Google Now was named "Innovation of the Year" by *Popular Science* magazine.[105]

Nest Labs, which was acquired by Google in 2014 for $3.2 billion, makes smart home devices such as thermostats and smoke detectors that are designed explicitly to solve very human frustrations. For example, why should you have to go through the irritating process of programming a thermostat? Why can't it just learn and adapt to your daily behaviors? And if a smoke detector's sensor gets triggered by mistake, why can't you silence the alarm simply by waving at it? The *Wall Street Journal* described Nest's approach to innovation as follows: "First, find the most annoying, obvious problem that millions of people deal with every day. Then ask if things really have to be that way."[106] Once Nest has zeroed in on some common frustration it wants to solve, the company combines smart software with network connectivity, along with cool design, to transform what is usually a boring and unfriendly appliance into something that wows customers with its intelligence, simplicity, and beauty.

While most of us love to use smartphones and tablets, these mobile devices still present us with a few major aggravations. First and foremost is insufficient battery life. Some innovative companies are looking into possible solutions. StoreDot, a startup in the field of nanotechnology, has developed a groundbreaking new kind of battery for mobile devices, which can be charged in less than a minute. TAG Heuer, the maker of luxury watches, has taken a different approach with the Meridiist Infinite. This pricey, solar-powered phone has invisible photovoltaic cells built into its screen that automatically recharge the device from natural or artificial light. There are all kinds of other inventions to overcome mobile battery life problems, such as portable power packs, charging mats, hand-wound dynamos, and even a pedal-powered phone charger that connects to your bicycle.

Another gripe is that many mobile apps—such as chat, streaming media, or banking—don't work without an Internet connection, which is especially irksome when travelling in certain places such as deep underground on the subway. To address this problem, a California-based software company called Couchbase has designed a mobile solution that allows apps to work without Internet connectivity by embedding a database and sync capability directly into their software (rather than storing and accessing the data on a cloud server). In 2014, Couchbase signed a deal with Beats Electronics, now owned by Apple, to enable users to enjoy the company's streaming music service even when they are not connected to the Internet.

A team of researchers at the University of Illinois and Northwestern University is working on a stretchy, stick-on skin patch (much like a Band-Aid) that incorporates off-the-shelf sensors and microchips to wirelessly monitor your health more accurately than wristwatch-type devices.

Goodyear has developed a self-inflating tire that uses a built-in sensor to continuously monitor the tire's air pressure while you drive. If it gets too low, the regulator automatically opens a valve to allow air into a pumping tube, which then inflates the tire to its optimum pressure. All of this happens without ever stopping the vehicle or bothering the driver.

In 2012, Ukrainian students created sensor-equipped gloves that can recognize the sign language used by speech- and hearing-impaired people and translate it into text on a smartphone app, which subsequently converts it into spoken words. For the first time in history, this allows the voiceless to verbally communicate with people who don't understand sign language.

UK-based quantum physicist and pet owner Nick Hill came up with the solution to a nagging problem of his own. It seemed that every neighborhood critter liked using the cat flap on his back door to wander in and out of his home. The answer was to design an electronically activated flap that only opens when it recognizes the ID microchip on his kitty's collar. It turns out this idea appealed to a lot of other pet owners, too, so Hill decided to found a startup to manufacture and sell the system. Since 2008, his company has already shipped hundreds of thousands of units.

Every day seems to bring news of another breakthrough application for 3D printing technology. So far, the process has been used to produce everything from toys to jewelry, fashion accessories, musical instruments, automotive and aerospace parts, home decor, building materials (and even houses), food, medical equipment, prosthetic body parts, and replacement knees, hips, and vertebrae. Now, scientists are working hard on the next frontier: 3D-printed human organs. Researchers have already been able to use the machines to print small strips of organ tissue from human cells. The promise is that, within a few years, they will be able to reproduce whole artificial organs—hearts, kidneys, livers, lungs—for use in surgical transplants. In 2013, doctors were able to give a 2-year-old girl in Illinois a new windpipe built from her own stem cells. And bioengineers in Kentucky predict that it will be possible to print a whole "bioficial" human heart in the next decade.

LESSONS
TO TAKE AWAY

Innovators look at things from the customer's perspective. (They uncover unsolved problems, common frustrations, and unvoiced needs, then design solutions from the customer backward.)

Make the customer your starting point for idea generation. (Try to emulate P&G's attitude that "The Consumer Is Boss." Develop a deeper understanding of your customers' needs through listening, observing, and interacting.)

Customers don't always know what they want. (Market research, customer questionnaires, and focus groups will only get you so far. Immerse yourself in the customers' environment and try to make their needs, frustrations, and feelings your own.)

Ask yourself what's wrong with it. (Think about the annoyances or inconveniences your customers might be experiencing with your products and services. Identify the "pain points" and look for ways to solve them.)

Focus on particular customer groups. (Try to understand the special needs of certain market segments, demographic groups, or even individuals. Put yourself in their shoes and show empathy for their situation.)

Innovate for local needs and tastes. (What works well in your home market might flop in another geography. Dig deep to identify local requirements and preferences, then use these insights to rethink, redesign, or tailor your offerings.)

Match what is possible with what is needed. (Work hard to innovate from both the technology side and the customer side. Try to get better at bringing the two sides together.)

Part Four

How big ideas are built

The Archimedes Principle

There is a common myth about innovation that **big ideas** simply come to us out of nowhere in a sudden **flash of inspiration.**

For over two thousand years, ever since Archimedes is supposed to have leapt out his bath crying "Eureka!," this has been the way we characterize these magical moments. But even though it might feel sometimes as if ideas just pop into our heads out of the blue, we are now beginning to understand that there is much more involved in the process.

The fact is, creative ideas don't just occur to us spontaneously from one moment to the next. Our minds actually build them from a unique chain of associations and connections, sometimes over a considerable period of time.

When we examine the creative process in more detail, we discover that breakthrough thinking is usually built on an illuminating insight (or a series of insights) into a situation or a problem that inspires an unexpected leap (or leaps) of association in the mind, resulting in a completely novel configuration of previously existing ideas. This fresh combination of thoughts, in which various, perhaps unrelated concepts and domains click together in a whole new relationship, is what suddenly manifests itself as a big idea or creative solution. That's the famous Eureka moment when a light bulb seems to switch on in our heads.

Consider Archimedes himself. The "Eureka!" story may well be mythical. But in many ways it aptly illustrates how the creative process often works. In the legend, the Greek polymath didn't simply sit down in the bath one day and say, "Hey, I've just had a great idea for measuring the density of an irregular-shaped object!" Rather, he had been intensely focused for quite a while on solving exactly this problem.

According to the story, King Hiero II of Syracuse suspected he had been cheated by his goldsmith, and he asked Archimedes to come up with a way to verify his hunch. After giving the goldsmith a bar of pure gold to make him a new crown, which was to be shaped like leaves in honor of the gods who had given him victory in battle, the king wondered if some of the gold had been secretly substituted with silver in the finished product. Hiero asked Archimedes how to determine if all the gold had really been used in the crown, without melting it down or damaging it in any way. To answer this question, Archimedes needed a way to calculate the crown's density, which would be an important indication of its purity (since silver and other metals are less dense than gold). But at the time nobody knew how to measure the density of an irregular-shaped object. So this was the complicated challenge he was mentally wrestling with.

When Archimedes stepped into the Syracuse public bath, therefore, he may have been seeking a way to relax, but his mind was subconsciously still working on the problem. And as he sat in the water, submerged his limbs, and watched the water level rise, he realized that the volume of water he was displacing had to be equal to the volume of the body part he was immersing.

This brilliant but incredibly simple insight provided the basis for his breakthrough solution, because water displacement offered him a way to measure the volume of the crown, regardless of its shape. Once Archimedes had the volume, he could divide the weight of the crown by this value, and thus arrive at the density. Then all he had to do was compare it to the density of a bar of pure gold (using the same water displacement method) to find out if the two values matched. As the story goes, Archimedes' innovation revealed that the king's goldsmith had indeed been dishonest. And today we still use water displacement to measure the volume and density of an object.

What was the process through which Archimedes came to his famous solution?

1. Archimedes decided to focus his mind on a specific challenge.

2. As a mathematician and physicist, he must have reviewed everything he and anyone else knew on the subject to find some clues.

3. He grappled with the problem, surely exploring a range of possible solutions, none of which gave him the answer he needed.

4. At some point Archimedes probably reached a creative impasse—a state of frustration at not being able to solve the problem despite all his efforts.

5. He took a break. He chose to unplug himself from his mental fixation and just relax by taking a bath. And while in that state of mental and physical comfort his unconscious mind was free to entertain fresh thoughts, and to integrate them with previous thoughts—not obsessively this time, but playfully.

6. This is when he gained the insight. Just like the rest of us, Archimedes had observed changes in water level every time he had gotten into a bath. But this familiar cause and effect relationship had never had any special significance for him— that is, until he started looking at it in the particular context of the problem he was trying to solve. Pondering the king's challenge had given him a receptive frame of mind—a solution-seeking perspective that enabled him to notice things he would otherwise have taken for granted. Suddenly the rise in the level of the water had a new meaning, because it was directly related to the volume of whatever was submerged in the bath.

7. Following immediately on Step Six (so that the two steps actually seemed like one), the new insight inspired Archimedes with a big idea—water displacement could be used to measure the volume of the crown (or any irregular-shaped object, for that matter), which would mean that its density could be calculated! This moment of rapid and exhilarating transition—from unsolved to obvious—was what became known as the "Eureka moment."

8. Archimedes initiated experiments to see if his new idea actually worked—if it was a practical solution to the problem, and could be implemented effectively.

In many ways, these eight steps are typical of the way breakthrough thinking often happens, as we shall see in the following examples.

How Big Ideas Are Built

Rethinking the
Universe

From the most advanced scientific circles to the cheapest tourist T-shirts, Albert Einstein is commonly regarded as the epitome of genius. But how did he actually arrive at his brilliant new theories and mathematical formulas? Did they just come to him in a sudden flash of inspiration? Or were they pieced together systematically in his mind over a longer period of time? Indeed, were his scientific breakthroughs built on illuminating insights that recombined previously existing ideas? Let's consider the process through which Einstein reinvented physics.

Just like Archimedes, we find that Einstein would concentrate obsessively—sometimes for many years—on solving a single problem. He would consider the work of his predecessors and peers—from Isaac Newton to James Clerk Maxwell, David Hume, Ernst Mach, Hendrik Lorentz, Henri Poincaré, and Max Planck—either building on or refuting their ideas. He would explore radical new concepts through his famous thought experiments, like riding across the universe on a light beam, or being in an elevator in free fall. But finding the answers to his mind puzzles about space and time was difficult intellectual work, and there were occasions when

he ran out of steam. Thankfully, however, Einstein knew how to unwind. For example, he loved sailing, taking long walks around town, playing the violin, and—like Archimedes—relaxing in the bath (sometimes for hours on end). When he came up with his theory of special relativity, and shortly afterward with $E = mc^2$, he had probably also been greatly helped by the dullness of his day job—an assistant clerk at the patent office in Bern, Switzerland—which must have given him plenty of opportunities to daydream.

Einstein's world-changing theory didn't just occur to him one lucky day while he was sitting at his desk staring idly out of the window. By his own account, he had been thinking about it for at least seven years, starting during his diploma course at the Swiss Federal Polytechnic in Zürich, where he studied mathematics and physics (and took special interest in extracurricular books on advanced physics theories). As a student, Einstein became captivated by James Clerk Maxwell's mathematical equations for electrodynamics, which had been published just a few decades earlier. These equations—based on a revolutionary theory of electromagnetic waves—represented a completely new understanding of physics. In his groundbreaking work, Maxwell was the first to describe light as electromagnetic radiation with a constant speed in a vacuum, represented by the symbol c.

The fascination for Einstein was that Maxwell's equations seemed to contradict the accepted laws of mechanics as formulated by Galileo and Newton, because electromagnetism—in particular light—simply didn't behave as those classical laws predicted. According to Galilean–Newtonian relativity, light should have different speeds when measured from different inertial frames of reference—that is, observation points moving at constant speeds relative to each other. So how could the speed of light always be the same, regardless of the motion of the observer relative to the light source?

The conventional wisdom of the day was that light waves travelled through an invisible, zero-density transmission medium called ether (or aether), which was supposed to be omnipresent throughout the universe, filling every space. So it was assumed that the fixed speed of light predicted by Maxwell's equations had to be relative to the ether at a preferred state of rest. It was also assumed that as observers moved their position (or their inertial frame of reference) relative to the ether, they would see light moving at different speeds.

But in 1887, less than 10 years before Einstein started his diploma course, two American physicists, Albert Michelson and Edward Morley, conducted an experiment to measure the speed of light from different directions relative to the ether. And they were amazed to discover that the speed of light was always constant, in every direction. Rather than embracing these results as an important achievement, the scientific community put them down to a failed experiment, one that had revealed nothing about the ether and its preferred state of rest—which, after all, was supposed to be the whole point of the exercise. A few physicists even tried to explain away the controversial new findings by offering their own misguided theories about ether, which only added to the confusion.

So by the turn of the twentieth century, the apparent incompatibility between Newtonian laws of mechanics on the one hand, and the work of Maxwell, Michelson, and Morley on the other, had become the great conundrum of physics. And it was exactly this seemingly unsolvable puzzle that the young graduate Albert Einstein ambitiously determined he would try to solve.

It turned out to be a long, hard, and confusing struggle that ended up leading him nowhere. And the more he pursued it, the more the solution eluded him. The frustrating thing was that everything seemed to be scientifically indisputable (Newton's laws of mechanics, Maxwell's speed of light as confirmed by Michelson and Morley, and the idea of the ether), yet the whole equation didn't work. So something clearly had to be wrong. But what was it? Einstein still didn't know, but he somehow sensed that the answer, when found, would fundamentally change the whole of physics. That's why he continued to obsess about it to the point where, in the spring of 1905, he "wondered if this was the path to insanity" and even "feared for his health."[1] At the tender age of 26, after working on the problem for many years with no results, Einstein found himself in an intellectual and emotional crisis with almost no hope of ever cracking the puzzle. That is when, on the verge of giving up on the entire thing, he decided to visit his close friend and colleague at the patent office, Michele Besso, to explain his epic struggle. Ironically, it was just after this conversation that he found the solution.

Essentially, Einstein's breakthrough came from applying the perceptual lens of innovation called Challenging Orthodoxies, which we first identified in Part One of this book and examined in more detail in Part Three.

Einstein asked himself the following questions: What if Newton's laws of mechanics are not as fixed as everyone has believed for centuries? What if time and space are not absolute? What if they are variable, and the only universal constant is in fact the speed of light? What if Maxwell's theory of electrodynamics needs to be modified to apply to any inertial frame of reference, rather than just relative to the ether? And what if the Michelson–Morley experiment didn't fail? What if their findings were actually correct, and it is the concept of the ether that is wrong?

By looking at the whole issue through this contrarian lens, Einstein was able to apply fresh thinking to the problem. He began to develop some radical new questions about time and space that

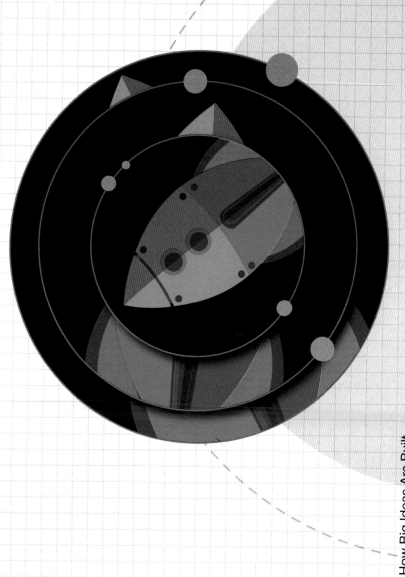

few had ever dared ask before: What if we challenge the assumption about simultaneity? What if two events at different places that supposedly occur at exactly the same time actually occur at different times depending on the frame of reference (or motion) of the observer? In other words, what if time cannot be absolutely defined? What if a clock were perceived to slow down or speed up depending on how fast you were moving through space relative to other observers? And what if space itself behaved differently if you were traveling close to the speed of light? What if moving objects appeared to become much shorter in length, and increased infinitely in mass? And what if none of these phenomena depend on an ether? What if the mysterious ether is just a myth?

Einstein later recalled how the decisive insight about simultaneity inspired his fundamentally new theory of physics:

"Today everyone knows, of course, that all attempts to clarify this paradox [of light that leads to special relativity] satisfactorily were condemned to failure as long as the axiom of the absolute character of time, or of simultaneity, was rooted unrecognized in the unconscious. To recognize clearly this axiom and its arbitrary character already implies the essentials of the solution of the problem."[2]

"After seven years of reflection in vain (1898–1905), the solution came to me suddenly with the thought that our concepts and laws of space and time can only claim validity insofar as they stand in a clear relation to experiences; and that experience could very well lead to the alteration of the concepts and laws. By a revision of the concept of simultaneity into a more malleable form, I thus arrived at the special theory of relativity."[3]

Albert Einstein

Once this key insight opened Einstein's eyes to see the solution to the problem, he was able to get to work immediately on the mathematical details, and in just five weeks he produced what is arguably the greatest scientific paper of the twentieth century: "On the Electrodynamics of Moving Bodies."

Of course, Einstein went on to many other outstanding scientific achievements, and if we examine the thinking processes behind all of these subsequent successes we find a similar approach—almost a recipe for creative genius—recurring time and time again. It's the same eight-step process we previously identified in the story of Archimedes, as shown graphically on the following pages.

Again, what this teaches us is that big ideas need more than a moment. There is a definite thinking process involved in constructing a breakthrough. And Einstein provides us with an excellent model of the master idea-builder.

CHALLENGING ORTHODOXIES

8 Steps to Building a Breakthrough

Frame a specific challenge and focus on solving it.

Research the subject. Learn from the work of others.

Relax. Detach from the problem. Let it incubate in the unconscious mind.

Come to an illuminating insight that fundamentally shifts your perspective.

The 4 Lenses of Innovation

Immerse yourself in the problem. Explore possible solutions.

Reach a roadblock. Feel the creative frustration.

Build the insight (or insights) into a big idea—a new combination of thoughts.

Test and validate the new idea—try to make it work.

How Big Ideas Are Built

Inventing the
20th Century

Let's look at one more example of this process in action. Consider Thomas Edison—perhaps the most prolific innovator of all time. Did the man who is said to have "invented the twentieth century" follow the same eight steps to innovation success? Absolutely. Here's how he usually worked:

Frame a specific challenge and focus on solving it.

In his biography of Edison, Neil Baldwin writes of the great genius's "consuming obsession."[4] After identifying an opportunity he wanted to pursue—something he believed would solve an important problem—Edison and his team at Menlo Park would focus on it intensively, working around the clock for months on end in the relentless search for a solution.

Research the subject. Learn from the work of others.

As a foundation for each project, Edison first studied the subject exhaustively. He once said to a reporter, "When I want to discover something, I begin by reading up everything that has been done along that line in the past—that's what all these books in the library are for. I see what has been accomplished at great labor and expense in the past. I gather data of many thousands of experiments as a starting point, and then I make thousands more."[5]

Immerse yourself in the problem. Explore possible solutions.

Edison's endless "trial and error" experiments were designed to persistently and inexhaustibly try every conceivable possibility until the desired solution was found. He and his fellow engineers famously tried over 3,000 different filament materials in the development of their incandescent light bulb. Less well known is the fact that Edison's team also conducted close to 50,000 experiments in the quest to develop the first alkaline storage battery.

Reach a roadblock. Feel the creative frustration.

With so many experiments leading Edison and his team down blind alleys, there were inevitably times when they felt a deep sense of frustration. Edison expressed it as follows: "In trying to perfect a thing, I sometimes run straight up against a granite wall a hundred feet high. If, after trying and trying, I can't get over it, I turn to something else."[6]

Relax. Detach from the problem. Let it incubate in the unconscious mind.

For Edison, turning to "something else" often meant taking a temporary pause from the project and reading a book on something entirely different, using one activity "as a relief from another," as Michael Gelb and Sarah Miller Caldicott recount in *Innovate Like Edison*.[7] He also knew how to punctuate periods of intense concentration with relaxing breaks. There would be midnight lunches with the whole team at one long table, where they would eat pie, drink beer or coffee, tell jokes, smoke cigars, and sing humorous songs while someone played the pipe organ that was a permanent fixture in the lab. Edison also believed it was important to take time off for what he called "loafing"—he particularly enjoyed walking, gardening, and fishing. On occasions, he is known to have sat for hours with a baitless hook just staring into the rippling water.

Then there were the naps. A couple of times a day, Edison would usually climb on top of his desk and curl up there, resting for a brief while to revitalize himself (his wife Mina later had a cot brought to his office). In 1910, Frank Dyer, one of Edison's Menlo Park experimenters (known affectionately as "muckers"), coauthored a two-volume biography called *Edison: His Life and Inventions* with Thomas Martin.[8] In the book, the authors explain that during Edison's naps, "he would use several volumes of *Watt's Dictionary of Chemistry* for a pillow." His employees used to say that he "absorbed the contents during his sleep, judging from the flow of new ideas he had on waking."

6 **Come to an illuminating insight that fundamentally shifts your perspective.**

Edison surrounded himself with a rich source of potentially inspiring insights. For example, his Menlo Park laboratory contained a dizzying selection of machines, materials, and chemicals that could be employed and recombined in all kinds of different ways to create new inventions. One of the materials one could commonly find laying around was carbon. In fact, the Lab used to produce its own lampblack—a soot-like material of almost pure carbon that was scraped off the glass of kerosene lamps that were left burning continuously in a little shed nearby.

And so it was that after trying all kinds of different filament materials in the development of the light bulb—from paper and cardboard to fishing line, twine, cedar shavings, platinum, coconut hair, and fibers from vines and bamboo—the legend is that Thomas Edison happened to be sitting one night in his laboratory working on another project, while unconsciously rolling a piece of lampblack between his fingers as one might doodle with a pen. The lampblack, which was mixed with tar, became very malleable, and as he continued to roll it the material turned into a fine thread. As he glanced down at his fingers, it suddenly occurred to Edison that the carbon lampblack might actually make an effective filament.

In a moment, we'll look in more detail at this insight and how Edison used it to solve his light bulb puzzle. In the meantime, consider how, while working on one challenge, Edison would sometimes come to an insight that opened up an unexpected opportunity in another field.

For example, his first great invention at Menlo Park came out of his efforts to increase the efficiency of telegraph machines by finding a way to automatically record and resend messages. His experiments were focused on a system that would emboss the telegraphic signals on a circular paper disk as they came in over the wire. This disk could then be removed and used in a second machine that would pick up the embossed recording and repeat the Morse code messages to other recipients. Edison discovered that with this system he could speed up the transmission speed of the telegraphic signals from around forty words a minute to several hundred words a minute.

But that wasn't all. He also discovered that when the machine was working at high speed it emitted a noise that reminded him of very rapid speech. While listening to that sound, the insight came to him that an adapted version of this embossing system might actually be able to record and play back the human voice!

LEVERAGING RESOURCES

These are very good examples of looking at something through the third lens of innovation—Leveraging Resources—which is about understanding how existing competencies and assets could be used in different ways, or in novel combinations, to create new value.

How Big Ideas Are Built

219

7 Build the insight (or insights) into a big idea—a new combination of thoughts.

Let's go back to that legendary piece of lampblack that Edison had been rolling between his fingers. As usual, there is much more background to the story. The fact is that Edison had considered using a carbon filament earlier on in the light bulb project—carbon produces a good deal of heat and light when it burns. The trouble is that it usually burns up in just a few seconds due to oxygen in the atmosphere, which initially made carbon useless for the light bulb project because a lamp would need to stay illuminated for hours. Edison had therefore focused instead on platinum because of its higher melting point. But experiments showed that platinum also absorbed oxygen from the atmosphere as it was burning, and was therefore melting at a lower temperature, which is why Edison began working with a new technology—vacuum—to remove all the air from the glass chamber of the bulb. Although this improved the performance of the platinum filaments, they were still impractical for commercial use because they were too expensive and had very low electrical resistance, requiring big and costly copper-wire conductors. What Edison needed was a slow-burning material for the filaments that was cheap enough to make his bulbs affordable, and that had high electrical resistance in order to reduce the cost of the electricity distribution system itself.

Hence, the thousands of experiments with alternative materials, including 40 different metals and fibers from a thousand species of bamboo. Edison had even appointed someone "to ransack the jungles of the Far East" in his search for the perfect bamboo fiber. Some of these materials didn't work at all. Some burned too quickly. Some overheated. Some were just not bright enough, or glowed with the wrong color. None of them gave Edison the lighting effect he was looking for.

So when Edison looked down at that thread of lampblack in his fingers, his real insight was this: If carbon were placed in the newly developed vacuum bulb it would theoretically burn for a longer period of time due to the absence of oxygen, and might therefore now be a viable option. His breakthrough idea was that carbon might even be the ideal solution for the filament, since it was cheap, easy to manufacture, and had high electrical resistance.

"Take an insight and work it into a form useful to the world."

Scott Berkun

What about the other insight described earlier—that an adapted version of Edison's telegraph recording system might be able to record and play back the human voice?

Building on this insight, Edison's combinational idea was to build a machine that could record and replay telephone messages. Why would this particular opportunity occur to him? Let's look at the context. First, Edison had spent his early career as a telegraph operator, and had gone on to invent a series of devices related to telegraphy—including improved telegraph printers, a telegraphic stock ticker, and the quadruplex telegraph, which could transmit and receive four messages simultaneously on the same wire. Thus, for many years he had lived and worked almost exclusively in the world of telecommunicated messages, and Edison routinely chose to pursue what Steven Johnson, author of *Where Good Ideas Come From*, calls "the adjacent possible"—new solutions based on his existing know-how, or a recombination of technologies he was already using.[9]

Second, Alexander Graham Bell had recently invented the telephone (which was basically an acoustic telegraph). Voice transmission via telegraph wires was already recognized by some forward thinkers as the "next big thing." In fact, Edison had just patented a carbon button transmitter to improve the acoustic quality of Bell's invention, thus making phone conversations more understandable. So during that period (the spring and summer of 1877) Edison was already commercially involved in the new science of sound, and was aware of the potential large-scale transition from written (Morse code) messages to spoken ones.

Third, he was always on the lookout for practical ideas that could be turned into things people would want to buy. If there was commercial potential in a machine for recording and repeating telegraph messages, what about a device for business organizations that could record and play back the new telephone messages?

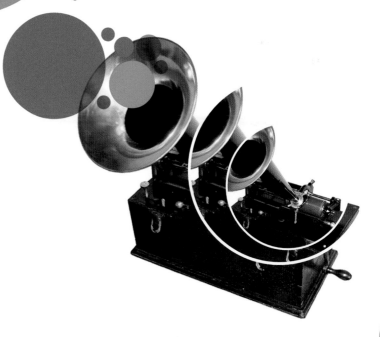

When we understand this context, it becomes clear that Edison wasn't only building on an insight from the lens of Leveraging Resources (using his skills and assets associated with telegraphy, recording, and acoustics in new and different ways). He was also utilizing insights from two of the other lenses of innovation: "Harnessing Trends" and "Understanding Needs."

LEVERAGING RESOURCES

HARNESSING TRENDS

UNDERSTANDING NEEDS

Looking for opportunities to ride the exciting new wave of telephony and sound transmission, which was quickly gaining momentum.

Trying to anticipate emerging market requirements that telephony would create (or inefficiencies on which he could improve).

{ It was actually by combining or "crashing" these three distinct kinds of insights that Edison came up with his idea for the world's first voicemail system. }

8 ✓✓✓ ▶ **Test and validate the new idea—try to make it work.**

How would Edison know if a carbon filament might be the answer to his light bulb puzzle? After holding the lampblack over a Bunsen burner to turn it into carbonized wire, Edison and his team installed it in the bulb, connected the battery cables, and turned on the power. The filament burned brightly for about 30 seconds, then began to spark and die. But Edison wasn't discouraged. He realized that the piece of lampblack probably still had some oxygen from the atmosphere trapped inside it. So he searched for something simpler to carbonize, and decided on sewing thread. One of his assistants ran to a woman neighbor and came back with a spool of blue cotton thread, which they proceeded to bake and blacken until it was pure carbon with no oxygen in it at all. This hair-thin wire was clamped into the bulb and, once switched on, it began to glow with an even brightness, not for 30 seconds, or even 30 minutes, but for over 40 hours! The electric light bulb was born.

And what about the idea for a telephone recording device? With his usual passion, Edison quickly launched an experiment to see if the system could actually work. In just a matter of weeks he and his team had built a prototype based on a cylinder wrapped in tin foil, on which he hoped he could engrave the movements of a diaphragm as it reacted to vibrations imparted by the human voice. Then, using a stylus to read these recordings and reproduce the original movements of the diaphragm, his theory was that he could play back the spoken words.

Not sure at all whether the device would work or not, Edison set up a trial and famously shouted "Mary had a little lamb" into the mouthpiece. He and his colleagues were astonished to find that the machine reproduced his words almost perfectly. What he had in fact invented was not a telephone message recorder, or a "talking machine" as some later called it, but the world's first phonograph, a product that went on to launch the recorded music industry.

Unpacking the
creative process

Archimedes. Einstein. Edison. Their genius seems to have followed a formula. And we discover this same eight-step model when we examine countless other cases of successful invention and innovation. In fact, if we look at any creative business today—e.g., advertising, design, architecture—or at countless R&D labs around the world, we are likely to find some variation of this basic methodology being employed every day in the deliberate search for original or breakthrough solutions.

For well over a hundred years, scientists, psychologists, and practitioners have been reflecting on and studying how creativity works, and their conclusions all point to the same basic process.

It was back in the late nineteenth century that a German physiologist by the name of Hermann von Helmholtz first began to describe creative thinking as a multistage activity. He defined three distinct phases in the act of creation:[10]

1) *Saturation*—exploring a topic through information gathering

2) *Incubation*—unconsciously joining the dots between thought elements

3) *Illumination*—the moment when a new, recombinant idea is born

French polymath and scientific philosopher Henri Poincaré (whose own theory of relativity was a major inspiration for Einstein's), described the path to innovation in similar terms in his 1904 tome *The Foundations of Science*, but added a fourth stage to the process—verification.[11] His model was as follows:

1) Working consciously on a particular problem until reaching an impasse.

2) Temporarily relaxing and thinking of something else in order to allow for unconscious incubation.

3) Experiencing "sudden illumination" when the mind's "unconscious machine" produces an inspired new idea out of all the previous conscious work.

4) Verifying to check the validity of the creative result.

In 1926, after decades of studying the way people think, a British social psychologist by the name of Graham Wallas came to an almost identical conclusion about how breakthrough ideas are built. In his book *The Art of Thought*, published that very year, he likewise described creative thinking as a sequence of phases, but his was a five-stage model:[12]

1. Preparation

Having decided to focus on solving a particular problem, we first investigate it "in all directions" to gather existing knowledge and clues to possible answers, putting ourselves in a frame of mind that is receptive to new ideas.

2. Incubation

Next we switch off the conscious, deliberate search for a solution and instead let the unconscious mind process the problem, either by turning our attention to some other pursuit or by simply relaxing from all conscious mental work.

3. Intimation

We begin to feel that an idea is bubbling up from the unconscious into the conscious, but it is not yet tangible enough for us to grasp or define.

4. Illumination ///////

This is the point where we suddenly come to a flash of insight and a new idea is born. Wallas describes this stage as "the culmination of a successful train of association" in which previously unconnected elements seem to "click" into an inspiring new configuration that offers an illuminating solution to the problem. Interestingly, Wallas observes that "sometimes the successful train seems to consist of a single leap of association, or of successive leaps which are so rapid as to be almost instantaneous."[13]

5. Verification ///////

Finally, we try to consciously test the validity of the new idea to see if it actually works and is fit for purpose.

Wallas's model, which is commonly treated as just four stages, with "intimation" being included in the illumination stage, has long been accepted as the standard description of the creative process, and it remains at the core of most creativity training programs being offered around the world today.

However, Wallas was by no means the last word on the subject. In 1939, an American advertising executive called James Webb Young published *A Technique for Producing Ideas*, in which he argued:[14]

"The production of ideas is just as definite a process as the production of Fords; that the production of ideas, too, runs on an assembly line; that in this production the mind follows an operative technique that can be learned and controlled; and that its effective use is just as much a matter of practice in the technique as is the effective use of any tool."

Preparation ▶ Incubation ▶ Illumination ▶ Verification

Young argued that what is most valuable in mastering the creative process is "how to train the mind in the *method* by which all ideas are produced" (italics mine). And what exactly is this method? Essentially, Young echoed both Poincaré and Wallas with his five-step technique for producing creative ideas:[15]

1 Gathering raw material from which to build new combinations of thought

2 Digesting the material to see how individual facts or ideas might fit together

3 Unconsciously processing the problem while doing something else—e.g., working, listening to music, going to the movies, reading a book, sleeping

4 Experiencing a sudden "aha!" moment when you least expect it, as a new combination of thoughts is formed from all the raw material in the mind

5 What Young calls "the cold, gray dawn of the morning after," when your new idea has to meet reality by submitting it to criticism, verification, improvement, and adaption to match the particular need

Young believed that "an idea is nothing more nor less than a new combination of old elements," and that the capacity to build these creative combinations "depends largely on the ability to see relationships" between different facts, concepts, and other elements. Thus, he asserted, producing ideas is chiefly about searching for and spotting these novel relationships.

Young compared the process to what happens inside a kaleidoscope, where every turn of the crank moves tiny pieces of glass into a new configuration, revealing a seemingly infinite number of different geometrical patterns when viewed through the prism. He wrote, "The greater the number of pieces of glass in it the greater become the possibilities for new and striking combinations." Hence, he argued, it is necessary to gather a lot of good raw material at stage one of the creative thinking process, in order to create a large number of potential new relationships between these elements, leading to different kinds of combinations and ultimately to more original ideas.

Over two decades after James Webb Young, another American advertising executive, Alex Osborn, made his own contribution to the field of understanding creativity. Osborn was the original "O" in the global ad agency network BBDO, and the inventor of creative techniques like brainstorming and CPS (Creative Problem Solving). In 1953, he published *Applied Imagination*, in which he outlined a seven-step model for creative thinking:

1. *Orientation:* identifying the problem to be solved
2. *Preparation:* gathering data that are relevant to the issue
3. *Analysis:* studying the relevant data and other material
4. *Ideation:* creating a lot of alternative ideas (divergent thinking)
5. *Incubation:* stepping back from the problem to allow illumination
6. *Synthesis:* putting all the puzzle pieces together (convergent thinking)
7. *Evaluation:* judging and verifying the final ideas

In 1962, American psychologist Jacob Getzels, who has been called "one of the fathers of creativity research,"[16] wrote the seminal book *Creativity and Intelligence*,[17] followed in 1976 by *The Creative Vision*,[18] in which, improving on Osborn's model, he proposed that the first stage of creativity is about finding or formulating the *right* problem to be solved. In fact, his central argument was that correctly understanding the problem is the key to creatively solving it.

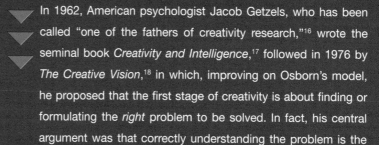

"The creative process is chaos wrapped around structure and held together by a sprinkle of magic dust."
Steve Zelle, idApostle

In more recent years, several other authors have published works on the subject, but most of their models for the creative thinking process add up to variations on the same theme. So after more than a century of examining how we come up with breakthrough ideas, the unanimous conclusion seems to be that there is definitely a linear process involved, and that this process consists of a series of clearly defined and similarly described stages. But is this really the way innovation always happens? Is it absolutely necessary to go through every single step of this process, in exactly the right order, to produce a winning idea? Let's consider a few cases.

" Say goodbye
to the bag "

What about James Dyson's invention of the Dual Cyclone bagless vacuum cleaner back in the late 1970s and early 1980s? If we break down the process by which he developed this idea into its individual stages, it would look something like this:

Frame a specific challenge and focus on solving it

While renovating a country house, Dyson became frustrated with his Hoover vacuum cleaner because it kept losing suction as the bag filled up with dust. He reasoned that there must be a way to build a better vacuum cleaner. So he decided to figure out how.

Come to an illuminating insight that fundamentally shifts your perspective

Shortly afterward, Dyson was visiting a local sawmill when he noticed large centripetal separators (or industrial cyclones) removing sawdust from the air, and realized that this was a much more efficient way to collect dirt and dust.[19]

Build the insight (or insights) into a big idea—a new combination of thoughts

Dyson's big idea was to try to scale down an industrial cyclone and install it on a domestic vacuum cleaner to replace the conventional dust bag and improve suction power.

Test and validate the new idea—try to make it work

After working on his idea for five years, and putting it through a stunning 5,127 prototypes,[20] Dyson was finally ready to launch the G Force Dual Cyclone—the first vacuum cleaner without a bag—which eventually went on to revolutionize the market and make him a billionaire.

Notice that Dyson seems to have skipped or shuffled a few steps in the creative process. Where, for example, was the initial preparation and research stage—all the information gathering and study, the investigation "in all directions" to learn from the work of others? Instead of feeding the front end of the creative process, this stage actually came at the end, after the idea itself, when Dyson was working on the development of his prototypes. If, at the very beginning, he had spent time intensely studying other vacuum cleaners and how they worked, he would probably have focused on trying to make an improved dust bag, rather than on how to get rid of it.

Notice, too, that when Dyson walked into that sawmill, he wasn't on some kind of field trip aimed at deliberately searching out possible solutions. He wasn't there to collect raw material for the ideation process. He hadn't organized a "divergent thinking" brainstorming session to try to create a lot of alternative ideas.

He wasn't trying to step back from the problem and relax, or to overcome a creative impasse, by doing something different. But he had clearly identified a problem he was interested in solving, and while he was busy with other things, his mind was unconsciously incubating or processing it. Thus, when he entered that sawmill and noticed the industrial cyclone, Dyson was in a frame of mind that was open to any new thought or understanding—any new insight—that might help him solve his problem.

What Dyson's story illustrates is that innovation doesn't always follow the same linear model for creative thinking. There are many cases like this one where some stages of the process may be present, but others might be skipped altogether. And those that are present may be sequenced very differently than prescribed. Let's look at a few more examples.

What about some of the other cases of breakthrough innovation we looked at earlier in the book?

Take Curves, the international women-only fitness franchise. How did Gary and Diane Heavin come to this big idea? Did they start by specifically looking for a way to reinvent the fitness industry? Did they first do a lot of formal research into customer needs and market trends? Did they go out and look at some of the most successful fitness clubs to see if they could learn from the work of others? Did they generate a ton of different ideas to explore many possible creative solutions? Did they hit a roadblock in their innovation efforts and then try to detach and let the whole thing incubate in their minds? No. They simply began to notice that quite a number of their female customers were feeling uncomfortable about training in a fitness club full of men. This key insight—based on observation and empathy alone—led them to think about a simple but revolutionary solution to the problem: a fitness club with "no makeup, no men, and no mirrors."

When Michael Dell started building and selling personal computers to his fellow university students in the 1980s, was he consciously looking for a way to change the whole PC industry? How did he come to his disruptive and highly innovative business model? Again, we have to ask ourselves, Where was

the multistaged model of creative thinking, or what James Webb Young called "the method by which all ideas are produced?" Dell may well have framed a challenge—in his case how to make personal computers available at a price that he and other poor students could afford. But in many ways he already knew the answer. Most of the information gathering and the study of relevant data had actually preceded that step. By the time he attended college, Dell was already quite a computer expert. At the tender age of 15 he had bought an Apple computer just so he could take it apart and see how it worked. For several years, he had researched the subject as a hobby and had learned how the PC manufacturers made their products. He knew where he could obtain all the necessary parts to build a computer and, more importantly, how to put those parts together. That's how he had discovered that the price of an assembled computer was five times higher than the price of the parts that went into it. This insight, combined with the knowledge that dealers were pushing up the purchase price by putting a high margin on the products, led him to think about setting up a computer manufacturing business of his own that sold directly to customers. There were no deliberate attempts at ideation. There was no creative impasse. There was no attempt to step back from the challenge and let it incubate in the mind (because the incubation period had been going on for years, and the solution seemed immediately obvious). All Dell did initially was find a way to leverage his existing knowledge and skills to make some extra money at college. It was only when things started taking off, and he took on more and more accounts from outside the university, that he realized there was an opportunity to set up a real business. In his first year after dropping out of college and registering what was originally called "PC's Limited," he made $6 million in sales.

IKEA's innovative business model is best known for its flat-packaged, self-pickup, ready-to-assemble furniture. But where did the idea originally come from? As it turns out, the company stumbled upon this concept in the mid-1950s when an early coworker removed the legs of an IKEA table in order to fit it into a car for transport. It wasn't the output from an ideation session or a long creative thinking process aimed at how to upend the furniture industry by dramatically reducing costs and prices.

As we learned from the story of Netflix's origins, founder Reed Hastings had not been grappling for some time with the challenge of how to create a better video rental service. He had actually just sold his own company and was simply irritated with paying late return fees at his local video store. His insight, which occurred while driving from the store to the gym, was that a flat monthly membership fee (like the ones charged by fitness clubs) might also work for a video rental business. So he might have been briefly focused on how to address his own frustration and think about a more customer-friendly business model, but the insight came to him within minutes, dispensing with the preliminary need for research, or for an incubation period.

Similarly, Jeff Bezos wasn't consciously looking for a new business idea in 1994 when he read in a trend report that Internet usage was increasing exponentially. Thus, in this instance, the inspiring insight came first, followed closely by the idea of starting a Web-based retail business. Next came the decision to frame a specific challenge and focus on solving it—what would be the most appropriate product category to build an Internet company around? This is when Bezos began to research the subject, immersing himself in it, and exploring possible solutions. Initially listing 20 products that he could potentially market online, he methodically evaluated each option on the list and finally selected books because it seemed like the easiest kind of product to order, store, and ship.

There are countless other examples illustrating how the creative process can often work differently. In cases like these, we find that some stages of the generally accepted creative thinking models may have been evident, but not necessarily all of them, and not in the order that is conventionally described.

So what should we conclude about how creative ideas have their genesis? Is there really a "method by which all ideas are produced," as James Webb Young asserted more than six decades ago? Certainly, Archimedes, Einstein, and Edison seemed to follow quite similar steps to their breakthrough solutions, essentially corresponding with the linear, multistage models of the creative process that have been defined and refined over the past hundred years.

In contrast, many other inventors, entrepreneurs, and innovators came to their ideas in ways that deviated quite obviously from these standard models. Their approach to innovation was more intuitive than deliberate; more serendipitous than systematic. But, as we found out when we unpacked these latter cases, there was nevertheless a stepwise process involved in discovering and developing each of these opportunities, even though several of the steps may have been in a different order than prescribed in most models, or simply skipped altogether.

It turns out, then, that the production of ideas is not quite "as definite a process as the production of Fords," to use James Webb Young's assembly line analogy. However, there are some common steps that seem to recur in every case, whether the innovators in question were deliberately trying to follow "an operative technique," or instead were just following their creative instincts. It's definitely not wrong to consciously set up the front end of the creative process in the most effective way by framing a specific challenge and focusing on solving it, researching the subject to learn from the work of others, immersing yourself in the problem and exploring possible solutions—probably reaching a roadblock or creative impasse at some point—and then detaching from the problem to let it incubate in the unconscious mind. Anyone who has ever spent time in R&D, new product development, advertising or design, or who has ever worked on solving some creative challenge of their own, will no doubt immediately identify with this sequence of steps. But this doesn't mean it's the only way to generate a big idea. Everyone knows that innovation sometimes happens, at least partly, by chance. As we have clearly seen, it's not always necessary to follow each one of these preliminary steps, in this particular order, to discover a new opportunity, although several or all of the steps may still occur at some point further downstream.

If we strip the whole creative process down to its absolute basics, however, we find that there are in fact only two constants: two elements that can never be skipped and that always occur in exactly the same order. In fact, these two critical elements are indispensable to every single innovation story in the world.

One element is the big idea. Obviously, at the heart of every significant innovation there is a compelling and value-creating idea of some kind—a new combination of thoughts. *The other element is the illuminating insight (or insights)*. Without fail, every big idea was preceded by at least one insight—a new and penetrating understanding into a situation or problem. These two elements of the creative thinking process—the *insight* and the *idea*—are invariably present in each case, and are always inextricably connected. Why? Because if there was one universal law of innovation, it would be this: Powerful new ideas are never simply snatched out of the air. They are always inspired by insights.

LESSONS
TO TAKE AWAY

Creative ideas don't just occur to us spontaneously. (Our minds actually build them from a unique chain of associations and connections, sometimes over a considerable period of time.)

Archimedes, Einstein, and Edison seem to have employed a similar eight-step creative process:

(1) Frame a specific challenge and focus on solving it.
(2) Research the subject. Learn from the work of others.
(3) Immerse yourself in the problem. Explore possible solutions.
(4) Reach a roadblock. Feel the creative frustration.
(5) Relax. Detach from the problem. Let it incubate in the unconscious mind.
(6) Come to an illuminating insight that fundamentally shifts your perspective.
(7) Build the insight (or insights) into a big idea — a new combination of thoughts.
(8) Test and validate the new idea — try to make it work.

* Most common models for the creative process add up to variations on the same theme. (For well over a hundred years, scientists, psychologists, and practitioners have been studying how creativity works, and their conclusions all point to the same basic process.)

* That doesn't mean that the creative process is fixed. (Some innovators come to their ideas in ways that deviate from these standard models. Their approach to innovation is more intuitive than deliberate; more serendipitous than systematic.)

* However, there are always two constant elements to the creative process. (One element is the big idea. The other element is the illuminating insight or insights that served to inspire that idea.)

What exactly is an insight?

Talk to cognitive scientists and they will tell you an insight is the moment you spontaneously come to an understanding of a previously incomprehensible concept, or you suddenly grasp the solution to a seemingly unsolvable problem. In their classical laboratory experiments, usually with college students or members of the general public, they typically ask people to solve a creative puzzle like how to connect nine dots in a diagram using just four straight lines and without lifting the pencil from the paper, or how to attach three candles to a wall and light them up using just three tacks and three matches.

These puzzles might seem simplistic, but they are actually designed to be difficult and frustrating, inevitably leading subjects to an impasse that forces them to go back, challenge their original assumptions, and think "outside the box," hopefully opening their eyes at some point to the solution. Some modern neuropsychologists actually scan the brain activity of the subjects while they are performing these tasks, to try to observe what happens in the neural circuits of the human mind as a person finally figures out how to crack the puzzle. This enlightening moment of "insight," which may be accompanied by a feeling of great joy, satisfaction, or relief, is often described in the scientific literature as the Eureka moment, the "aha!" experience, or the epiphany.

But are we to believe that solving brainteaser puzzles in a university lab under controlled conditions can teach us a lot about the role of insights in building innovative ideas in the real world?

Cognitive psychologist Gary Klein doesn't think so. In his brilliant book, *Seeing What Others Don't: The Remarkable Ways We Gain Insights*, he argues that the only way to truly understand how insights work is to study "the way people think in natural settings, rather than how they are forced to think in laboratory experiments using artificial tasks."[21] His naturalistic investigation of insights, which focused on 120 real-life cases of innovation, discovery, or invention, looked at how individuals actually came to the insights that inspired their breakthroughs.

What Klein found was that the accepted scientific view of insight, which he defines as "moving from an impasse state to a solution state"[22] (along the lines of Graham Wallas's staged model of the creative process, and the lab-based experiments just described), turns out to be way too narrow. In case after case of remarkable insights, he discovered that the people involved had not necessarily set out to address a particular challenge, done any deliberate preparation, reached an impasse while trying to solve a problem, or had any time for incubation. Thus, the definition of insight as "moving from an impasse state to a solution state," while relevant in some instances, actually creates an incomplete understanding about how insight works.

Common to all of Klein's insight examples, however, was the unexpected "flash of illumination" where a new idea or solution suddenly became apparent. In Graham Wallas's famous model, which corresponds with the standard scientific definition of insight, this illumination stage was the magical Eureka moment when we come to the "happy idea," or see the solution for the very first time. This definition has popularized and perpetuated the notion that the insight is the moment an idea is born, or at least the moment we recognize an idea's potential for solving a particular problem, or for doing something in an original or better way. But Klein poses a different theory: "Perhaps the 'aha' experience, when everything finally snaps into place, marks the culmination of the insight process. Perhaps it isn't the insight itself."[23]

Let me build on Klein's theory. What if the insight, the formation of a new idea, and the "aha!" experience are not necessarily the same thing at all? What if these are actually separate and consecutive steps in the creative process, but are so closely linked, and often appear to happen so simultaneously, that to the innovator—and to the scientific researcher—they may appear to be one?

Wallas himself hinted at this when he described an idea as "the culmination of a successful train of association," and wrote that "sometimes the successful train seems to consist of a single leap of association, or of successive leaps which are so rapid as to be almost instantaneous."[24]

{ "Perhaps the "aha" experience, when everything finally snaps into place, marks the culmination of the insight process. Perhaps it isn't the insight itself." }

Gary Klein, PhD

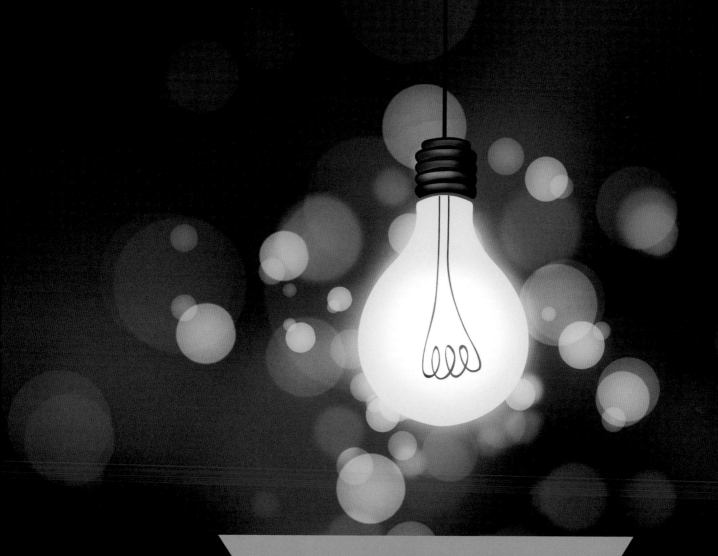

What actually happens when we experience a "Flash of Illumination"?

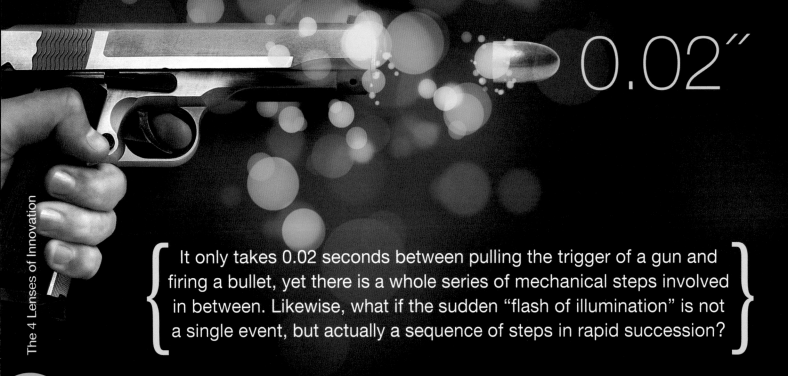

The reason this all seems like one instantaneous event is that the human brain works incredibly quickly. In August 2013, researchers at the Okinawa Institute of Technology in Japan and Forschungszentrum Jülich in Germany found that it took 82,944 processors from the fourth fastest supercomputer in the world—the K computer at the Riken research institute in Kobe, Japan—working for a full 40 minutes just to simulate one single second of human brain activity.[25] That should give us an impression of how blindingly fast our brains can process information, make novel associations and connections, form them into ideas, and recognize the potential of these new thought combinations.

We might compare it to what happens when a gun is fired. The movement of the trigger sets a spring in motion (the firing pin), which releases the hammer, which strikes the primer of the cartridge, which in turn ignites the gunpowder, creating an explosion that propels the bullet through the barrel and out of the gun. All of this happens in about 0.02 seconds, making the experience feel instantaneous. Nevertheless, there is a whole series of mechanical steps involved in the process between pulling the trigger and the bullet exiting the barrel.

0.02″

{ It only takes 0.02 seconds between pulling the trigger of a gun and firing a bullet, yet there is a whole series of mechanical steps involved in between. Likewise, what if the sudden "flash of illumination" is not a single event, but actually a sequence of steps in rapid succession? }

The 4 Lenses of Innovation

Likewise, I believe there is much more to the mysterious "flash of illumination" than has previously been thought. I propose that, while it might appear to be a singular stage in the creative process, it may in fact be composed of several successive steps that follow each other so quickly that they seem to take place all at once. Until now, the popular creative thinking models have thrown all of these steps into the same pot. The "illumination" stage is supposed to be simultaneously the moment of insight, the moment a "happy idea" pops into our heads, and the moment we suddenly see the solution with all clarity, perhaps accompanied by a feeling of elation. But in fact, if we unpack the creative process in more detail, we might be surprised to find that there are as many as four distinct steps involved at this stage, all of which seem to happen in just one instantaneous "flash." Analogous to the process of firing a gun, my theory suggests that there is a trigger (the insight) that sets off a mechanism (the leap of association) that produces a result (the new idea), which in turn creates an experience (the Eureka moment).

Thus, in my eight-step model of the creative process, the insight is not the grand finale, the culmination point, the flash of genius when all the pieces "click" together and we suddenly become aware of a breakthrough solution. Rather, it is the point immediately preceding all of that—the step that catalyzes the "leaps of association" that act as precursors for a new idea. The insight, in other words, is not the end in itself but the means to an end. It is the trigger that sets things in motion.

Here's the distinction: An insight is not a new idea—or even the recognition of a new idea—it is a fresh thought or an illuminating understanding that *inspires* a new idea.

Think about how we commonly use the term *insight* in business. Marc Pritchard, global brand building officer at Procter & Gamble, the world's largest consumer products company, describes insights as "human truths, motivations, and tensions," which his company's brands set out to address.[26] He talks about customer insight as the "spark" that "'can create big ideas," and refers to "fresh creative ideas that are powered by insights, that are powered by the way people think and feel."[27] Many other companies similarly refer to insight as "a deep understanding of customer behavior," or "a thorough understanding of customer problems, needs, and wants." No doubt your own company sometimes commissions in-depth research to deliver you insights into customer needs and behaviors, or into emerging market trends. You may also use data mining to help you discover statistical insights that will influence your business decisions, help you improve operations, reveal new sales opportunities, and give you a competitive edge.

Insights are the triggers that can lead to big ideas

Do insights come from
breakthrough thinking?

Consider the countless books, magazine articles, websites, or surveys that promise us "expert insights" on all manner of management topics like leadership, performance excellence, social media marketing, supply chain management, or the future of a particular industry.

The Drucker School of Management has a channel on YouTube called **Drucker Insights**, providing many volumes of video interviews and lectures featuring the management wisdom of legendary thought leader Peter Drucker. Microsoft runs a series of live online events called **Microsoft Insights**, designed to share information on emerging opportunities in the technology field. Zappos, the online shoe and apparel retailer, runs a special website called **Zappos Insights**, offering tips, training, and boot camps on how to create a fun workplace culture like their own—one that empowers employees and encourages happiness. Facebook offers a service called **Facebook Insights,** which gives developers, page managers, and marketers key page-performance metrics for tracking and improving user engagement. In fact, type the word *insights* into Google, and you will find thousands of search results offering insights on everything from the global financial crisis to sleeping disorders, improv jazz, children's temperaments, the sex life of dolphins, or dating Irish men.

What do all these "insights" have to do with the famous "aha!" experience described in the scientific literature—the sudden epiphany when we move "from an impasse state to a solution state?" Are we really all talking about the same thing?

When P&G's marketing executives talk about a "customer insight," for example, they are obviously not referring to a Eureka moment or an epiphany experienced by the customer. Rather, they mean an illuminating *piece of information* about the customer's interests or behavior that gives *them* a new and penetrating understanding about how to better address that customer's needs.

Or does breakthrough thinking
come from insights?

So what are we to conclude from all this? Is an insight simply a new piece of data or information that will teach us something we didn't know? Or is it the surprising new understanding—the shift in mental perspective—that we gain from that piece of information? Or is it the moment when the new understanding or perspective inspires us with an exciting and original idea? Or is it the exhilarating experience of suddenly knowing with all certainty that this new idea represents the solution to a particular problem we have been unsuccessfully grappling with? How can an insight be all of these things at the same time? To use the language of systems theory, how can an insight simultaneously be the input, the throughput, and the output in the creative process? It's more than a little confusing.

Either millions of people from many different fields are incorrectly using the word *insight*. Or it's a term that has been spread so thinly that everyone is using it correctly to describe different things. When you hear cognitive scientists talk about insights, you would have to conclude that they mean moments of sudden realization that come from breakthrough thinking. But when the term is used by business executives, marketing professionals, innovation practitioners, R&D managers, and creative people in the advertising and design business, it's obvious that they mean the exact opposite—that breakthrough thinking comes from insights.

These varying definitions of insight are now so deeply entrenched that I suppose everyone is right at some level. But in terms of developing a workable theory of innovation, and then using that theory to improve our ability to actually innovate, we do need to agree on a practical definition of insights, and on exactly how and where they work in the creative process.

A practical definition of insights

Look up the word *insight* in a dictionary, and you will find it defined as "a new and penetrating understanding about a particular situation or a problem." It's about grasping or discerning the true nature of something; suddenly noticing or perceiving a matter clearly or deeply; literally seeing *into* a situation (hence in-sight) in a way that sheds light on or helps solve a problem.

In their article, *Unleashing Hidden Insights*, Marco Vriens (from Microsoft) and Rogier Verhulst (from LinkedIn) define an insight as "a thought, fact, combination of facts, data and/or analysis of data that induces meaning and furthers understanding of a situation or issue."[28] It is something that has the potential of "redirecting the thinking about that situation or issue, which then in turn has the potential of benefiting the business."

Executives at Mars, the global chocolate manufacturer, refer to the process of discovering insights as "peeling back the onion," in the sense that it is about looking beyond the obvious by methodically removing successive layers of shallow, superficial information in an effort to drill down to the deeper and more profound truths about something."

In *The Art of Insight*, Charles Kiefer and Malcolm Constable wrote that insights "result in a dramatically improved understanding of a situation or problem such that we see things more deeply and more accurately than before."[29] That's why Jeremy Bullmore, member of the Advisory Board at WPP, the multinational

"A good insight is like a refrigerator, because the moment you look into it, a light comes on."

Jeremy Bullmore, WPP

marketing communications company, says that "a good insight is like a refrigerator, because the moment you look into it, a light comes on."[30]

A great example of an illuminating insight is Professor Theodore Levitt's famous remark: "People don't want quarter-inch drills. They want quarter-inch holes." For his marketing students at Harvard Business School 40 or 50 years ago, this fresh understanding represented a drastic shift in mental perspective. It immediately altered their perception by allowing them to see the marketing challenge in a completely different light.

Thus, I like to think of an insight as a striking realization that fundamentally changes our thinking. It can often come from an illuminating new piece of information that either prompts us to look at an issue from a completely different angle, or that connects with existing information in a way that brings us to a startling new conclusion. But sometimes these novel thoughts or realizations just seem to surface in our heads quite suddenly without the recent addition of any new information, particularly after a period in which the unconscious mind has been incubating previous knowledge, information, interests, and experiences.

Simply put, an insight is something you previously didn't know, or didn't yet think about, that has the power to surprise and inspire you. And what role do such insights play in the creative thinking process? As Scott Gray, head of planning at digital marketing agency Quirk, puts it, "Insights are to an idea what firelighters are to a fire. They represent the best way of generating great ideas that inspire success."[31]

A new and penetrating
understanding
about a situation
or a problem

Something
you previously didn't know,
or didn't yet think about,
that has the power to surprise and
inspire you

Understanding
Ideation

In *Seeing What Others Don't*, Gary Klein defines insights as "discontinuous discoveries"[32]—pieces of information that unexpectedly shift our viewpoint, or our set of beliefs, in a way that is transformative. These revised understandings disrupt or restructure the normal patterns of thinking in our minds, creating entirely different associations or connections, thus enabling us to envisage completely new ideas and solutions.

To return to James Webb Young's metaphor of the kaleidoscope from earlier in the book, it is as if a powerful insight turns the crank in our minds, so that existing facts and concepts click together in a new combination, revealing a strikingly novel relationship between these elements. In other words, the insight (the new understanding) is the catalyst for change. This causes a shift in our thinking patterns—a leap (or several leaps) of association—that connects various elements (thoughts, concepts, data) in a totally new relationship. The result is a new combination of thoughts—which we call an "idea"—that suggests an original, exciting, or better course of action. The recognition of that idea and its breakthrough potential is the moment when we suddenly "see" the answer with all certainty and clarity. This is what I believe to be the Eureka moment (literally meaning "I have found it!").

When we put this all together, what we have is a new model for understanding the flash of illumination that we have all experienced at various times of our lives, but have so far found difficult to explain, and even more difficult to replicate or to induce. It's a model, built on the principles of systems theory, that clearly defines the **input** (an insight), the **throughput** (a leap of association), and the **output** (a new idea), as well as the resulting **experience** (a Eureka moment) involved in this stage of the creative process. I believe it gives us a workable theory of innovation from which we can begin to build a methodology for systematically generating high-quality insights and then using these insights to provoke breakthrough ideas.

| INPUT | > | THROUGHPUT | > | OUTPUT | > | EXPERIENCE |

| INSIGHT | > | LEAP OF ASSOCIATION | > | NEW IDEA | > | EUREKA MOMENT |

A new and penetrating understanding that allows us to see a problem or situation in a different light

A shift in our thinking patterns that connects various elements (thoughts, concepts, data) in a totally new relationship

A fresh and different pattern of thoughts that suggests an original, exciting, or better course of action

An exhilarating moment of awareness when we recognize the breakthrough potential of a new idea with all certainty and clarity

Stepping stones
for creative thinking

There is another metaphor I sometimes use when describing insights. The great Hungarian author and philosopher, Arthur Koestler, whose book *The Act of Creation* made an important contribution to the study of the creative process, once described words as "stepping stones for thought." Similarly, I like to think of insights as "stepping stones for creative thinking." Just as a large, flat stone (or a series of stones) allows us to cross easily from one side of a stream to another, insights allow us to make the necessary leaps of association that lead us to big ideas.

In my own eight-step model of the creative process (shown on pages 214 and 215), you may recall that I clearly separated the insight from the idea, as follows:

Come to an illuminating insight that fundamentally shifts your perspective

Build the insight (or insights) into a big idea—a new combination of thoughts

Let's go back and briefly review some of the innovation stories we looked at earlier in the book in an effort to not just distinguish between the insight and the idea in each of these cases, but also to understand how the insights became the stepping stones to these big ideas.

Archimedes and the king's crown

Insight The amount of water displaced by a submerged object corresponds directly to its volume

Idea Water displacement could be used as an accurate method to measure the volume, and therefore calculate the density, of an irregular-shaped object

Einstein's theory of special relativity

Insight Two events at different places that supposedly occur simultaneously actually occur at different times depending on the observer's frame of reference

Idea A new concept of physics in which space and time appear to behave differently relative to different observers, when an object approaches the speed of light

Edison's ideal light bulb filament

Insight Although carbon burns up very quickly in the atmosphere due to oxygen, it would theoretically burn much slower in an oxygen-free vacuum bulb

Idea A cheap, high-resistance light bulb filament based on carbonized sewing thread

Edison's "talking machine"

Insight If it's possible to record and resend telegraph messages by embossing them on a circular disk, it might also be possible to record and play back the human voice

Idea A phonograph machine for recording and replaying voice messages, based on the success of Alexander Graham Bell's newly invented telephone

Dyson's bagless vacuum cleaner

Insight Large centripetal separators (or cyclones), used in industrial settings, seem to be a very efficient way to collect dirt, dust, and debris

Idea Scale down an industrial cyclone and install it on a vacuum cleaner to replace the conventional dust bag and improve the suction power

Try this Innovation Quiz

Can you distinguish between the insight and the idea in the following cases? Try to also define which of the "Four Lenses" was involved in each example.

Classic	Page
Curves—women-only fitness clubs	232
Dell—made-to-order computers	232
Amazon.com—an online bookstore	233
IKEA—ready-to-assemble furniture	233
Netflix—unlimited rentals for a flat-fee	233
Modern	
Beats by Dre—designer headphones	104
Nest—intelligent home appliances	198
Waze—GPS-navigation with social media	143
Kono—cone-based pizza concept	190
Dutch Boy—Twist & Pour paint container	187

Improving your capacity
for radical innovation

Now that we understand insights as the raw material out of which big ideas are built, we can begin to discuss a practical methodology for improving our capacity to innovate.

Companies often ask themselves why their innovation efforts seem to produce so few truly game-changing ideas. On the surface, they may appear to be doing everything right. They identify very relevant strategic challenges. They collect and collate lots of industry data, market research reports, trend surveys, technology road maps, and customer data to help them understand these selected areas of focus. They organize brainstorming sessions facilitated by creativity consultants, or launch open innovation campaigns across and beyond the company, or invest in longer-term R&D activities in an effort to generate new ideas and opportunities. Yet all too often these initiatives yield nothing more than lukewarm ideas for incremental improvements rather than radical new concepts that could create dramatic revenue growth and perhaps even revolutionize an industry. So where are things going wrong?

The answer is that you can't produce big, breakthrough ideas unless you first generate the right kinds of insights. It's like a farmer hoping to reap a bountiful harvest without first sowing the right seeds. We need to understand that the output is dependent on the input. Investing time, money, and effort in innovation without

first building a rich portfolio of insights is mostly a fruitless exercise. People are being asked to make giant leaps in creative thinking but without the intellectual stepping stones they need to get them from here to there. Their companies expect to get out-of-the-box ideas without developing the fresh and inspiring perspectives that can help people see out of the box in the first place.

> You can't harvest big ideas unless you sow the right seeds

When we examined creativity as a linear process earlier in the book, we found that the only real constant in every innovation case is the presence of an illuminating insight (or a series of insights) that leads to a big idea. So if we want to significantly improve our capacity to innovate—as organizations, teams, or individuals—where would be the best place to concentrate our efforts?

The late Eli Goldratt, originator of the revolutionary Theory of Constraints, used to argue that the key to improving the through-put of any system is to find and remove the core bottlenecks. He compared each organizational process to a chain composed of many links, where the strength of the chain is obviously deter-mined by the weakest link. Clearly, even if we tripled the strength of any (or all) of the other links, this would not affect the perfor-mance of the chain. The only way to improve its overall strength would be to focus on improving the chain's fundamental weak-ness. Similarly, the key to improving the performance of the creative thinking process is to concentrate on strengthening the weakest link in the chain—the key constraint on the system. And what is that constraint? In most organizations, it's either a lack of high-quality strategic insights, or the failure to use those insights effectively to drive innovation.

That's why it doesn't help companies a great deal to become better at all the other steps in the creative process, like iden-tifying the most important strategic challenges, doing intensive background research on a particular subject, organizing ideation sessions, evaluating ideas, and so forth. For that matter, it doesn't make much difference how good they are at implementing and eventually commercializing those ideas, either, because there is little point at being very good at implementing ideas with low potential impact on the business.

Instead, most organizations need to focus on improving their ability to generate truly inspiring insights and to use them as the building blocks for innovation. First, because it's the single most important factor in producing big ideas. Second, because it's usually their weakest capability—it's the core bottleneck in their efforts to create the next breakthrough business opportunity.

What's the weakest link **in your company's creative** thinking process

How **powerful** are your insights?

"But wait," you might say. "Our company already puts a great deal of effort into generating insights. We do a lot of market research and conduct focus groups. We go to industry conferences to keep our finger on the pulse of change. We work with trend forecasters and scenario planners to help us manage our way to the future. Who says we don't have enough insights?"

All of the above might be true. However, ask yourself: How fresh and inspiring are the insights you are generating? How deep and meaningful are they? How differentiated are they from the insights your competitors are using in their own innovation efforts? Would they *surprise* your competitors? Are they novel and unique? Are they proprietary? Are they powerful enough to open up significant new opportunities for innovation? Are they shared across the firm so everyone can use them to trigger their creative thinking? Or do your insights get stuck on the desks—or in the heads—of just a few of your people, like your marketing executives or R&D staff? Do you have a robust and continually updated portfolio of strategic insights that is truly driving your innovation efforts? Are you using those insights as the essen-

tial basis for imagining new offerings, marketing strategies, processes, customer experiences, and business models? Or is there a disconnect somewhere between the insights you generate and the new ideas you produce?

When I talked earlier about the constraint on creative thinking in most organizations, I never said it was a lack of insights. I said it was a lack of *high-quality* insights, or the failure to use those insights effectively to drive innovation. **What most large companies are missing is a systematic methodology and an organized process for generating, capturing, sharing, and using powerful insights at the very front end of their innovation efforts.** They may well invest time and money in acquiring insights of some sort, but are they the right kinds of insights for disrupting the rules of the game? Do these insights challenge convention and stretch people's thinking along new lines, or do they merely restate the obvious? Do they uncover the deeper implications and unexploited opportunities inherent in emergent discontinuities? Do they cast light on trends that competitors have either overlooked or ignored? Do they point to completely new ways of leveraging the company's skills and assets, or other resources that exist outside the organization? Do they offer profoundly new perspectives on customer needs, provoking breakthrough solutions for transforming the customer experience?

These are the kinds of insights companies should be actively accumulating and then using to fuel the front end of their innovation process. As we have learned, the only way to produce ideas radical enough to drive dramatic growth, open up unexploited market spaces, and disrupt existing industry business models is by first generating the high-quality raw material—the powerful insights—that can serve to trigger those ideas. And the great news is that your company can now deliberately and systematically discover such insights using the Four Lenses methodology described in this book.

Earlier in the book, we looked at many examples of these lenses in action, demonstrating how they may be used effectively as a catalyst for innovation. We considered several successful companies that challenged deep-seated orthodoxies and thereby reshaped their industries. We saw how others achieved market dominance by harnessing nascent trends that had the potential to change the competitive rules. We examined firms that leveraged their core competencies and their assets in unconventional ways, or that combined their resources with those of other organizations, in order to open up exciting new business opportunities. And we learned from companies that recognized unsolved customer problems, unmet needs and wants, and then worked hard to design innovative solutions from the customer backward. Now it's time to put these lessons into practice inside your own company.

Working with the
FOUR LENSES

In my experience with companies all around the world, the best way to apply the Four Lenses methodology is systematically. You might want to try some of the following recommendations, all of which are market-proven ways to dramatically improve your organization's ideation efforts.

Let's start with the ideal scenario: It's time to create some innovative new growth opportunities for your company's future. First, create a core group from across the organization that can devote some time to this critical challenge. Divide the group into four teams—one for each lens. Aim for somewhere between six and 12 people per team. If you are using a bigger group, it's fine to have two, three, or even more teams per lens. With some companies, I have sometimes had as many as five or six teams working on each particular lens, so 20 or more teams in total. The goal is for each team to try to generate some important new strategic insights using one of the lenses. So some people will be challenging deep-seated orthodoxies about who your customers are, what you offer them, how you deliver value, how you make money, and how you differentiate from the competition. Others will be identifying and analyzing trends that have the potential to bring exciting new benefits to customers or even to upend your industry, with a particular focus on developments that competitors have so far overlooked or ignored. The third group will be looking for ways to leverage your company's resources into adjacent or perhaps radically different kinds of opportunities, or to make combinations between your own resources and those of external organizations in order to create new value for customers. The fourth set of people will be searching for deep, unarticulated customer needs that could form the basis for compelling new offerings or quantum leap improvements to your existing products and services.

How much time will the teams have for their respective assignments? That depends on how strategically important this process is to your company. Some firms give their discovery teams several months, others allocate less time—a few weeks, or maybe just a few days. As a rule of thumb, the more time your teams are given, the more thorough their work will be, usually resulting in a correspondingly higher quality of insights. Whatever you decide

in terms of time allocation, at the end of the discovery period your aim is to receive from each team a collection of new and penetrating understandings that have the power to inspire some big ideas.

Next is when the sparks begin to fly. Having compiled a portfolio of strategic insights from all the teams, it's time for the ideas to start flowing (often the individual teams have already begun to develop some novel ideas anyway because their insights will quite naturally stimulate fresh creative thinking as they work). What you want the teams to do now is switch their attention from gathering insights to building the insights they have already generated into radical new ideas. At this point, what I

often do is recompose the teams specifically for ideation, so that we get representatives from each of the Four Lenses in the newly formed teams. That means the ideation process can be approached from all four perspectives. The teams then begin to "crash" or combine insights from the various lenses (it's what I like to call "creative chemistry") to produce a slew of unexpected ideas and business opportunities.

Another thing you can do at this stage is widen the number of participants involved in the ideation process. For example, some companies host an innovation event where they invite a large number of employees to come together and review and discuss all the insights from the Four Lenses, hoping to generate and capture a

"It's many…insights coming together that
bring big ideas into the world."

Scott Berkun

lot of new ideas on this occasion. Others make the insight portfolio available online to employees across the organization, asking them to submit ideas that these new understandings may inspire. Still others organize a series of ideation sessions with more teams of people, using the insight portfolio to drive new thinking. Later, of course, there is a lot of work to do in clustering ideas that reinforce each other, grouping them into domains, further improving the creative output, and finally sifting through this pool of potential opportunities to select the ideas your company wants to seriously consider for experimentation and development.

Of course, not everything has to be done on such a grand scale. The Four Lenses can also be employed by a single business unit, division, geographical region, organizational function, department, project group, or team. The principle is exactly the same. Whether there are many people involved in the process, or just a handful, the aim is to develop new perspectives using the Four Lenses, which then translate into a number of high quality strategy insights, which in turn begin to inspire some game-changing ideas.

There are times when a company requires some disciplined blue-sky thinking to reinvigorate an aging business model. At other times, what is needed is a way to apply the power of strategic creativity to a specific and narrowly defined business objective. The Four Lenses give you the perfect tool for both. They can help your company gain a wider perspective—for example, when you are searching for a whole new strategic direction for the business—or they can help you focus your ideation on some predefined corporate challenge, customer issue, industry problem, or emerging opportunity domain. You can use the lenses as and when you need them—let's say for a particular project—or you can use them on an ongoing basis to ensure that your company is continuously feeding the front end of your innovation pipeline with a robust and up-to-date portfolio of insights, ideas, and strategic options. The fact is, you can teach literally anyone, anywhere in your organization, to use the Four Lenses every single day to bring more creativity to whatever they do, enabling them to come up with ideas that might—who knows?—actually influence the destiny of your company.

CHALLENGING
ORTHODOXIES

HARNESSING
TRENDS

LEVERAGING
RESOURCES

UNDERSTANDING
NEEDS

This book has taken us on quite a journey.

In our search for a practical methodology for creative thinking, we have considered everything from the beliefs of ancient civilizations to the practices of today's most cutting-edge companies. In between, we have looked at the innovative thinking patterns that became prevalent during the Renaissance, the kinds of cultural environments that allow creativity to flourish, the inner workings of the human mind, the specific steps that led great thinkers—as well as accidental innovators—to their discoveries, and the pivotal role that insights play in the creative process.

My goal in writing this book was to somewhat demystify the front end of innovation. For thousands of years, people have perpetuated the belief that it takes a rare kind of genius to produce great ideas. What I have argued on these pages is that everyone possesses the capacity to be creative. All we have to know is how to bring out the potential genius that is already inside each one of us.

An analogy I often use is cooking. A lot of people still believe it's a skill you either naturally possess or you don't. But nothing could be further from the truth. I happen to be a big fan of the British celebrity chef, Jamie Oliver. Before I started watching Jamie's TV shows over a decade ago, I shared the belief that somehow cooking was some kind of mystical art for which

anywhere near edible. But week after week, I would watch him prepare mouth-watering meals in just a few easy steps, and it wasn't long before I was in the kitchen trying these recipes for myself. Lo and behold, with Jamie's training and a bit of practice I began to learn the principles and routines that have turned me into quite an experienced hobby chef myself.

It's similar with home improvement and maintenance. In the old days, we used to call in professionals to do a lot of the building, modifying, and repair jobs around the house that a large number of people now do for themselves. All it took was some guidance from the experts, in the form of DIY books, TV shows, or more recently YouTube videos, along with the right tools, and millions have discovered they had an "inner builder" just waiting to be unleashed.

Innovation is actually no different. With some expert guidance, the proper tools, and a little practice, literally anyone can improve their creative thinking skills. Once we accept that creativity is not a birthright of exceptional people but a skill that can be taught and acquired, we can begin to seriously tap into the latent innovation potential inside all of us and across our organizations. I sincerely hope this book has been a helpful step in the right direction.

Christopher Morley, the American journalist, novelist, essayist, and poet, once wrote that "the real purpose of books is to trap the mind into doing its own thinking."[33] If these pages have inspired you to think in radical and innovative new ways, I will consider the

LESSONS
TO TAKE AWAY

Insight is a term that is commonly used in a wide variety of ways. (Some see it as the culmination of creative thinking, others as the starting point. This book presents insights as the input for innovation.)

Insights are the precursors or triggers for new ideas. (Nobody ever simply snatches an idea out of the air. In case after case, we find that creative ideas are always inspired by insights.)

An insight is a new and penetrating understanding about a situation or a problem. (It's something you previously didn't know, or didn't yet think about, that has the power to surprise and inspire you.)

Think of insights as stepping stones for creativity. (You can't get to the other side—the production of new and original ideas—without first generating the right kinds of insights.)

Insights restructure the normal patterns of thinking in our minds. (They create entirely different associations or connections, thus enabling us to envisage completely new ideas and solutions—perhaps the answer to a puzzle or an unexpected opportunity.)

This helps us understand the "flash of illumination." (Insights catalyze the "leaps of association" in our minds that produce new ideas. The instant recognition of an idea's potential is the "Eureka moment.")

We now have a systematic methodology for discovering high-quality insights. (The Four Lenses provide you with an organized process for generating and using powerful insights at the very front end of your innovation efforts.)

Part One: The Mind of the Innovator

1. "Guardian Angel," *World Heritage Encyclopedia,* accessed October 25, 2014, http://www.worldheritage.org/articles/Guardian_Angel.

2. Weihua Niu and Robert J. Sternberg, "The Philosophical Roots of Western and Eastern Conceptions of Creativity," *Journal of Theoretical and Philosophical Psychology* 26 (2006): 18–38, doi:10.1037/h0091265.

3. David S. Landes, *The Unbound Prometheus: Technological Change and Industrial Development in Western Europe from 1750 to the Present* (New York: Press Syndicate of the University of Cambridge, 1969), 24.

4. W. W. Tarn, "The Hellenistic Ruler-Cult and the Daemon," *The Journal of Hellenic Studies* 48, no. 2 (1928): 206–19.

5. Władysław Tatarkiewicz, *A History of Six Ideas: An Essay in Aesthetics,* trans. from the Polish by Christopher Kasparek, The Hague: Martinus Nijhoff, 1980.

6. Frans Johansson, *The Medici Effect: Breakthrough Insights at the Intersection of Ideas, Concepts and Cultures* (Boston: Harvard Business School Press, 2004), 3.

2. Harnessing Trends

7. Petrarch (1367), "Apologia cuiusdam anonymi Galli calumnias" ("Defence against the calumnies of an anonymous Frenchman"), 1367, in *Opera Omnia* (Basel, 1554), 1195. This quotation comes from the English translation of Mommsen's article, where the source is given in a footnote. Cf. also D. Marsh, ed., *Invectives* (Cambridge, MA: Harvard University Press, 2003), 457.

8. Petrarch (1343), *Africa,* IX, 451–7. This quotation comes from the English translation of Theodore Mommsen, "Petrarch's Conception of the 'Dark Ages,'" *Speculum* 17, no. 2 (Cambridge, MA: Medieval Academy of America, 1942): 226–42.

9. Carol E. Quillen, *Rereading the Renaissance: Petrarch, Augustine, and the Language of Humanism* (Ann Arbor: University of Michigan Press, 1998), 12.

10. Rudolf Pfeiffer, *History of Classical Scholarship 1300–1850* (Oxford: Oxford University Press, 1976), 1; Gilbert Highet, *The Classical Tradition* (Oxford: Oxford University Press, 1949), 81–88.

11. *NSA Family Encyclopedia,* s.v. "Petrarch, Francesco" (Standard Education Corp., 1992, vol. 11), 240.

12. Ernst Cassirer et al., "Renaissance or Prenaissance," *Journal of the History of Ideas* 4, no. 1 (Philadelphia: University of Pennsylvania Press, 1943): 69–74; Mommsen, "Petrarch's Conception."

13. Robert Black, *Renaissance Thought* (London: Routledge, 2001), 24.

3. Leveraging Resources

14. Henri-Jean Martin, "The Arrival of Print," in *The History and Power of Writing* (Chicago: University of Chicago Press, 1995), 217.

15. Karl Schorbach and Douglas Crawford McMurtrie, *The Gutenberg Documents* (New York: Oxford University Press, 1941), 111–12.

16. Heinrich Wallau, *The Catholic Encyclopedia,* vol. 7, s.v. "Johann Gutenberg" (New York: Robert Appleton Company, 1910).

17. Hellmut Lehmann-Haupt, *Gutenberg and the Master of the Playing Cards* (New Haven: Yale University Press, 1966).

18. Joseph Needham, *The Shorter Science and Civilisation in China,* vol. 4 (Cambridge: Cambridge University Press, 1994), 14.

19. Philip B. Meggs and Alston W. Purvis, *Meggs' History of Graphic Design* (Hoboken, NJ: John Wiley & Sons, Inc., 2012).

20. Paul Lester, *Visual Communication: Images with Messages* (Belmont, CA: Wadsworth, 1994), 151.

21. From *Lives of the Most Eminent Painters, Sculptors, and Architects,* published 1500. Quoted from Martin Roberts, *Italian Renaissance* (London: Longman, 1992).

22. Jim Atkins, "Adventures in Architecture: The Series. Il Duomo: Brunelleschi and the Dome of Santa Maria del Fiore, Episode 7: The Machines," *AIArchitect* 15 (July 25, 2008), http://info.aia.org/aiarchitect/thisweek08/0725/0725p_duomo.cfm.

4. Understanding Needs

23. Helen Gardner, *Art through the Ages* (New York: Harcourt Brace & World, 1970), 450–6.

24. Daniel Arasse, *Leonardo da Vinci* (Old Saybrook: Konecky & Konecky, 1998), 95.
25. Tina Seelig, *InGenius: A Crash Course on Creativity* (New York: HarperOne, 2012), 75.

Time for an Innovation Renaissance

26. Seelig, *InGenius*, 9–10.
27. Paul Johnson, *Creators: From Chaucer and Dürer to Picasso and Disney* (New York: HarperCollins, 2006), 3.
28. Nancy Andreasen, *The Creating Brain: The Neuroscience of Genius* (New York: Dana Press, 2005), 114, 181.

Part Two: The Power of Patterns

The Pattern Recognition Principle

1. Ray Kurzweil, *How to Create a Mind* (New York: Penguin, 2012), 38.

The Pattern of the Crowd

2. Alexandra Jerselius, "Hyper Island Executive Study: Personality Trumps Skill in Search for Talent," *Our Community* (blog), April 1, 2014, https://www.hyperisland.com/community/news/hyper-island-executive-study. The study, *Tomorrow's Most Wanted,* was conducted by Hyper Island in cooperation with Edelman in Stockholm, Sweden, over a three-month period in 2013, and polled over 500 international respondents; around half of those polled were in leadership positions.
3. Dimensional Research, *Customer Service and Business Results: A Survey of Customer Service from Mid-Size Companies,* April 2013, https://d16cvnquvjw7pr.cloudfront.net/resources/whitepapers/Zendesk_WP_Customer_Service_and_Business_Results.pdf; Amy Gesenhues, "Survey: 90% of Customers Say Buying Decisions Are Influenced by Online Reviews," *CMO Zone* (blog), *Marketing Land,* April 9, 2013, http://marketingland.com/survey-customers-more-frustrated-by-how-long-it-takes-to-resolve-a-customer-service-issue-than-the-resolution-38756.

Resistance to Change

4. George Humphrey, *The Story of Man's Mind* (Boston: Small, Maynard and Company, 1923), 109.

Sharpening Our Perceptive Powers

5. Brian Todd and Dugald McConnell, "Autopilots May Dull Skills of Pilots, Committee Says," *CNN Travel,* September 2, 2011, http://edition.cnn.com/2011/TRAVEL/09/01/airlines.autopilot/.
6. Andy Pasztor, "Pilots Rely Too Much on Automation, Panel Says," *The Wall Street Journal*, November 17, 2013, http://online.wsj.com/news/articles/SB10001424052702304439804579204202526288042.
7. Tom Costello (Nov 19, 2013), "Airline pilots depend too much on automation, says panel commissioned by FAA" *NBC News* http://www.nbcnews.com/news/other/airline-pilots-depend-too-much-automation-says-panel-commissioned-faa-f2D11625301.
8. Carl Honore, *Under Pressure: Rescuing Our Children from the Culture of Hyper-Parenting* (New York: HarperOne, 2009), 49.

Part Three: Looking through the Four Lenses

"Here's to the Crazy Ones"

1. George Bernard Shaw, *Maxims for Revolutionists, an Appendix to Man and Superman* (Cambridge: Cambridge University Press, 1903).
2. *Steve Jobs: Visionary Entrepreneur*, an extended version of *Steve Jobs: Secrets of Life* (Menlo Park, CA: Silicon Valley Historical Association, 1994).

What Exactly Is an Orthodoxy?

3. George Orwell, *Nineteen Eighty-Four* (London: Secker and Warburg, 1949), 37.

Meet the Challengers

4. Josh Sanburn, "How Dr. Dre Made $300 Headphones a Must-Have Accessory," *Time*, January 16, 2013, http://business.time

.com/2013/01/16/how-dr-dre-made-300-headphones-a-must-have-accessory/.

On a Path of Disruption

5. Chris Anderson, "Elon Musk's Mission to Mars," *Wired*, October 21, 2012, http://www.wired.com/2012/10/ff-elon-musk-qa/.

6. SpaceX, "Production at SpaceX," September 24, 2014, http://www.spacex.com/news/2013/09/24/production-spacex.

7. NASA, "NASA Awards Space Station Commercial Resupply Services Contracts," (Contract Release C08–069, December 23, 2008), http://www.nasa.gov/home/hqnews/2008/dec/HQ_C08–069_ISS_Resupply.html.

8. CNN Library, "International Space Station Fast Facts," last modified September 20, 2014, http://www.cnn.com/2013/10/22/world/international-space-station-fast-facts/.

9. Ajai Raj, "Elon Musk: SpaceX Wants to Build a City on Mars," *Business Insider*, September 12, 2014, http://www.sfgate.com/technology/businessinsider/article/Elon-Musk-SpaceX-Wants-To-Build-A-City-On-Mars-4979634.php.

10. Jerry Hirsch, "Tesla Quietly Becomes One of California's Bestselling Luxury Cars," *Los Angeles Times*, August 27, 2013, http://articles.latimes.com/2013/aug/27/autos/la-fi-hy-prius-tesla-lead-california-car-sales-20130823.

11. "Video: The Tesla Model S Is Our Top-Scoring Car," *Consumer Reports*, May 9, 2013, http://www.consumerreports.org/cro/news/2013/05/video-the-tesla-model-s-is-our-top-scoring-car/index.htm.

12. Edward Niedermeyer, "Tesla Is a Car, Not a Revolution," *Bloomberg View*, February 28, 2014, http://www.bloombergview.com/articles/2014–02–28/tesla-is-a-car-not-a-revolution.

13. Mike Isaac, "Elon Musk Shakes Off the Electric Car Naysayers (Video)," *All Things D,* May 29, 2013, http://allthingsd.com/20130529/elon-musk-shakes-off-the-electric-car-naysayers-video/; "Elon Musk at D11: Full Session," *The Wall Street Journal* video, 1:09:24, May 30, 2013, http://www.wsj.com/video/elon-musk-at-d11-full-session/1F7C3196–2B5D-4A1F-9FD0-B8DF95FFC97D.html.

14. Ibid.

15. Mark Rogowsky, "Tesla Sales Blow Past Competitors, but with Success Comes Scrutiny," *Forbes*, January 16, 2014, http://www.forbes.com/sites/markrogowsky/2014/01/16/tesla-sales-blow-past-competitors-but-with-success-comes-scrutiny/.

16. Jeff Cobb, "Tesla Sells 25,000th Model S," *HybridCars* (blog), January 6, 2014, http://www.hybridcars.com/tesla-sells-25000th-model-s-globally/.

17. Chris Woodyard, "Nevada, Tesla Announce Huge 'Gigafactory' Deal," *USA Today*, September 5, 2014, http://www.usatoday.com/story/money/cars/2014/09/04/tesla-gigafactory-reno/15095411/.

18. Rolfe Winkler, "Elon Musk Electrifies Techies," *The Wall Street Journal,* June 3, 2013, http://blogs.wsj.com/moneybeat/2013/06/03/elon-musk-electrifies-techies/.

19. Jon Favreau, "Elon Musk," *Time*, April 29, 2010, http://content.time.com/time/specials/packages/article/0,28804,1984685_1984745_1985495,00.html.

Innovation Means Shifting Assumptions

20. Kim Bhasin, "Nike Has Gone All-In on Its Game-Changing Flyknit Racer," *Business Insider,* February 14, 2013, http://www.businessinsider.com/nike-has-gone-all-in-on-its-game-changing-flyknit-racer-2013–2.

21. Alysha Khan, "Modern Day Willy Wonka Engineers Sweet Success with Specialty Candy Stores," *Sun Sentinel,* June 15, 2013, http://articles.sun-sentinel.com/2013–06–15/business/fl-itsugar-candy-specialty-20130615_1_candy-bar-u-s-candy-industry-susan-whiteside.

22. Michael Smith, "GE Bringing Ultrasound to PGA Tour Events," *Street & Smith's Sports Business,* May 5, 2014, http://www.sportsbusinessdaily.com/Journal/Issues/2014/05/05/Marketing-and-Sponsorship/GE-ultrasound.aspx; "GE Healthcare," *Fast Company*, March 2013, 136.

23. Danielle Sacks, "Chipotle: Exploding All the Rules of Fast Food," *Fast Company,* March 2012, 125.

24. Gabe Gagliano, "HBO GO Interactive Features Coming to the iPad," *Tech of the Hub*, March 28, 2012, http://www.techofthehub.com/2012/03/hbo-interactive-features-coming-ipad-exclusive.html.

25. Julie Zeveloff, "A Chinese Company Plans to Build the World's Tallest Building in Just 90 Days," *Business Insider*, June 18, 2012, http://www.businessinsider.com/a-chinese-company-plans-to-build-the-worlds-tallest-building-in-just-90-days-2012–6.

26. Mary Quinn O'Connor, "Buy American: No Need to Go Truffle Hunting in Europe," *Fox News*, March 8, 2012, http://www.foxnews.com/leisure/2012/03/08/eating-expensive-fungus/.

27. "50 Most Innovative Companies: #15 NFL," *Fast Company*, March 2012, 98.

Ready to Rethink Everything?

28. Matthew May, "How WellnessMart Untangled Health Care," *Upstart Business Journal,* November 15, 2012, http://upstart.bizjournals.com/resources/author/2012/11/15/how-wellnessmart-untangled-health-care.html?page=all.

29. Lucas Mearian, "3D Printer Creates Lithium-Ion Batteries the Size of a Grain of Sand," *Computerworld*, June 19, 2013, http://www.computerworld.com/article/2497979/emerging-technology/3d-printer-creates-lithium-ion-batteries-the-size-of-a-grain-of-sand.html.

30. Daniel Michaels, "For Diners Dangling from a Crane, May We Suggest the Hanger Steak?" *The Wall Street Journal*, May 22, 2013, http://online.wsj.com/articles/SB10001424127887324787004578497090113579334.

31. Pascal Rossignol, "A Representative from European Helicopter Maker AgustaWestland Presents Project Zero at the Le Bourget Airport Near Paris," *Orlando Sentinel*, June 20, 2013, http://touch.orlandosentinel.com/#section/-1/article/p2p-76381098/.

32. Tesco, "Tesco Homeplus Expands Number of Virtual Stores," press release, February 7, 2012, http://www.tescoplc.com/index.asp?pageid=17&newsid=593.

33. "Tesco Builds Virtual Shops for Korean Commuters," *The Telegraph,* June 27, 2011, http://www.telegraph.co.uk/technology/mobile-phones/8601147/Tesco-builds-virtual-shops-for-Korean-commuters.html.

34. Kristine Lofgren, "World's First Algae-Powered Building by Splitterwerk Architects Opens in Germany," *Inhabitat,* March 5, 2013, http://inhabitat.com/splitterwerk-architects-design-worlds-first-algae-powered-building-for-germany/.

35. Tom Murphy, "4 Questions to Consider When Buying Eyewear Online," *Boston Globe*, April 11, 2013, http://www.bostonglobe.com/business/2013/04/10/questions-consider-when-buying-eyewear-online/5MGZrsl4zp59ftEDb0i8dL/story.html.

36. Ryan Kim, "At Warby Parker, the Power of Branding Is Easy to See," *Gigaom*, March 26, 2012, https://gigaom.com/2012/03/26/at-warby-parker-the-power-of-branding-is-easy-to-see/.

37. Juliet Mann, "Don't Cry over Spilt Milk—It Could Become a Skirt," *CNN World,* July 6 2012, http://www.cnn.com/2012/07/05/world/europe/qmilch-milk-sustainable-fashion/index.html.

Seeing the Future in the Present

38. John Naisbitt, *Mind Set! Reset your Thinking and See the Future* (New York: HarperCollins, 2006).

39. *The Economist,* "Books of the Year 2003," December 4, 2003. He is reported to have first said this in an interview on *Fresh Air*, NPR, August 31, 1993; he repeated it, prefacing it with, "As I've said many times" in "The Science in Science Fiction," *Talk of the Nation*, NPR, November 30, 1999, audio (timecode 11:55), http://www.npr.org/templates/story/story.php?storyId=1067220.

40. Willard Van Orman Quine, in Andrew Bailey, *First Philosophy: Knowledge and Reality: Fundamental Problems and Readings in Philosophy* (Peterborough, Ontario: Broadview Press, 2004), 300.

41. Emily Greene Balch, "Toward Human Unity or beyond Nationalism," Nobel lecture, April 7, 1948, Oslo, Norway, http://www.nobelprize.org/nobel_prizes/peace/laureates/1946/balch-lecture.html.

A Global "Change Bomb"

42. "Eastman Kodak Company, Market Capitalization, 2005, Q1," *Wikinvest,* accessed October 21, 2014, http://www.wikinvest.com/stock/Eastman_Kodak_Company_(EK)/Data/Market_Capitalization/2005/Q1.

43. Jordan Weissmann, "What Killed Kodak?" *The Atlantic,* January 5, 2012, http://www.theatlantic.com/business/archive/2012/01/what-killed-kodak/250925/.

44. Chris Mallon, "Nokia's Enterprising Value," *The Motley Fool*, January 27, 2004, http://www.fool.com/investing/general/2004/01/27/nokias-enterprising-value.aspx.

45. Jefferson Graham, "App Store for iPhone Already a Hit with Developers," *USA Today*, July 10, 2008, http://usatoday30.usatoday.com/money/industries/technology/2008–07–09-apple-apps-store-iphone-ipod_N.htm.

46. Apple Press Info, "Apple's App Store Marks Historic 50 Billionth Download," May 16, 2014, http://www.apple.com/pr/library/2013/05/16Apples-App-Store-Marks-Historic-50-Billionth-Download.html.

The Race for Tomorrow

47. Scott Allison, "The Responsive Organization: Coping with New Technology and Disruption," *Forbes*, February 10, 2014, http://www.forbes.com/sites/scottallison/2014/02/10/the-responsive-organization-how-to-cope-with-technology-and-disruption/.

48. Victoria Barret, "Why Salesforce.com Ranks #1 On Forbes Most Innovative List," *Forbes*, September 5, 2012, http://www.forbes.com/sites/victoriabarret/2012/09/05/why-salesforce-com-ranks-1-on-forbes-most-innovative-list/.

49. C. K. Prahalad, "Strategies for Growth," in *Rethinking The Future*, ed. Rowan Gibson (London: Nicholas Brealey Publishing, 1996), 73.

Learning to Ride the Waves

50. Jon Kabat-Zinn, *Wherever You Go, There You Are: Mindfulness Meditation in Everyday Life* (New York: Hyperion, 1994), 30.

Meet the Trend Surfers

51. "Bill Gates Time Line" *Forbes*, June 16, 2006, http://www.forbes.com/2006/06/16/cz_rr_ck_billgatesslide.html; "Microsoft Corporation," *Reference for Business: Encyclopedia of Business*, 2nd ed., accessed Oct 19, 2014, http://www.referenceforbusiness.com/businesses/M-Z/Microsoft-Corporation.html.

52. "Bill Gates Time Line."

53. Benjamin Romano, "Gates' Big-Picture Memos Shaped Microsoft, Changed Tech World," *Seattle Times*, June 27, 2008, http://seattletimes.com/html/microsoft/2008020208_microsoft27.html.

54. Bill Gates, "The Internet Tidal Wave," internal Microsoft memo to executive staff and direct reports, May 26, 1995, http://www.usdoj.gov/atr/cases/exhibits/20.pdf.

55. Ibid.

56. "Microsoft Announces Record Fiscal Year Revenue and Income," *Microsoft News Center*, July 18, 2000, http://news.microsoft.com/2000/07/18/microsoft-announces-record-fiscal-year-revenue-and-income/; "Bill Gates Time Line."

57. John Mackey, *Conscious Capitalism: Liberating the Heroic Spirit of Business* (Cambridge, MA: Harvard Business Review Press, 2013), 14.

58. "Jeff Bezos—Person of the Year," *Time*, December 27, 1999, http://content.time.com/time/covers/0,16641,19991227,00.html (cover), and http://content.time.com/time/magazine/article/0,9171,992927,00.html (article).

59. Joanna Stern, "Jeff Bezos Says Washington Post Could Take a Page from Amazon," *ABC News*, September 25, 2013, http://abcnews.go.com/Technology/jeff-bezos-washington-post-page-amazon/story?id=20364644.

The Man from the Future

60. Matt Peckham, "The First Macintosh: 'The Computer for the Rest of Us,'" *Time*, October 5, 2011, http://techland.time.com/2011/10/05/the-10-most-memorable-apple-commercials/slide/macintosh-the-computer-for-the-rest-of-us/.

61. Steve Jobs, "Steve Jobs Speaks Out: On Catching Tech's Next Wave," *Fortune*, March 7, 2008, http://archive.fortune.com/galleries/2008/fortune/0803/gallery.jobsqna.fortune/13.html.

It's Happening Now!

62. Zoe Flood, "Kenya's Mobile Innovation Brings Digital Money Closer," *BBC News*, July 3, 2014, http://www.bbc.com/news/business-28142515.

63. Nigam Arora, "Seeds of Apple's New Growth in Mobile Payments, 800 Million iTune Accounts," *Forbes*, April 24, 2014, http://www.forbes.com/sites/nigamarora/2014/04/24/seeds-of-apples-new-growth-in-mobile-payments-800-million-itune-accounts/.

The Next Big Thing for Your Business

64. Peter Harrop, Raghu Das, and Guillaume Chansin, *Wearable Technology 2014–2024: Technologies, Markets, Forecasts*, IDTechEx, July 2014, http://www.idtechex.com/research/reports/wearable-technology-2014–2024-technologies-markets-forecasts-000379.asp.
65. Jon Phillips, "Wearables Sales Tripled in a Year—and Will Grow 500 Percent by 2018, Study Says," *CIO*, April 10, 2014, http://www.cio.com/article/2377173/consumer-technology/wearables-sales-tripled-in-a-year—and-will-grow-500-percent-by-2018—study-says.html.
66. Chip Cutter, "Mary Meeker: The Future Is 'Wearables, Drivables, Flyables, Scannables,'" *LinkedIn*, May 29, 2013, https://www.linkedin.com/pulse/article/20130529152733–13780238-mary-meeker-the-future-is-wearables-drivables-flyables-scannables.

Repurpose, Redeploy, and Recombine

67. Seth Golden, "Coca-Cola's Decade-Long Struggle to Fix Its Declining CSD Business," *Seeking Alpha*, April 7, 2014, http://seekingalpha.com/article/2128453-coca-colas-decade-long-struggle-to-fix-its-declining-csd-business.
68. Joseph Schumpeter, *Theory of Economic Development* (New Brunswick, NJ: Transaction Publishers, 1934), 65–66.
69. Andrew Hargadon, *How Breakthroughs Happen* (Cambridge, MA: Harvard University Press, 2003), 31.

How Would You Define Google?

70. Philip Elmer-DeWitt, "Steve Jobs to Larry Page: 'You Guys Are Doing Too Much,'" *Fortune*, July 7, 2014, http://fortune.com/2014/07/07/steve-jobs-to-larry-page-you-guys-are-doing-too-much/.

71. Adam Lashinsky, "Larry Page: Google Should Be Like a Family," *Fortune*, January 19, 2012, http://fortune.com/2012/01/19/larry-page-google-should-be-like-a-family/.

Extending the Boundaries of the Business

72. Peter Cohen, "Macworld Expo Keynote Live Update," *MacWorld*, January 9, 2007, http://www.macworld.com/article/1054764/live-update.html.
73. Christian Sylt, "The Secrets behind Disney's $2.2 Billion Theme Park Profits," *Forbes*, July 14, 2014, http://www.forbes.com/sites/csylt/2014/07/14/the-secrets-behind-disneys-2–2-billion-theme-park-profits/.
74. Jason Lasecki, "Adventures by Disney Named World's Leading Luxury Tour Operator," *Disney Parks Blog,* December 13, 2012, http://disneyparks.disney.go.com/blog/2012/12/adventures-by-disney-named-worlds-leading-luxury-tour-operator/.
75. "Pirates of the Caribbean" franchise total grosses, *Box Office Mojo*, accessed October 18, 2014, http://www.boxofficemojo.com/franchises/chart/?id=piratesofthecaribbean.htm.

Stretching into New Spaces

76. Julia La Roche, "Dan Loeb Unveils a New Bet on a Dutch Nutrition Company," *Business Insider*, July 18, 2014, http://www.businessinsider.com/third-point-buys-royal-dsm-2014–7.
77. Ibid.
78. B. U., "Shop Horror," *The Economist*, July 21, 2014, http://www.economist.com/blogs/schumpeter/2014/07/tesco.
79. "Corning Inc.—Company Profile, Information, Business Description, History, Background Information on Corning Inc.," *Reference for Business: Encyclopedia of Business,* 2nd ed., accessed October 18, 2014, http://www.referenceforbusiness.com/history2/5/Corning-Inc.html#ixzz3GXcoxE3M.

Unlimited Potential for Growth

80. Richard Branson, "Richard Branson on Branding," *Entrepreneur,* March 30, 2011, http://www.entrepreneur.com/article/219405.

81. Richard Branson, "Don't Be Afraid to Diversify," *Richard* (blog), accessed October 18, 2014, http://www.virgin.com/richard-branson/dont-be-afraid-to-diversify.

82. Richard Branson, *Losing My Virginity: How I've Survived, Had Fun, and Made a Fortune Doing Business My Way* (New York: Three Rivers Press, 1998), 144.

83. Des Dearlove, *The Unauthorized Guide to Doing Business the Richard Branson Way* (West Sussex, UK: Capstone Publishing, 2010), 71.

Exploiting Underutilized Assets

84. Lydia Leong, et al. *2014 Cloud Infrastructure as a Service Magic Quadrant* (Stamford, CT: Gartner Inc., May 28, 2014), http://aws.amazon.com/resources/gartner-mq-2014-learn-more/.

85. Alex Williams, "Amazon Web Services Wins Again in Battle to Build the CIA Cloud," *TechCrunch*, October 7, 2013, http://techcrunch.com/2013/10/07/amazon-web-services-wins-again-in-battle-to-build-the-cia-and-nsa-cloud/.

86. Shane Smith, "Redbox Passes 500 Million Rentals," *Inside Redbox*, September 22, 2009, http://www.insideredbox.com/redbox-passes-500-million-rentals/.

87. Ben Fritz, "Redbox Tries to Break Out of Its Box," *The Wall Street Journal,* May 20, 2014, http://online.wsj.com/news/articles/SB10001424052702304422704579574191322689248.

What Else Could We Do with This?

88. "John Stith Pemberton," *American Civil War Story,* accessed October 19, 2014, http://www.americancivilwarstory.com/john-stith-pemberton.html.

89. James Hamblin, "Why We Took Cocaine out of Soda," *The Atlantic,* January 31, 2013, http://www.theatlantic.com/health/archive/2013/01/why-we-took-cocaine-out-of-soda/272694/.

90. "Percy Spencer, Microwave Inventor," *Invention at Play,* Lemelson Center for the Study of Invention and Innovation, accessed October 19, 2014, http://www.inventionatplay.org/inventors_spe.html.

91. Jeff Suess, "Play-Doh Began as Wall Cleaner," *Cincinnati.com,* January 24, 2013, http://www2.cincinnati.com/blogs/ourhistory/2013/01/24/play-doh-began-as-wall-cleaner/.

92. Pamela Cyran and Chris Gaylord, "The 20 Most Fascinating Accidental Inventions," *Christian Science Monitor*, October 5, 2012, http://www.csmonitor.com/Innovation/2012/1005/The-20-most-fascinating-accidental-inventions/Play-Doh.

93. Emma Stoye, "Cyanoacrylate," *Royal Chemical Society's Chemistry World*, June 12, 2013, http://www.rsc.org/chemistryworld/2013/06/cyanoacrylate-superglue-adhesive-glue-podcast.

94. Chih-Chang Chu, J. Anthony von Fraunhofer, and Howard P. Greisler, eds., *Wound Closure Biomaterials and Devices* (Boca Raton, FL: CRC Press, 1996), 331.

Leveraging Resources from Others

95. Scott Mendelson, "Box Office: 'How To Train Your Dragon 2' Crosses $500M Following China Debut," *Forbes*, August 15, 2014, http://www.forbes.com/sites/scottmendelson/2014/08/15/box-office-how-to-train-your-dragon-2-crosses-500m-worldwide-following-china-debut/.

Innovating from the Customer Backward

96. A. G. Lafley and Ram Charan *The Game Changer: How Every Leader Can Drive Everyday Innovation* (London: Profile Books, 2008), 33.

97. Ibid.

98. Ibid., 48–49.

99. Ibid., 59–63.

100. "WWDC 1997: Steve Jobs about Apple's Future," YouTube video, 1:11:09, video of Steve Jobs at Apple's Worldwide Developers Conference, October 19, 2011, https://www.youtube.com/watch?v=qyd0tP0SK6o.

Do Customers Really Know What They Want?

101. Also cited in David Sturt and Todd Nordstrom "Delight Your Customers by Giving Them What They Didn't Ask for," *Forbes*, January 3, 2014, http://www.forbes.com/sites/davidsturt/2014/01/03/delight-your-customers-by-giving-them-what-they-didnt-ask-for/.

102. Edward R. Murrow, 1955, NBC; as cited in Kathleen Constable, *A Stranger within the Gates* (Lanham, MD: University Press of America, 2000), 3.

103. Gijs van Wulfen, *Creating Innovative Products and Services* (Surrey, England: Gower Publishing, 2011), 103.

104. Vern Burkhardt, "Design Thinking for Innovation: Interview with Tom Kelley," *IdeaConnection*, June 28, 2009, http://www.ideaconnection.com/open-innovation-articles/00126-Design-Thinking-for-Innovation.html.

Matching What Is Possible with What Is Needed

105. Jacob Ward, "Innovation of the Year: Google Now," *Popular Science*, November 16, 2012, http://www.popsci.com/bown/2012/product/google-now.

106. Farhad Manjoo, "Behind the Best Innovations: Obvious, Annoying Problems," *The Wall Street Journal*, October 9, 2013, http://online.wsj.com/news/articles/SB10001424052702304500404579125131894144044.

Part Four: How Big Ideas Are Built

Rethinking the Universe

1. Einstein, interview by David Reichinstein, in Reichinstein, Albert Einstein sein Lebensbild und seine Weltanschauung, Prague: Ernst Ganz, 1935), 22. See also Peter Michelmore, *Einstein: Profile of the Man* (New York: Dodd, Mead and Company, 1962), 44.

2. The remark is in a voice recording, transcribed and presented in the German in F. Herneck, "Zwei Tondokumente Einsteins zur Relativitätstheorie," *Forschungen und Fortschritte* 40 (1966): 133–35; and translated in John Stachel et al., *The Collected Papers of Albert Einstein Volume 2, The Swiss Years: Writings, 1900–1909*, 264.

3. Albert Einstein, *Autobiographical Notes* (Munich: Paul List Verlag, 1949), 51.

Inventing the Twentieth Century

4. Neil Baldwin, *Edison—Inventing the Century* (New York: Hyperion, 1995), 213.

5. Dagobert D. Runes, ed., *The Diary and Sundry Observations of Thomas Alva Edison* (New York: Philosophical Library, 1948).

6. Michael J. Gelb and Sarah Miller Caldicott, *Innovate Like Edison: The Five-Step System for Breakthrough Business Success* (New York: Penguin, 2007), 118. Originally from Lawrence Frost, *The Thomas A. Edison Album* (Mattituck, NY: Amereon, 1984).

7. Gelb and Caldicott, *Innovate Like Edison,* 118.

8. Frank Dyer and Thomas Martin, *Edison, His Life and Inventions* (New York: Harper Brothers, 1929), Chapter XXII.

9. Steven Johnson, *Where Good Ideas Come From: The Natural History of Innovation* (New York: Riverhead, 2010), 23.

Unpacking the Creative Process

10. Betty Edwards, *Drawing on the Right Side of the Brain Deluxe: The Definitive 4th Edition* (New York: Jeremy P. Tarcher, 2012).

11. Henri Poincaré, *The Foundations of Science*, trans. George Bruce Halsted (New York: Science Press, 1913), 33.

12. Graham Wallas, *The Art of Thought* (London: Jonathan Cape, 1926), 10, 99, 102.

13. Ibid., 94.

14. James Webb Young, *A Technique for Producing Ideas* (1940; repr., New York: McGraw-Hill, 2003), 5.

15. Alex F. Osborn, *Applied Imagination: Principles and Procedures of Creative Thinking* (New York: Scribner's, 1957).

16. "Jacob W. Getzels, Creativity Scholar, 1912–2001," University of Chicago News Office, April 10, 2001, http://www-news.uchicago.edu/releases/01/010410.getzels.shtml.

17. Jacob Getzels, *Creativity and Intelligence* (New York: John Wiley & Sons, Inc., 1962).

18. Jacob Getzels, *The Creative Vision* (New York: John Wiley & Sons, Inc., 1976).

"Say Good-Bye to the Bag"

19. Charlie Burton, "The Seventh Disruption: How James Dyson Reinvented the Personal Heater," *Wired UK,* October 22, 2011, http://www.wired.co.uk/magazine/archive/2011/11/features/the-seventh-disruption-james-dyson/viewall.

20. Alison Beard, "James Dyson: The Extended Life's Work Interview," *Harvard Business Review,* accessed October 19, 2014, http://hbr.org/web/2010/07/dyson2.

What Exactly Is an Insight?

21. Gary Klein, *Seeing What Others Don't: The Remarkable Ways We Gain Insights* (New York: PublicAffairs, 2013), 26. (The book is also known as *Everything That Follows Is Different: The Disruptive Power of Insight.*)
22. Ibid., 22.
23. Ibid.
24. Wallas, *The Art of Thought*, 94.
25. Markus Diesmann and Abigail Morrison, "Largest Neuronal Network Simulation to Date Achieved using Japanese Supercomputer," press release, August 2, 2013, http://www.fz-juelich.de/SharedDocs/Pressemitteilungen/UK/EN/2013/13–08–02Largest-Simulation.html.
26. "Procter on Purpose: Marc Pritchard of Procter & Gamble Seeks Deeper Brand Meaning," *The Hub Magazine*, May/June 2011, http://www.hubmagazine.com/html/2011/hub_42/may_jun/2372305742/procter-gamble_marc-pritchard/.
27. Marc Pritchard, "Quote of the Week," BrandAds, accessed October 18, 2014, http://brandads.com/quote-of-the-week/marc-pritchard/.

A Practical Definition of Insights

28. Marco Vriens and Rogier Verhulst, "Unleashing Hidden Insights," *Marketing Research*, Winter 2008, https://www.ama.org/Documents/MRWinter08Vriens.pdf, 13.
29. Charles Kiefer and Malcolm Constable, *The Art of Insight* (San Francisco: Berrett-Koehler Publishers, 2013), 24.
30. Jeremy Bullmore, "Why Is a Good Insight Like a Refrigerator?", WPP, accessed October 17, 2014, http://www.wpp.com/wpp/marketing/marketresearch/why-is-a-good-insight-like-a-refrigerator/.
31. "Strategy: An A-Z of Business Quotations" *Schumpeter* (blog), *The Economist*, October 19, 2012, http://www.economist.com/blogs/schumpeter/2012/10/z-business-quotations-1.

Understanding Ideation

32. Klein, *Seeing What Others Don't*, 23.

Working with the Four Lenses

33. For Christopher Morley quotes, see http://www.goodreads.com/author/quotes/30802.Christopher_Morley and http://www-stat.wharton.upenn.edu/~steele/Rants/Academic-Resarch-Quotes.html.

All images used in this book are either original illustrations by Adriana Matallana, images owned by Rowan Gibson, copyrighted images from stock companies that have been purchased and used with permission, the property of other companies used with permission, or are images obtained from the public domain that do not require specific permission for use. A list of credits for these images includes the following:

PREFACE

Page xvi. Portrait photo by Eduardo Lopez.

PART ONE

Page xvi. Reworked brain image, original is a copyrighted image from Shutterstock (Image ID: 145505737), used with permission.

Page 3. Prometheus, Marie-Lan Nguyen, public domain:
http://commons.wikimedia.org/wiki/File:Prometheus_Adam_Louvre_MR1745.jpg.

Page 7. The Gonzaga Family and Retinue Detail 146574 Fresco Palazzo Ducale Camera Degli Sposi Bridal Chamber Mantua Italy, Andrea Mantegna, public domain:
www.findfreegraphics.com/image-83/mantegna.htm.

Page 8. Vitruvian Man, Leonardo da Vinci, public domain via Wikimedia Commons:
http://upload.wikimedia.org/wikipedia/commons/1/17/Vitruvian.jpg.

Page 13. Astronomer Copernicus-Conversation with God, Jan Matejko, public domain via Wikimedia Commons:
http://upload.wikimedia.org/wikipedia/commons/8/88/Jan_Matejko-Astronomer_Copernicus-Conversation_with_God.jpg.

Page 14. Christopher Columbus, Sebastiano del Piombo, public domain via Wikimedia Commons:
http://upload.wikimedia.org/wikipedia/commons/5/5d/Christopher_Columbus.PNG.

Page 17. Francesco Petrarca, Unknown, public domain via Wikimedia Commons:
http://upload.wikimedia.org/wikipedia/commons/5/59/Francesco_Petrarca00.jpg.

Page 21a. Gutenberg Bible, public domain via Wikimedia Commons:
http://upload.wikimedia.org/wikipedia/commons/2/27/Gutenberg_bible_Old_Testament_Epistle_of_St_Jerome.jpg.

Page 21b. Johannes Gutenberg, public domain via Wikimedia Commons:
http://upload.wikimedia.org/wikipedia/commons/d/d7/Johannes_Gutenberg.jpg.

Page 23a. Gutenberg Bible, David Ball, This work is licensed under the Creative Commons Attribution-ShareAlike 3.0 License. This licensing tag was added to this file as part of the GFDL licensing update:
http://upload.wikimedia.org/wikipedia/commons/b/b0/Gutenberg_Bible.jpg.

Page 23b. Color palette, Mlaoxve, public domain via Wikimedia Commons:
http://commons.wikimedia.org/wiki/File:Oil_painting_palette.jpg.

Page 23c. First printing machine, Natalisha9162 (own work), CC-BY-SA-3.0, (http://creativecommons.org/licenses/by-sa/3.0), via Wikimedia Commons:
http://upload.wikimedia.org/wikipedia/commons/6/63/First_Printing_machine.png.

Page 23d. Wine press, free download:
http://all-free-download.com/free-vector/vector-clip-art/wine_press_clip_art_18726.html.

Page 25. Florence Cathedral dome, Frank K., via Wikimedia Commons:
http://upload.wikimedia.org/wikipedia/commons/a/a6/View_of_the_Duomo%27s_dome%2C_Florence.jpg,
(http://creativecommons.org/licenses/by/2.0).

PART TWO

PART THREE

Page 107. Rocket, NASA, public domain via Wikimedia Commons: http://upload.wikimedia.org/wikipedia/commons/b/bc/ COTS2Dragon.6.jpg.

Page 108. Tesla Car, Copyrighted image from Shutterstock (Image ID: 186846827), used with permission.

Page 111a. Nike shoe, Mogi, Creative Common: https://www.flickr.com/photos/_mogi/8546705594/in/photostream.

Page 112a. Copyrighted image from Corbis (Image ID: 42–49886853), used with permission.

Page 112b. Copyrighted image from Corbis (Image ID: 42–58701386), used with permission.

Page 112c. Candy Closeup, by Evan Amos (Own work), via Wikimedia Commons: http://upload.wikimedia.org/wikipedia/commons/9/98/ Rock-Candy-Closeup.jpg; CC-BY-SA-3.0 (http://creativecommons.org/licenses/by-sa/3.0).

Page 113a. Sky City photo, property of BROAD Group, used with permission.

Page 113b. Truffle, public domain via Wikimedia Commons: http://upload.wikimedia.org/wikipedia/commons/2/26/ Truffe_noire_du_P%C3%A9rigord.jpg.

PART FOUR

Page 205. Archimedes Bath, public domain via Wikimedia Commons: http://upload.wikimedia.org/wikipedia/commons/4/47/Archimedes_bath.jpg.

Page 208. Albert Einstein, by Lucien Chavan, public domain via Wikimedia Commons: http://upload.wikimedia.org/wikipedia/commons/8/87/Einstein_patentoffice_full.jpg.

Page 216. Thomas Edison, By Louis Bachrach, Bachrach Studios, restored by Michel Vuijlsteke, public domain via Wikimedia Commons: http://upload.wikimedia.org/wikipedia/commons/9/9d/ Thomas_Edison2.jpg.

Page 221. Phonograph, by Norman Bruderhofer, www.cylinder.de (own work (transferred from de:File:Phonograph.jpg)), http://upload.wikimedia.org/wikipedia/commons/a/a0/EdisonPhonograph.jpg; GFDL (http://www.gnu.org/copyleft/fdl. html) or CC-BY-SA-3.0 (http://creativecommons.org/licenses/by-sa/3.0).

Page 223. Phonograph, by Norman Bruderhofer, www.cylinder.de (own work (transferred from de:File:Phonograph.jpg)), http://upload.wikimedia.org/wikipedia/commons/a/a0/EdisonPhonograph.jpg; GFDL (http://www.gnu.org/copyleft/fdl. html) or CC-BY-SA-3.0 (http://creativecommons.org/licenses/by-sa/3.0/).

Page 226. Graham Wallas, public domain via Wikimedia Commons: http://upload.wikimedia.org/wikipedia/commons/7/70/ Graham_Wallas.jpg.

Page 227. Ford assembly, by Literary Digest 1928–01–07, Henry Ford Interview, photographer unknown, public domain via Wikimedia Commons: http://upload.wikimedia.org/wikipedia/commons/8/86/ Ford_Motor_Company_assembly_line.jpg.

Page 231a. James Dyson, By Michiel Hendryckx (own work), via Wikimedia Commons: http://upload.wikimedia.org/wikipedia/commons/a/af/ James_Dyson_4.jpg; CC-BY-SA-3.0 (http://creativecommons.org/licenses/by-sa/3.0.

Page 231b. Dyson Vacuum Cleaner, by Arpingstone, this work has been released into the public domain by its author, via Wikimedia Commons: http://commons.wikimedia.org/wiki/File:Dyson.cleaner. dc07.arp.jpg.

Page 238. Gary Klein, portrait photo by Steve Ziegelmeyer.

INDEX

A

Act of Creation, The (Koestler), 248
AgustaWestland, 114–115
Alberti, Leon Battista, 13, 28
Alcohol Free Shop, 186
Alexander, Susan Rice, 113
Allen, Paul, 130
All Things Digital (2013), 108
Amazon
    creativity and, 233
    Harnessing Trends and, 134–136, 146
    Leveraging Resources and, 160–161, 168
    power of patterns and, 64
    Understanding Needs and, 181, 198
amputation, alternative treatments and, 37
Anderson, Chris, 106
Andreasen, Nancy, 50
Andreessen, Mark, 134
Android (Google), 126
Android Wear (Google), 147–148, 156–157
animation, of films, 138
Apple
    Challenging Orthodoxies, 92, 93, 104
    Harnessing Trends, 120–121, 126, 130, 137–141, 146
    Leveraging Resources, 160, 174
    power of patterns and, 84
    Understanding Needs, 183, 198, 199
Applied Imagination (Osborn), 229
Arasse, Daniel, 31
Archimedes Principle, 204–207, 249
Architectura, De (Vitruvius), 27
architecture, Brunelleschi and, 24–28
Art of Insight, The (Kiefer, Constable), 244
Art of Thought, The (Wallas), 226–227
Art through the Ages (Gardner), 31
assets
    exploiting underutilized assets, 168–169
    as resources, 152, 159
    See also Leveraging Resources
association, insight and, 238, 246–247
Audi, 187
automaticity, 69
automation addiction, 81
automobiles
    air conditioning in, 187
    smart, 144

B

Baldwin, Neil, 216
Ballmer, Steve, 131
banking industry, 145–146

Barnes & Noble, 135

BASF, 173

batteries, for mobile devices, 114, 198–199

Beats by Dre, 104

Beats Electronics, 199

Bell, Alexander Graham, 221

Besso, Michele, 211

Bezos, Jeff, 64, 134–136, 168, 181, 233. *See also*
    Amazon

"big ideas," different routes to, 232–234. *See also*
    creativity; insight

Bosch, 186

Boscolo, Rossano, 190

brain
    brainteaser puzzles and insight, 236 (*See also*
        insight)
    creative process and, 224–229 (*See also* creativity)
    functional fixedness and, 70–71
    pattern-recognition principle and, 68–69
    perception and creativity, 66–67

Branson, Sir Richard, 166–167

breakthrough ideas
    creativity and, 207, 214–215
    insight and, 241, 242–243, 248

Brin, Sergey, 104, 157, 158

British Airways, 148–149

Brunelleschi, Filippo, 13, 24–29

BSB (Broad Sustainable Building), 113

bubble wrap, 172

Bullmore, Jeremy, 244–245

Burj Khalifa (Dubai), 113

business boundaries, extending, 160–162,
    163–165

C

calculators, 38

Caldicott, Sarah Miller, 217

Canada, consumers' cultural needs and, 192

Canon, 163–164

Canute (King of Denmark and England), 129

Cassiodorus, 5

castello (machine), 27

cat doors, 200

centipede effect, 75

CGI rendering, 138

Challenging Orthodoxies, 92–117
    advantage of, 102–104
    creativity and ideas, 211
    disruption and, 100–101, 105–110
    othodoxy, defined, 96–97
    othodoxy and need to challenge, 98–101
    overview, 92–95, 117
    rethinking for, 114–116
    shifting assumptions for innovation, 111–113
    working with, for insight, 254–258

change
    rate of, 122
    Renaissance and radical change, 40–45
    resistance to, 74–77
    trends as patterns of change, 126–129, 130–136
    understanding, 120–121
    See also Harnessing Trends

China, consumers' cultural needs and, 191, 192–193

Chipotle, 112

Chotukool (Godrej & Boyce), 190

Chrome (Google), 156

clocks
Brunelleschi and, 24
Galileo and, 35
Coca-Cola, 153, 170
coffee, 186
cognition. *See* brain
Cohen, Jack, 163
Columbus, Christopher, 14
competencies, as resources, 152, 159. *See also* Leveraging
Resources
conformity, orthodoxy and, 97
Constable, Malcolm, 244
Constantine, Mark, 103
"Consumer Is Boss, The" (P&G), 178–179
Coover, Harry, 171–172
Copernicus, 12
Corning, 164
Couchbase, 199
"cradles of creativity," 49–52
"crazy ones," as innovators, 92–95
Creating Brain: The Neuroscience of Genius, The
(Andreasen), 50
Creative Vision, The (Getzels), 229
creativity, 202–235
Archimedes Principle, 204–207, 249
Challenging Orthodoxies for, 12–14
Children and, 111, 162
different routes to "big ideas," 232–234
Dyson and, 230–231, 249
Edison and, 216–223, 249
eight steps of, 207, 214–215, 241, 248
Einstein and, 208–213, 249
Harnessing Trends for, 15–19 (*See also* Harnessing Trends)

historical perspective, 2–10
illuminating insight and, 234 (*See also* insight)
overview, 235
perceptive powers and, 66–67, 80–83
process of, 224–229
Creativity and Intelligence (Getzels), 229
Creators (Johnson), 50
culture, corporate, 44
cultural needs, understanding, 191–193
Curves, 64–65, 189, 232
"Customer Obsession" (Amazon), 181

D

Daedalus (Greek mythological character), 3–4
"daemon," 4–5
"Dark Ages," 16
Da Vinci, Leonardo, 31–34, 80
Dell, Michael, 102, 232–233
Dell (computer company), 102, 232–233
dentistry innovation, during Renaissance, 38
Descartes, R., 13
digital cameras, miniaturized, 173
Dimensional Research, 73
Dinner in the Sky, 114
disruption
Challenging Orthodoxies, 100–101, 105–110
Harnessing Trends and discontinuity, 126–129
diversification, of business, 166–167
Drucker, Peter, 242
Drucker Insights, 242
DSM, 163
Dual Cyclone (Dyson), 230–231

Duomo (Florence Cathedral), 24–25
Dutch Boy (Sherwin-Williams), 187
Dyer, Frank, 218
Dyson, James, 64, 230–231, 249

E

Eastman Kodak, 120, 126, 171–172
Echo (Amazon), 136
Edison: His Life and Inventions (Dyer, Martin), 218
Edison, Mina, 218
Edison, Thomas, 164, 216–223, 249
efficiency, 152–154
Eilmer of Malmesbury, 9
Einstein, Albert, 82, 208–213, 249
electronic books (e-books), 135
English Learning Centers (Walt Disney Company), 162
Enterprise, 103
ESPN, 64
Eureka moment, 205, 207, 236, 238, 241–242, 246–247, 259
"Eureka story" (Archimedes Principle), 204–207
Europe, consumers' cultural needs and, 192
experience, 246–247

F

Facebook, 120, 143, 144, 146, 242
Fauchard, Pierre, 38
Febreze (P&G), 191
Federal Aviation Administration, 81, 136
Fire Phone (Amazon), 136
"flash of illumination," 238–241
Florence Cathedral, 24–25
Flyknit (Nike), 111

Flywheel, 136
Ford, Henry, 183
foreign travel, Petrarch and, 15
Foundations of Science, The (Poincaré), 225
Four Lenses of Innovation
    applying to organizational culture, 54–57
    overview, 40–45
    as power tool for creative thinking, 84–85 (See also patterns)
    working with, for insight, 254–258
    See also brain; Challenging Orthodoxies; creativity; Harnessing Trends; insight; Leveraging Resources; mind of innovator; patterns; Understanding Needs
frames, 68
functional fixedness, 70–71
future, making changes to. *See* Harnessing Trends

G

Galileo Galilei, 2, 10, 12, 28, 34–36, 72, 209
Game Changer, The (Lafley), 180
"Gang of Four," 146
Gardner, Helen, 31
Gartner, 168
Gates, Bill, 130–131
Gelb, Michael, 217
General Electric (GE), 112, 122, 143
General Mills, 171
genius, etymology of, 4–5
Getzels, Jacob, 229
Ghiberti, Lorenzo, 24
Gibson, William, 119
Gigafactory, 109

Godrej & Boyce, 190
Goldratt, Eli, 251
Goodyear, 200
Google
    Challenging Orthodoxies, 104
    Harnessing Trends, 126, 144, 146, 147–148
    Leveraging Resources, 155–158
    Understanding Needs, 183, 198
GPS automotive navigation systems, 176
Graham, Martha, 118
Gray, Scott, 245
Greece (ancient), 3–4
growth potential, of business, 166–167
Grupo Matarromera, 168
guardian angels, concept of, 4–5
Gutenberg, Johannes, 20–23

H

hair care, 195–196
"Happiness Blanket" (British Airways), 148–149
Hargadon, Andrew, 154
Harnessing Trends, 118–151
    changing the future and, 137–141, 142–143,
        144–146
    creativity and ideas, 222
    overview, 118–119, 151
    as "race to future," 122–125
    recognizing trends, 147–150
    trends as patterns of change, 126–129, 130–136
    understanding change for, 120–121
    working with, for insight, 254–258
Harvard University, 114, 245

Hastings, Reed, 142, 188, 233
HBO GO, 112
health clubs, for women, 64–65, 189, 232
health food stores, in U.S., 132
Heavin, Diane, 64–65, 232
Heavin, Gary, 64–65, 232
Herd mentality, 73, 84
Heinz, 188
hierarchy, organizational culture and, 47
Hiero II (King of Syracuse), 205
Hill, Nick, 200
Homeplus, 115
How Breakthroughs Happen (Hargadon), 154
How to Create a Mind (Kurzweil), 68
humanism, 8, 16, 28, 31
Humphrey, George, 75
Huygens, Christiaan, 35
Hyper Island, 72
hyper-reflection, 75–76

I

IBM, 130, 178–181
Icarus (Greek mythological character), 3–4
ideation, 246–247. See also creativity; insight
IDEO, 184
IKEA, 102–103, 233
illumination, of ideas, 225, 227, 234, 238–241
iMac (Apple), 138
Imperial Billiards, 168–169
incubation, of ideas, 225, 226
India, consumers' cultural needs and, 190, 191
individualism, creativity and, 8–10, 49

"Industrial Internet," 143

inertia, 100, 124

InGenius (Seelig), 34, 49

ink, printing press invention and, 22

Innovate Like Edison (Gelb, Caldicott), 217

innovation

    as "accidental," 170–173 (*See also* Leveraging Resources)

    "crazy ones" as innovators, 92–95 (*See also* Challenging Orthodoxies)

    generating new patterns for, 78–79 (*See also* patterns)

    insight and capacity for radical innovation, 250–251 (*See also* insight)

    making radical change for, 40–45

    organizational culture and, 46–57

    production distinguished from, 154

    See also brain; Harnessing Trends; mind of innovator; Understanding Needs

innovators. *See* mind of innovator

input, 246–247

insight, 236–259

    breakthrough thinking and, 242–243

    capacity for radical innovation and, 250–251

    defined, 236, 242–243, 244–245

    ideation and, 246–247

    Innovation Quiz, 249

    overview, 236–241, 259

    power of, 252–253

    stepping stones for creative thinking, 248–249 (*See also* creativity)

    working with Four Lenses for, 254–258

institutional patterns of behavior, 72–73

Internet

    advent of, 131, 134

    "Internet of Things"/"Industrial Internet," 143

"Internet Tidal Wave, The" (Gates), 131

intimation, ideas and, 226

iPhone (Apple), 126, 139–140, 174

iPod (Apple), 138–139, 174

isochronism, 35

Italy, Renaissance period in, 6

IT'SUGAR, 111

Ive, Jonathan, 138

J

Japan, consumers' cultural needs and, 191

Jobs, Steve

    Challenging Orthodoxies, 92, 93, 104

    Harnessing Trends, 120–121, 130, 137–141

    Leveraging Resources, 160, 174

    power of patterns and, 84

    Understanding Needs, 181, 182, 183

    See also Apple

Johansson, Frans, 6

Johnson, Paul, 50

Johnson, Steven, 221

K

Kabat-Zinn, Jon, 129

kaleidoscope metaphor (Young), 228, 246

Kelley, Tom, 184

Kengen, 169

Kepler, J., 12

ketchup bottles, 188
Kiefer, Charles, 244
Kimberly-Clark, 172
Kindle (Amazon), 135
King Island Cloud Juice, 169
Kleenex, 172
Klein, Gary, 236–241, 246
Kodak. *See* Eastman Kodak
Koestler, Arthur, 248
Kono Pizza, 190
Kraft Foods, 192–193
Kurzweil, Ray, 68
Kutol, 171

L

Lafley, A. G., 189–191
Landes, David, 4
Lego Movie, The, 176
Lego (toy), 175–176
Leonardo da Vinci, 31–34, 80
Leveraging Resources, 152–177
    competencies and assets as resources, 152, 159
    creativity and ideas, 222
    efficiency and, 152–154
    exploiting underutilized assets, 168–169
    extending boundaries of businesses, 160–162, 163–165
    Google's business model, 155–158
    growth potential and, 166–167
    innovation as "accidental," 170–173
    minds of innovators and, 20–29
    overview, 177

    recombination and, 174–176
    working with, for insight, 254–258
Levitt, Theodore, 245
LIBRIé (Sony), 135
light bulb, invention of, 218, 220, 223, 249
LinkedIn, 120
Listerine, 172–173
"Living It" (P&G), 179
L'Oréal, 193
Loughborough University, 189
Lucasfilm, 138
Lush, 103
Luther, Martin, 12

M

Machiavelli, Niccolò, 13
Macintosh (Apple), 130, 137, 174
Mackey, John, 132–133
market research. *See* Understanding Needs
Mars, 244
Martin, Thomas, 218
"Matching What Is Possible with What Is Needed" (P&G), 195
Maxwell, James Clerk, 209–210
McCauley, Richard, 114
McDonald's, 153, 165, 168, 191–192
McFie, Duncan, 169
McLean, Malcolm, 188
McVicker, Joe, 171
medical innovation, during Renaissance, 36–37, 38
Medici Effect, The (Johansson), 6

Medici family, 6
Menander, 4
mental inertia, 100, 124
Meridiist Infinite, 199
Michelson, Albert, 210
Microsoft, 130–131, 140, 242
microwave ovens, 170
Middle East, consumers' cultural needs and, 191
milk yarn fabric, 115
mind of innovator, 1–59
    Challenging Orthodoxies and, 12–14
    creative genius and, 2–10
    Four Lenses of Innovation, overview, 40–45
    Harnessing Trends and, 15–19
    innovation renaissance, 46–57
    Leveraging Resources and, 20–29
    overview, 58–59
    Understanding Needs and, 30–39
    See also brain; creativity; insight
Mind Set! Reset Your Thinking and See the Future (Naisbitt),
    119
"Miracle on the Hudson," 81
mobile applications ("apps")
    Harnessing Trends and, 120–121
    Understanding Needs for, 198–200
mobile banking, 145–146
Model S (Tesla Motors), 108–109
Morley, Christopher, 258
Morley, Edward, 210
Moro, Carlos, 168
Mosaic (Netscape), 131, 134
movable type, 20–23
M-Pesa, 146, 165

Murrow, Edward R., 182
muses, 4
Musk, Elon, 106–110

N

Nabopolassar (King of Babylonia), 2
Naisbitt, John, 119
needs, understanding. See Understanding Needs
Nest Labs, 157, 198
Nestlé, 165, 186
Netflix, 103, 142, 188, 233
Netscape, 131, 134
New Product Development, 46, 179, 234
Newton, Isaac, 13, 100
NeXT, 138
"NFL Now," 113
Nielsen, 144
Nike, 111, 142
Nineteen Eighty-Four (Orwell), 96
Nintendo, 103
Nokia, 120, 139
nonalcoholic adult drinks, 186
Northwestern University, 200

O

Olay Body Wash (P&G), 195
Ollila, Jorma, 120
"On the Electrodynamics of Moving Bodies" (Einstein),
    212
open innovation, 196,
oral care products, 194–195

Oreos (Kraft Foods), 192–193

organizational culture

applying Four Lenses to, 54–57

building a pro-innovation culture, 53

collective "brain" of organizations and, 98

as "cradle of creativity," 49–52

institutional patterns of behavior, 72–73

overview, 46–48

orthodoxies, challenging. See Challenging Orthodoxies

Orwell, George, 96

Osborn, Alex, 229

output, 246–247

P

pacifier thermometers, 189

Page, Larry, 104, 155, 158

"pain points," of customers, 185

paint can design, 187

Pandora (Greek mythological character), 4

Pantene Pro-V (P&G), 195–196

paper, printing press invention and, 22

Paracelsus, 12

Paré, Ambroise, 36

Pascal, Blaise, 38

pattern of the crowd, 72

patterns, 61–88

defined, 65

Four Lenses of Innovation as power tool for creative thinking, 84–85

functional fixedness and, 70–71

innovation and, 78–79

institutional patterns of behavior, 72–73

orthodoxies as, 96–97

overview, 86–87

pattern-recognition principle, 68–69

perceptive powers and creativity, 66–67, 80–83

perspective and, 62–65

resistance to change and, 74–77

Pausanias, 4

PayPal, 106

peer-to-peer lending companies, 146

Pemberton, John, 170

pendulums, 35

perceptive powers, creativity and, 66–67, 80–83

Pérez, Antonio, 120

perspective, patterns and, 62–65

Petrarch, 12, 15–17

Pfizer, 172

Pirates of the Caribbean (film series), 162

Pixar, 138, 160, 174–175

pizza, in a cone, 190

Plato, 4

Play-Doh, 171

Plutarch, 4

PocketPaks Breath Freshening Strips (Listerine), 172–173

Poincaré, Henri, 225

Popular Science, 198

PortalPlayer Inc., 174

Post-It (3M), 172

power tools, 186

Prahalad, C. K., 124

preparation, ideas and, 226

PriceWaterhouseCoopers, 135

Prime Pantry (Amazon), 136

printing press, 20–23

Pritchard, Marc, 241

Procter & Gamble (P&G)
    creativity and, 165, 173
    insight and, 241, 242
    Understanding Needs and, 178–181, 183, 190, 191,
        194–196

progress, humanist philosophy and, 31

Project Zero (AgustaWestland), 114–115

Prometheus the Titan (Greek mythological character), 3

prosthetic limbs, 37

Pulte Homes, 182

Q

Quirk, 245

Qzone, 120

R

"race to future," 122–125

radical innovation, capacity for, 250–251

Rainbow Crafts Company, 171

Raytheon Corporation, 170

recombination, 22, 23, 174–176

Redbox, 168

refrigeration, in India, 190

Renaissance
    Challenging Orthodoxies, 12–14
    concept of creativity and, 6–10
    as "cradle of creativity," 49
    Harnessing Trends and, 15–19
    Leveraging Resources and, 20–29
    radical change during, 40–45

Understanding Needs and, 30–39

RenderMan (Pixar), 138

research and development (R&D), consumer application
    and, 179–180, 194–200

resources, leveraging. See Leveraging Resources

retail, digital versus physical, 140–141

Ribbon Machine process (Corning), 164

Robb, Walter, 133

Rolls-Royce, 103

Rome (ancient), 4–5

Rubin, Jeff, 111

S

Safaricom, 146, 165

saturation, of ideas, 225

Sawhney, Mohanbir, 182

schemata, 68

Schumpeter, Joseph, 154

scripts, 68

sector (tool), 36

Seeing What Others Don't (Klein), 236–241, 246

Seelig, Tina, 34, 49

senior executives, recognizing change and, 122–125

Shaw, George Bernard, 93

Sherwin-Williams, 187

shipping containers, 188

sign language mobile apps, 200

skin patches, for health monitoring, 200

smart cars, 144

smart wristbands, 148

smoke detectors, 198

social media, Harnessing Trends and, 120

Socrates, 4
SolarCity, 106, 110
Sony, 135
sound transmission, early inventions, 219, 221–222, 223, 249
Southwest Airlines, 102
SpaceX, 106–110
special relativity theory (Einstein), 209–212, 249
Spencer, Percy, 170
Splitterwerk, 115
Starbucks, 142–143
StoreDot, 198–199
Story of a Man's Mind, The (Humphrey), 75
Sullenberger, Chesley "Sully," 81
Summer Infant, 189
Super Glue, 172
Swatch Group, 102

T

tablet computers, 140
TAG Heuer, 198–199
Technique for Producing Ideas, A (Young), 227–229
telecopes, 34–35
telegraph invention, 219, 220, 249
telephone invention, 221–222
Tesco, 115, 163
Tesla Motors, 106, 108–110
Theory of Constraints (Goldratt), 251
Theory of Economic Development, The (Schumpeter), 154
thermometers, medical, 189
thermoscope, 35

thermostats, for home, 198
"Think Different" (Apple marketing campaign), 92, 138
thinking. *See* brain; creativity; insight; mind of innovator
"third age suit" (Loughborough University), 189
3D printing, 136, 200
3M, 172
throughput, 246–247
tires, 200
Toffler, Alvin, 128
TomTom, 176
Toy Story (Pixar, Disney), 138
trends, harnessing. *See* Harnessing Trends
truffles (North Carolina grower), 113
"TV Everywhere," 112
"Twist & Pour" (Sherwin-Williams), 187
Twitter, 120, 143, 144

U

Understanding Needs, 178–201
    creativity and ideas, 222
    of cultural groups, 191–193
    identifying customers' needs, 182–184, 185–188
    innovators' minds and, 30–39
    overview, 178–181, 201
    research and consumer application, 179–180, 194–200
    of specific customer groups, 189–190
    working with, for insight, 254–258
University of Illinois, 114, 200
Unleashing Hidden Insights (Vriens, Verhulst), 244
US Airways, 81
USB flash drives, 173

V

vacuum cleaners, 64, 230–231, 249
Van Eyck, Jan, 22
Van Orman Quine, William, 119
Verhulst, Rogier, 244
verification, of ideas, 227
Vesalius, Andreas, 12
Vespucci, Amerigo, 14
Viagra (Pfizer), 172
video game companies, 144–145
Virgin Group, 166–167
Vitruvius, 27
von Helmholtz, Hermann, 224
Vriens, Marco, 244

W

Wallas, Graham, 226–227, 238
Walt Disney Company, 138, 148, 161–163, 174–175
Warby Parker, 115
"wave riders," 126–129
Waze, 143
wearable technology, 147–149
websites, interactive, 180

Weibo, 120
Welch, Jack, 122
WellnessMart, 114
Where Good Ideas Come From (Johnson), 221
Whole Foods Market, 132–133
Wii (Nintendo), 103
Windows (Microsoft), 131
Wood, Luke, 104
work environment. *See* organizational culture
wristbands, smart, 148

X

X.com, 106
Xerox, 174

Y

Young, James Webb, 227–229, 234, 246
YouTube, 144

Z

Zappos, corporate culture, 46, 82
Zappos Insights, 242
Zara, 103–104

ABOUT THE AUTHOR

Rowan Gibson is widely recognized as one of the world's foremost thought leaders on business innovation. The media have labeled him "Mr. Innovation," "the Innovation Grandmaster," "the W. Edwards Deming of innovation," and "a guru among the gurus." He is the author of two internationally bestselling books—*Rethinking The Future* and *Innovation to the Core*—which have been published in a total of 25 languages.

Over the last two decades, Gibson's international clients have included some of the world's largest and most successful companies. He teaches them how to seize new growth opportunities, create new markets, and even transform entire industries by recalibrating their management systems around the paradigm of innovation.

As one of today's most in-demand public speakers, Rowan Gibson has delivered keynote speeches, public seminars, and multiday innovation master classes in 60 countries around the world. In addition to his bestselling books, he has also authored numerous business articles, columns, and blogs, which have been read all over the globe. He has been interviewed frequently on television and radio, as well as online and in the international press. His media appearances include Forbes, CNN, *BusinessWeek*, *Harvard Business Review*, and BBC World.

Rowan Gibson is founder and President of Imagination Bridge, the global innovation consultancy, and cofounder of *Innovation Excellence*—the world's most popular innovation website. The portal, which builds on an international community with tens of thousands of members from over 175 countries, offers an arsenal of resources from today's innovation thought leaders and practitioners that is aimed at helping every company achieve innovation excellence. Follow the author on **Twitter: www.twitter.com/rowangibson.**

Author website: www.rowangibson.com

Book website: www.the4lenses.com

Consulting services: www.imaginationbridge.com

Web Portal: www.innovationexcellence.com